ALSO BY ANTHONY MCCARTEN

WARREN and

WARREN and BILL

Gates, Buffett, and the Friendship That Changed the World

ANTHONY McCARTEN

HARPER

An Imprint of HarperCollinsPublishers

HarperCollins books may be purchased for educational, business, or sales promotional use. For information, please email the Special Markets Department at SPsales@harpercollins.com.

FIRST EDITION

Designed by Leah Carlson-Stanisic

Library of Congress Cataloging-in-Publication Data has been applied for.

ISBN 978-0-06-303779-3

24 25 26 27 28 LBC 5 4 3 2 1

Human altruism which is not egoism is sterile.

—*Marcel Proust*

CONTENTS

PREFACE

Friends influence each other. Close friends of mine have, through their encouragement, seen me try surfing (disastrous), learn the guitar (more successful), take up tennis (forever grateful), try smoking dope (short-lived), end certain relationships and begin others (a speckled history), try to be a better person (work in progress), and even become a writer (jury, be merciful).

This book is about a friendship, one of the most impactful friendships of modern times. I am challenged, in fact, to think of another with such far-reaching reverberations in its impact on the world in the realms of finance, technology, and global philanthropy. Warren Edward Buffett and William Henry Gates III met in 1991; they played cards and golf, they joked and kidded around, swapped trade secrets, ate junk food. People seldom change, but when they do it is often only for a beloved partner or deep friend, and the change is impermanent—it requires the continued inflationary pressure of the other's existence. Warren and Bill's growing friendship brought with it inner and outer transformations, first in subtle, playful ways, and then in increasingly profound and far-reaching ones. Both men fed this bond with their most valuable commodity: their time (which both measure out by the teaspoonful). Soon their respective life partners were playing decisive roles in this unfolding buddy drama, leading to the establishment of the largest philanthropic enterprise of all time, the Bill & Melinda Gates Foundation, which holds, as of its last reporting, nearly $70 billion in assets. Until 2021, the foundation had only three trustees: Bill Gates, Melinda Gates, and Warren Buffett.

How did such an unusual union blossom from an unpromising beginning, a garden party at Bill's parents' vacation house outside Seattle to which Bill definitely didn't want to go after he learned Warren would be there? In what ways specifically did each man begin to influence the other? What aspects of character in one created a realignment in the other? And what does their giga-wealthy partnership mean for the rest of us and especially for the miseried millions in this unequal world ever more reliant on the generosity and judgment of the very very *very* rich?

My interest in Bill Gates arose in my student years when I wondered, with center-left bias and youthful indignation, how someone so wealthy could *not* want to devote himself entirely to the planet's salvation, to the alleviation of human suffering, to underwriting the general improvement of humanity's lot. Where was this man's *conscience*, I asked myself? Turns out, it was asleep, awaiting a fairy-tale awakening. Enter a beautiful princess, to plant upon the wet lips of the fairy-tale frog a royal and transmogrifying kiss. Awakened, spell broken, Billionaire Bill, before our eyes, was suddenly the Sir Galahad of global philanthropy. By 2000, Bill had stepped down from his role as Microsoft's CEO, bent no longer on monopolizing our digital future but on kissing the wounded, tending the doomed, aiding the flow of blood to the capillaries of the human corpus.

A decent man.

So, was meeting his former wife, Melinda, really the X factor that changed Bill, that accounted for such a Damascene conversion? Or had the seeds been sown earlier?

Bill remains a divisive figure. He has his fans but also his critics, long dug in and wildly armed. As I write this, the internet carries almost daily some zany conspiracy theory that places him on a spectrum somewhere between being a secret releaser of deadly viruses upon the earth so as to then reap money from selling vaccines to secretly being, well . . . a lizard. How the crowd loves a bogeyman, and Bill–despite his good works–has been cast in that role time and again (when the role hasn't gone to George Soros, that is). What does that *feel* like? To be so targeted and blamed? Does it wound him? What inner firewall makes him able to ignore the trolls?

My interest in Bill was furthered when I learned that he likes to play bridge, which is a confounding card game made up of bids and gambits, bluffs and marches. It is also one of the points of intersection with our second subject.

Warren Buffett, the seer of Omaha, is a very, very strong bridge player. One of his favorite partners is Bill. Why? They communicate silently, read the clues given off by the other assuredly, the key to a great bridge pairing. That is tough to beat. In addition, Warren has–in the decades since World War II (he was fifteen when the war ended)–managed to build a global empire worth, as of this writing, nearly $120 billion, making him the fifth richest man in the world, and at the same time remain not only liked but well liked, in some quarters even revered. Why is someone so enviably rich so enviably well liked? And why isn't Warren blamed for, say, releasing Covid-19 upon the earth? Why aren't the online trolls attacking him, saying that *he* is secretly a Komodo dragon? Why has envy, in his case, not taken the form of rage?

Part of the answer is that Warren is ahead of his critics. To those who say that the super-rich ought to pay much more in taxes, he agrees, has even argued for it, writing op-eds in the *New York Times* with headlines like "Stop Coddling the Super-Rich," calling on his government to hit both him and his kind where it hurts. Instead of playing the role of Louis XVI, he assumes the mantle of Robespierre. Warren can *afford* to pay much more in taxes, he assures us. He *wants* to pay more. Get rid of those unfair tax breaks that outrageously benefit those who least need further help. Folks, it's just the right thing to do.

A popular man.

(Bill is also happy to pay more in personal tax—even double—and believes he should have paid more in capital gains tax, too, even as he boasted in 2018 that he has paid more than anyone else: over $10 billion at the time. "If people want taxes at certain levels, great, set them at those levels," he's said publicly for at least a decade. And yet questions remain over untaxed money being able to be used for charitable donations, and their tax-deductible nature in general, especially when these are supermassive, and also around the corporate tax loopholes used by all the tech giants that partly allowed Bill and Warren and their ilk to become so megarich in the first place. It's worth noting that Bill's laudable donations to his and Melinda's foundation take the form of his untaxed shares in Microsoft, so might *their* money also be viewed—as some critics argue—as *our* money as well, subject to more public scrutiny and checks and regulation?)

Exhibit number 2: Warren's home. No castle. He has famously owned the same modest house since 1958. It has only a grass verge, one easily crossed. The man *invites* observation of his life and habits and business practices. He has nothing to hide. Cruise past Warren's place, as anyone can, and you might think that a kid with a paper route would not need a very strong arm at all to reach the porch with a bicycle-borne copy of the *Wall Street Journal*. Warren doesn't fear much. At ninety-three, he says he doesn't even fear the final auditor. Death, he posits, is simply one deal you can't finesse, leverage, or add nuance to. When the deadly dealer finally calls "Game over" and draws a horizontal line under the score sheet, Warren knows he will have to look down on his tabled cards—even more beloved to him than they are to Bill—and say, "Too good." His run, his great run, one of the greatest of all times, will be at an end. He will go into the ground or the air, as all the megarich have gone before him, with not a dime in his pocket, remembered only for the good or ill he did the public. As Warren himself has said, what will survive of us is not money, it's love: how much we gave, how much we received.

Plato wrote that there are three kinds of people: lovers of wisdom, lovers of honor, and lovers of gain. We should like to ask Plato, can a gainful person not in equal measure love and honor? Or an honorable one in equal measure love and gain? Can a single person not be a three-way lover, of gain, honor, and wisdom? This book will ask whether each single attribute excludes acquisition of the other two, or whether it's possible to defy Plato's axiom and be a paragon of all three.

I WILL ALSO survey, and offer some observations on, the current state of philanthropy in the modern era, especially the ambitious brand of "creative capitalism"—a term used by Bill Gates—which exploits market principles for the common good, connecting the promise of philanthropy with the power of private enterprise. So, whom does creative capitalism best serve? Whom does it fail? Human suffering is easily ignored because it is so prevalent, so *always*: like the sound of a twenty-four-hour gas flare, an intolerable noise so constant that, after a while, it's what silence becomes.

Why stray into this complex quagmire?

Philanthropy is a deeply divisive subject. It is likened in the minds of many of its critics to no more than an amnesty, which sees the superthieves elect to turn themselves in and return (some of) their ill-gotten gains without charges being laid. Others hold that criticism of any act of generosity is mean-spirited and counter-human—a form of "friendly fire" that takes out much-needed good guys.

Perhaps a study of the lives of the two greatest givers of *all* time can illustrate the true nature of philanthropy *in our* time.

THERE IS, IT seems to me, another reason these two men are worthy of our study.

For some years I have felt—despite the mass marches decrying income inequality, and the rescue of the word "socialist" from the trash bin of history—that we have actually been ignoring the very rich, in real ways, and at our peril. We have not been paying them the right kinds of attention, not been asking the right questions. We have been fixated on our own earthly complaints, our quarrels, daily needs, wants, hopes, rights, vacation plans, mortgages, relationships, jobs, debts, ailments, social media accounts, broadband speeds, flat tires, et cetera, ad nauseam, while, all the time, the very rich have quietly, immeasurably, grown richer, rivaling and sometimes smoothly surpassing many previous records of wealth in human history, such as Louis XIV of Versailles, the Romanovs at their most kleptomaniac, the industrious Carnegies and hoarding Vanderbilts and Rockefellers of the Gilded Age, the dynastic Windsors or various European nobles, a King Solomon or a Canute, or Cleopatra sloshing around in her bathtub full of donkey's milk. In the creeping decades of our distracted non-attention, the money, the money, the money has been rising, rising, rising to the top, in mind-boggling volume. Just how much money? In 2017, Oxfam reported that eight individuals have as much wealth as the poorest half of humanity. Let me repeat that. Not the top eight *hundred thousand* individuals on earth, not the top eight thousand, or eight hundred, or eighty: the top *eight*. These eight men—and we're talking men—to a man, had *half*—of *everything*.

As a forgotten poet once said: What the crap?

So, the rich, they are certainly not like you and me. Not anymore. They are now citizens of a country to which not even they are acclimated. They wake to challenges peculiar to them, to a climate so rare, a landscape so foreign, that there is little travel information available. How should they know how to set one foot in front of the other and avoid missteps made gigantic by their unique situation? For no road map was, or could ever be, issued for how you and seven pals—just enough guys for a game of pickup basketball—should rightly manage *half of everything*.

AS ARISTOTLE PUT it a few thousand years ago, "To give away money is an easy matter and in any man's power. But to decide to whom to give it, and how large, and when, and for what purpose and how, is neither in every man's power nor an easy matter." As long as *Homo sapiens* has had "money," we've wondered what the rich ought to do with theirs. It's a question difficult to disentangle from the matter of whether there ought to be rich people at all, but mingling the two questions tends to lead to a rhetorical dead end. Unless you sign off on Andrew Carnegie's 1889 take on what would be later called the trickle-down theory that society prospers when capitalists are left to their own devices—both in how they aggregate their wealth and how they give it away—the critique of inequality will wind up dominating any discussion about the nature and effects of giving by the already rich.

In 1916, John D. Rockefeller became the world's first billionaire. Think of a thousand millionaires decanted into one person: that was old Rockefeller, and this was back in the days when you could buy a whole house for a thousand bucks. Since then, the giga-rich club has been quietly increasing in membership at a surpassing rate. The thirty-seventh annual *Forbes* list of billionaires, published in 2023 tells us that we now have 2,640 billionaires. Bill Gates was in fact the first person to be worth over $100 billion, in 1999. As a jolly image, if turned into quarters, this treasure would fill to the brim eight cathedrals the size of St Paul's in London. If the average person in the United States (in 2023) pulls down $33 an hour, or just north of $1,300 a week, or over $68,000 a year *before* taxes, then this average person is but a single grain of sand, while Bill Gates is, mathematically, the moon.

This book concerns two lunar giants. It is about how their priorities have evolved as the years have flown by and their friendship has deepened. It is about their stories, as far as they are publicly known, and the times they have shared. And it is also about what they love, and the people whom they love and who love them.

In studying these men, this book will ask several tricky questions. How did the world get here? Is this state of affairs in any respects

fair? Is it sustainable? What is to become of a world where honest enterprise can result in public wealth coagulating in so few locations?
Are we safe in such a weighted world, safer than we've ever been, as
some thinkers and leaders claim, or are we headed for a reckoning?
Is the minting of billionaires an alert for a timely upgrade to the
world's core operating system, or do we need a new OS altogether, to
throw out the old one and build something new from scratch? Can
we trust these folks to do right by the rest of us, to be nice to us, now
that the world is literally in their debt and—to a worrying extent—
needful of their mercy? How many of them follow the diktat of steel
tycoon Andrew Carnegie, who in 1889 said that those who die rich
die in disgrace? Will the last checks written by any of these tycoons
actually—as Carnegie instructs they should—bounce?

PART I

1

WARREN, MEET BILL;
BILL, MEET WARREN

Bill Gates was annoyed. The view outside his helicopter was picture-postcard perfect–summer sun shining on the emerald-green water of Puget Sound–and Bill was annoyed to be viewing it, because he hadn't wanted to make this trip. It was July 5, 1991, and most of America was at play that Friday, nudging an extra-long weekend out of the national holiday, but he, Bill Gates, CEO of Microsoft, did not have "playtime" down in the planner his assistant filled out for him in minute-by-minute increments. He, Bill Gates, had work to do. He was, at the time, the second-richest man in America, according to *Forbes*, and instead of grinding away at whatever it took to become number one, he–Bill Gates!–was flying to his parents' vacation house on Hood Canal, because his mom was making him. *Come meet Warren Buffett*, she'd said–a demand, not an invitation. Bill couldn't see the point. Warren Buffett was yesterday's news. In eighth place on the *Forbes* list–not bad, admittedly, but definitely also-ran status. The guy was a stock picker. He wasn't creating the future, like Bill and his techie friends. (And enemies.) All Warren Buffett did, Bill told his mom, was buy and sell "pieces of paper." That was not real "value added." Mary Gates stood her ground.

Bill told his helicopter pilot he planned to be back in Seattle in two hours.

Warren Buffett was looking to make a quick exit, too. "What the hell are we going to spend all day doing with these people?" he complained to his traveling companion as they drove to the Gates compound. "How long do we have to stay to be polite?"

As the saying goes, "Behind every great man, there's a great woman." In 1991, Bill had his mom. Warren Buffett had a feminine coterie: his wife, Susan; his live-in partner, Astrid; and, of note on this particular day, Katharine Graham, known by intimates as Kay, the glamorous former publisher of the *Washington Post*, one of Warren's closest confidantes, and the person who'd dragged him out of Omaha for the Fourth of July. Warren and Kay were staying at the Bainbridge Island home of *Post* opinion editor Meg Greenfield, and it was she and Mary Gates who'd cooked up the scheme to introduce *Forbes* #2 and *Forbes* #8. Neither woman was confident the men would get along—more than likely, they'd bore each other, and Bill would get testy, and Warren would wander off in search of a fresh Cherry Coke. But it wouldn't be boring to watch.

The same gale that blew across the lawn finally carried the deafening noise of a chopper . . . *tha-thump, tha-thump, tha-thump*. The assembled party guests looked up: Bill was here.

WHAT DID BILL and Warren see in each other, when first they shook hands? Did Bill perceive a live facsimile of the beloved public Warren, American capitalism's twinkly-eyed grandpa? Or did he glimpse something a bit more ruthless, a bit Bill-like, behind those eyes? Did Warren recognize in Bill a younger version of himself, another dishabille workaholic with a mind forever running numbers?

Was Warren's greeting of Bill anything like how he would first greet another technology tycoon, Jeff Bezos, years later, hilariously throwing up his hands in mock alarm and shouting to Bezos: "Don't eat me! Don't eat me!" He might well have used the same line on Bill, given Microsoft's voracious appetite of that era.

At any rate, what was witnessed by the worried women looking on was Warren getting straight to the point. "So," he asked Bill, "how would you build IBM from scratch?"

Bill's eyes lit up.

With other party guests hovering nearby, Warren peppered Bill with questions, precisely the kind of questions that set Bill's heart aflutter. Warren wanted to know all about the software business. He wanted to understand how a young company like Microsoft was throwing Big Blue off its game. He wanted details about skill sets and pricing. He dug and dug, asking "amazingly good questions that nobody had ever asked," Bill recalled twenty-five years later. Bill advised Warren to dump some "peaked" stocks. Warren replied by pointing out that he'd gotten where he was by ignoring that kind of advice. Bill must have been stunned: Warren was the first person he'd met in a very long time with the authority to rebut him in this way.

They kept talking. "We talked and talked and talked and talked," says Warren. Bill was a good teacher. Warren was a keen student, eager to understand a business—tech—he'd stubbornly ignored up to that point. Bill and Warren talked so much that, frankly, it was rude. Mary and Bill Sr. had invited many of their high-powered friends to this gathering, and Bill and Warren ignored all of them, sneaking off like lovers for a walk on the pebble beach as the left-behinds eyed them, wondering what on earth they were talking so much about. "Probably joshing each other about their *Forbes* rankings," Meg Greenfield—known for her wryness—might have said to Kay as they eyed the two shabby figures standing at the water's edge. "Come on, let's play croquet."

The game ended. The sun set. At a certain point, the helicopter had to leave. Bill stayed.

FORMER *PC WEEK* journalist John Dodge covered Bill Gates extensively in the 1990s, and he's since written of the Microsoft founder's skills as a conversationalist, or lack thereof. Recalling a plane trip with Bill: "We talked tech the whole way. That's the way Gates was—tech and business talk only. Small talk was hard for him or just thoroughly meaningless." Sometimes, Dodge says, Bill would "stop talking and start rocking, signaling that the question was dumb."

A word on this rocking thing before we proceed. Bill Gates is famous for rocking. Not, like, *rocking out*, just rocking back and forth on his heels or in his seat, a thing he does when he's deep in thought. As John Seabrook described it in an article for *The New Yorker*:

> *While he is working, the dude rocks. Whether he is in business meetings, on airplanes, or listening to a speech, his upper body rocks down to an almost forty-five-degree angle, rocks back up, rocks down again. . . . And he rocks at different levels of intensity according to his mood.*

It's fair to assume, then, that tech and business were the near-exclusive topics of that long conversation between Bill and Warren the day they met. Which was probably fine by both of them; neither man was much for spilling his guts.

But there would have been plenty to spill that fine summer day.

Both tycoons had lately been thrust into the limelight. For Bill, that was bad news: Once celebrated as the booming tech industry's premier wunderkind, he was now accused of being a bully, a copy-cat, a budding monopolist. How, he might have asked Warren, had the investor managed the truly improbable feat of piling up billions of dollars while simultaneously polishing a persona straight out of a Frank Capra film? Stockholders swarmed the annual meetings of Berkshire Hathaway, the company Warren had taken control of in 1965, just to hear Warren Buffett wax dogmatic on the nature of a square deal. Picture Bill in a rare moment of candor complaining to Warren that all he truly wanted was to be seen for who he was—a problem-solver. Picture Warren comforting Bill by revealing that he, too, had once been accused of anticompetitive practices. *"Really?"* Bill replies, for the public had already forgotten whatever it knew about Warren Buffett's '80s-era newspaper war in Buffalo. But that's the thing, Warren explains to Bill: Today's villain is tomorrow's hero. That's how America works.

And Warren could have confessed his own simmering conflicts. It isn't easy, straddling two camps—one day you're golfing with a left-wing *Post* journalist, and the next day you're at a black-tie gala, gritting your teeth as your right-wing tablemates moan about welfare queens between bites of trout amandine. "I told 'em the real problem is *corporate welfare*," Warren recalls. "That shut 'em up."

The point is, Warren explains, it's confusing to be a man of the people among the powerful. The powerful don't seem to realize how lucky they are.

The conversation would, of course, turn to money. The getting and having of it. Bill Gates and Warren Buffett are among the very, very few who understand the unique pressures of owning a giant fortune. Everyone wants something from you—how do you say *no*? And how, when you say yes, do you personally decide what to give, and to whom?

An early theme of Warren's is that inherited wealth is a scourge. And yet instead of giving all your money away now, and so sparing your kids this living nightmare, the best idea, he long argued, is to wait till you're kaput. "Compounding," says Warren. Grow your stash, he advises, via the miracle that is compound interest, and there'll simply be more for your descendants to dole out when you're gone. Picture Bill running pro-and-con arguments for this through his linear mind and preparing to object—just as Warren adds that he also wished there were some kind of *system* for doing charity, so you could guarantee a return. *Yes! Yes!* Bill yelps, in his signature geeky squawk. *A system!* He starts nodding . . . and rocking.

Picture them comparing their brains. The uncanny ability to calculate vast sums in their heads. The comparative difficulty of figuring out people, with all their incalculable wants, needs, hurts, vanities. Picture them talking about bridge—as they maybe did even that first day; it's a game they both love.

None of the above is on the factual record, however. What *is* on the record: Eventually, Warren and Bill amble back from the beach and sit down to dinner. Bill's father poses a question to the assembled guests: What factor did they feel was most important in getting to where they'd gotten in life? They go around the table. Bill and Warren say the same thing: "Focus."

FOCUS. IT IS also known that on the day they met, Warren Buffett performed for Bill Gates the following analytical exercise. "He'll choose a year—say, 1970—and examine the ten highest market-capitalization companies from around then," Bill explains. "Then he'll go forward to 1990 and look at how those companies fared." Fun, right? More fun when he starts citing examples—with numbers—off the top of his head. Most people listening to this would tune out, scan the horizon, and wonder who was aboard passing ships. Not Bill. He says that Warren's "enthusiasm for the exercise was contagious." It was this kind of deep-in-the-weeds chitchat about business that kept Bill from coptering back to Seattle, and that formed the foundation of his long-lasting friendship with Warren. Both of these men had been thinking about this kind of thing, in this particular way, *forever*.

For Warren, it started at age six, with a stopwatch.

He'd pleaded for the stopwatch as a gift, and once he received it, he invented games to make use of it, like marble racing. He'd race marbles over and over, tracking each one's roll from bathtub edge to drain and recording the times down to the second. Soon, he was doing mental arithmetic in church, passing the boring parts of the service by noting the birth and death dates listed next to composers' names in the hymnal and seeing how long each one had lived. He'd measure their life spans against the average, seeing it as a test of the value of piety. In school, naturally, Warren proved to be gifted in math. Exceptionally so. But for him, math served a purpose: It helped you figure odds. And once you understand odds, you can place smart bets.

Math let you seize opportunities for profit, too. And what Warren Buffett loved most of all was making money. As a kid in Omaha during the Depression, he'd sell chewing gum and Coca-Cola door-to-door; the gum earned him two cents a pack, and six bottles of Coke netted a whole nickel. He'd store the coins in the nickel-plated money changer on his belt and record his takings in a ledger. Soon he got himself a job selling peanuts and popcorn to football fans at the University of Omaha. Other kids might have spent their hard-earned coins on candy or comic books; not Warren Buffett. He just kept squirreling them away.

"It's not that I *want* money," young Warren explained. "It's the fun of making money and watching it grow."

In 1940, Europe was at war, and Franklin Delano Roosevelt would be elected for an unprecedented third term as president, but what struck ten-year-old Warren Buffett's imagination with the most force that year was the trip he and his stockbroker father took to New York City. Top priority for the budding chewing gum magnate was a visit to the Stock Exchange; en route, he tagged along as Howard Buffett paid a call on Sidney Weinberg, senior partner at Goldman Sachs and, back then, as Buffett says, "the most famous man on Wall Street." Here the presence of young Warren was an unexpected boon: Weinberg might have been tempted to turn away a no-name Omaha broker like Howard Buffett, but, as Warren later recalled, he had a much harder time saying no when there was a cute kid in tow. Years later, when Buffett rescued Goldman Sachs from an imminent meltdown during the 2008 financial crisis, he looked back on this encounter with the man who'd restored the firm's battered reputation after the 1929 crash, and who posed to young Warren a question that would turn out to be one for the ages. "So," Weinberg asked, putting his arm around the gawky kid, "what stock do *you* like?"

In 1942, Warren Buffett dumped out his hoard of coins and birth-day cash. To his family's astonishment, he'd accumulated $120, a princely sum in those days. The problem was that the money wasn't *doing* anything; it was just sitting there. Warren had recently read—and reread and read again—the book *One Thousand Ways to Make $1,000*, and in it, he'd discovered the concept of "compounding." Compounding is the way you make money from money—you might stick it in the bank and let it accumulate interest. Or you can buy stocks, which is what Warren Buffett decided to do.

With his sister Doris as partner, Warren bought three shares of Cities Service preferred stock, a favorite stock of his father's, for $114.75—or $38.25 a share. Then he watched the market. Really watched it. The stock took a steep dip—cue heart palpitations—and then recovered, and Warren quickly sold when it hit $40 a share, net-ting him and Doris a profit of $5. "That's when I knew that he knew what he was doing," Doris Buffett told his authorized biographer Al-ice Schroeder.

Warren might have disputed his sister's confidence in him, be-cause Cities Service preferred soon after soared to $202 a share.

Buffett considers this episode one of the most significant of his life. It wasn't just that he'd sacrificed a hefty profit on the altar of his nerves—it was that he'd cost Doris that profit, too. Lesson learned: If you're going to invest on behalf of others, you'd better be damned sure of yourself. And the best way to be sure was to figure your odds.

If Warren comes across as the paradigmatic example of the Depression-era striver, all thrift and pluck, Bill represents another classic type: the nerd.

The word wasn't in common usage until the 1960s, and by the time it was, William Henry Gates III fit the bill to a T. The ability to cal-culate equations in your head? Check. Diminutive, squeaky-voiced, and supercilious toward peers with lesser IQs? Check. Flaunting an utter disregard for grooming or style? Check, for sure. As an elemen-tary school student, Bill favored shirts buttoned at the neck and trousers hiked up *over his waist*. Even his family nickname, Trey, could be misread as a dorky bilingual joke—he was William, and so was his father, and his father before that: uno, dos, trey. Despite these nerd qualifications, his parents were despairing of their son's lackadaisical approach to academics. More than once, Mary and Bill Sr., were called into school apropos one of Bill's pranks. They were clearly at pains to find some way of focusing their son: He was a wild man on water skis, but team sports didn't take; bored at school, he deigned to unleash the full power of his intellect only when his curiosity was piqued. To wit, the report he wrote in sixth grade, titled "Invest with Gatesway Incorporated," in which he imagined himself as a "young inventor" building a business on the back of his creation. "If my idea is good and I am able to hire good people," he wrote, "I should be successful."

The path to success opened for Bill a year after he penned that report. Mary and Bill Sr. decided, as Bill was entering seventh grade, to send him to Seattle's prestigious Lakeside School, a private academy that was then boys-only.

Ironically, had Bill been a better student and stayed in public school, he'd never have gotten his jump start on the computing revolution. Hardly anyone had access to computers in those days—early "computers" were hulking mainframe devices that wheezed in reply to punch-card commands fed to them by a small coterie of programmers. Like an oracle, a computer sat upon a pedestal, below which its root system of cables was planted, and like an oracle, it spat out cryptic responses to its supplicants' pleas to do this or do that. ERROR, it would say, and the unhappy programmer would shuffle back to their desk to scour pages of binary code to find their mistake. 1968, however, was a watershed year—Intel was founded that summer, Hewlett-Packard introduced its first programmable desktop calculator, and Stanford's Doug Engelbart demoed embryonic versions of a mouse, a word processor, email, and hypertext. The digital walls were crumbling as Lakeside School leased an ASR-33 teletype for its students' use that year.

This loud and ungainly machine had one magical power: It could connect, through its modem, to a mainframe. You'd type a few lines of primitive code into the ASR-33, send the command down the phone line to some General Electric Mark II mainframe or other, and—*presto!*—the ASR-33 printer would clatter out the mainframe's reply. Like, you might tell the mainframe to calculate the equation 2 + 2, and the number 4 would show up on the printer. (Of course, if your code was off, it would print out ERROR.) Because GE's Mark II spoke only one programming language, you did your coding in BASIC (Beginner's All-purpose Symbolic Instruction Code). Which meant that the command "Calculate 2 + 2" read as:

```
10 PRINT 2 + 2
20 END
RUN
```

Thirteen-year-old Bill Gates was Lakeside School's acknowledged BASIC master. In no time at all, he'd figured out how to use the language to create a digital game of tic-tac-toe. (Actually, that was the *second* program he wrote; the first converted numbers from one arithmetic base to another.) When the senior class president needed help with his BASIC, he was told to track down the pipsqueak who haunted the tiny office near the front doors of McAllister Hall—and lo and behold, there was Bill, hunched over the Teletype terminal, his feet swinging because they didn't reach the floor.

"When you use a computer, you can't make fuzzy statements," explains Bill of his love for the machine. "You make only precise statements."

Bill wasn't alone in his obsession. There were other computer nerds at Lakeside, tenth graders Paul Allen and Ric Weiland notable among them. In his memoir, Allen—future co-founder of Microsoft—remembers meeting Bill for the first time.

"I saw a gangly, freckle-faced eighth-grader edging his way into the crowd around the Teletype, all arms and legs and nervous energy," Allen writes. "You could tell three things about Bill Gates pretty quickly. He was really smart. He was really competitive; he wanted to *show* you how smart he was. And he was really, really persistent."

And even early on, Allen recalls, Bill had dollar signs in his eyes. He read his father's copies of *Fortune* "religiously," and one day he asked Allen what he imagined it would be like to run a Fortune 500 company. "I said I had no idea," writes Allen. "And Bill said, 'Maybe we'll have our own company someday.'"

WHEN YOU PUT young Warren and young Bill side by side, you see the type of focus they shared. It wasn't simply that both of them, from a young age exhibited hair-raising single-mindedness; it was also that they focused their obsessions on a goal, and it was the same goal: making money. Lots of it. As boys, Warren and Bill each proclaimed a wish to be super-successful and make a great deal of money; Bill mediated his number crunching through computing, whereas for Warren, the numbers themselves had an almost holy appeal. When he was seven years old, for instance, he had a near-death experience: hospitalized for a mysterious illness and refusing to eat, he healed himself by filling a page with numbers representing his future capital. "I don't have much money now," Warren told his nurse, "but someday I will and I'll have my picture in the paper."

The great thing about numbers is this: *they can be counted.* And counted *upon.* People are unpredictable, undependable, un-everything—calamity can strike at a moment's notice—but numbers you can track in a ledger; if you've got x dollars today and do y tomorrow to make more, they will almost always add up to the z figure you'd anticipated.

The numbers, and the money they represented, were a comfort and an escape for young Warren, a boy terrorized by his mother Leila's mood swings. A brilliant woman who'd grown up helping her

father publish a local paper, Leila Stahl Buffett learned to spell by
setting type. Later, she'd blame her migraines on a childhood spent
running the "jackhammer" of the family's Linotype machine. She
and Howard met as staffers at the student newspaper at the University of Nebraska, and in another, later era, Leila might have gone
on to become an editor or reporter—maybe at the *Washington Post*,
which her son would come, in time, to partly own. But like most
women in those days, she was bound for the home, and would translate her preternatural competence into picture-perfect housewifeli-
ness. But something darker lurked behind the scenes. Great verbal
thunderclaps would burst forth from Mother Buffett to shake which-
ever of her children was nearest. Doris, the eldest, took the majority of the verbal lashings; Roberta "Bertie," who joined the family
in 1933, managed to avoid much of her mother's ire. Warren often
found himself watching his mother's tirades, helpless to do anything
lest he, too, experience the ranting.

"There would be this flash, and then it didn't subside," Warren recalls of his mother's moods. "It was just endless."

Making money was therapeutic. It was something he could control. When Howard Buffett won a seat in the U.S. House of Representatives in 1942 and the family relocated to Washington, D.C.,
moneymaking was Warren's consolation for the loss of his Omaha
friends and family, and his sudden removal to a new school where
the other students looked down on him as a socially maladapt rube.
Among Warren's many D.C. hustles, the one he loved most was delivering the paper. Newspapers ran in his blood: Howard Buffett had
once hoped to be a reporter; Leila grew up covered in newsprint.
Warren relished throwing the papers, rising early to deliver the
Washington Post and the *Times-Herald*, and, adding an after-school
shift, the *Evening Star*. He mapped out his routes and raced to finish
them faster than he had the day before. It was like racing marbles in
the bathtub, only he was getting paid for it. To wit, when he filed his
tax return in 1944, he owed $7 in tax on $592.50 in income, a lot of

money back then. (He also declared $228 in interest and dividend income, and listed a $10 expense for "watch repair" and another $35 deduction for "Bicycle–Misc.") Not too shabby for a fourteen-year-old.

Then there was the income Warren didn't bother to report on his tax return: his ill-gotten gains from shoplifting. Warren had at last found a social niche—as a delinquent. On Saturdays, he and a pair of pals would raid the sporting goods section of the new Tenleytown Sears store.

Howard Buffett knew exactly the way to get his prodigal son back on the straight and narrow: threaten to take his money away. As Buffett recalls, his father told him he could either "do something in relation to [his] potential" or give up his paper route.

Warren figured he ought to do something in relation to his potential.

Staring at the sums he'd rigorously set down in his ledger, Warren decided it was time to start reinvesting his income. The holdings of Berkshire Hathaway today are about as eclectic as Warren's high school portfolio. Now it's See's Candies and GEICO insurance and Fruit of the Loom (and much, much, much more); back then, it was an Omaha hardware store, a Nebraska tenant farm, and starting businesses like a car-buffing operation in D.C., another that sold refurbished golf balls, and Buffett's Approval Service, which sold sets of collectible stamps. The real profit center, however, was the pinball machines.

A pinball machine is also a compounding machine. You buy it once, maybe pay for the odd repair, and then, literally, all a pinball machine does is take people's money. Coin after coin, game after game. One pinball machine pays for another pinball machine, and bingo! Now you've got two pinball machines swallowing change, and you can buy two more, and on and on, ad infinitum. Warren Buffett would have very happily supplied the entire Eastern Seaboard with his pinball machines had he been able to find enough suitable locations; as it was, he secured a nice little toehold in D.C. barbershops.

Sports betting was also included in the Buffett portfolio. In Omaha, Warren would go down to the track, but not to wager: rather, he'd pick up the "place" and "show" tickets people had discarded, not realizing they could collect on a horse's second- or third-place finish. Once he'd plucked the valuable scraps off the floor, his doting aunt Alice would cash out for him. (Kids weren't allowed to bet.) Later, Warren would discover another source of income from the track, handicapping horses and putting out a tip sheet, "Stable-Boy Selections."

Handicapping the stock market, Warren would find out, wasn't all that different from handicapping horses. And by the time he finished school back in Omaha in 1947, graduating sixteenth out of his class of 350 at Woodrow Wilson High, Buffett already knew that handicapping the market was what he was destined to do. He put "future stockbroker" under his picture in the yearbook and headed off to the University of Pennsylvania's Wharton business school.

What compounding was to Warren, coding became to Bill. He and the other Lakeside School programming prodigies had just gotten the hang of the Teletype when a Seattle area start-up, Computer Center Corporation, nicknamed C-Cubed, invited them to crash-test their machines—literally, their job was to run as many programs as they could, to see what prompted a crash. Bill and his pals, including Paul Allen, reveled in the free computer time—after school and on Saturdays, they'd design digital versions of blackjack, roulette, Monopoly. Bill's particular obsession was a war game he devised that was inspired by Napoléon. He'd type commands with a marker stuck in his mouth, rocking in his chair and tapping the keyboard with what Allen describes as an odd "six-finger, sideways scrabble."

Alas, all dreams must die. Or at any rate, go on hiatus. The C-Cubed honchos decided to call time on the crash-testing, at which point, Bill recalls, it was like, "OK, monkeys, go home." Bill and Paul scrambled for a workaround—they *needed* that computer. By that point, pretty much no one knew their way around the C-Cubed system better than they did—'twas a mere fillip to steal a few passwords from the administrators and shoplift computer time. And just as Warren's father had cottoned on to his son's scofflaw ways, the C-Cubed honchos picked up on the theft and updated their security software. The Lakeside gang cracked it in about an hour and a half. Proud of their accomplishment, they visited C-Cubed to demonstrate how they'd managed the feat. Ringleaders Bill and Paul were promptly banned from C-Cubed for three months.

As soon as that sentence had been served, Bill and Paul returned to C-Cubed with white flags in hand. Their days of hacking for personal benefit were over, they promised, but *surely* the skills they'd honed could be of use. Computer nerd fellowship prevailed: programmers Steve Russell and Dick Gruen took pity on the kids and put them to work.

Russell, a digital pioneer in his own right, who had created the *Spacewar!* video game while at MIT, had a particular affection for Bill. He found it remarkable that Bill, only a high school freshman at the time, could link certain types of bugs to specific programmers at headquarters: "Well, Mr. Faboli's code at this line, he's made the same mistake of not checking the semaphore when he's changing the status," Russell recalled as a typical example of Bill's error reports.

At least *someone* liked Bill. One former Lakeside student remembers him as "an extremely annoying person," and admits he took pleasure in giving him "a little bit of a hard time." But Bill gave as good as he got. He'd developed the charming tic of shouting "That's the stupidest thing I've ever heard!" at people; one hopes that *someone* had the wit to rejoin that it was statistically implausible for Bill Gates to continually hear ever-stupider things. Mellow Paul took Bill's churlishness in stride, volunteering alongside him at C-Cubed—right up until the day that brawny repo men arrived at the

C-Cubed office. The company was deeply in debt. "We're sitting there typing at the Teletypes, and these guys are coming in, taking the furniture," Bill recalls. Once the chairs were gone, Bill and Paul knelt by their terminals and kept typing, madly downloading the programs they'd written onto magnetic tape. The duo had learned much from the permanently shuttered C-Cubed—including, as Gates biographers Stephen Manes and Paul Andrews note, "how not to run a company."

The idea of running a company greatly interested Bill. As it did his recently acquired best friend, Kent Evans. A fellow habitué of the Teletype room in Lakeside's McAllister Hall, Kent Evans was chubby, frizzy-haired, gregarious, and quick to flash a smile that was lopsided due to his congenital cleft palate that had been "surgically repaired." He was also brash and uninhibited, upping the ante on Bill's headlong approach to whatever interested him. He and Bill pored over copies of *Fortune* together and came up with the name for Bill's first professional outfit: the Lakeside Programming Group, which he formed with Kent, Paul Allen, and Ric Weiland.

Their first gig came from Portland, Oregon–based Information Sciences, Inc., or ISI. The four boys were contracted to create a do-it-all payroll system, and the project was no joke: the task kept revealing new complexities. "You have these labor distribution reports," Bill later recalled, "and these quarterly tax reports, and health deduction reports . . ." And so on.

"It was a bitch of a program," seconded Paul.

The payroll system was still incomplete when Ric and Paul left for college. When LPG finally delivered a version of the program, ISI considered it unsatisfactory, and refused to dole out the agreed-upon free computer time. Towing Bill along, Kent stormed into the offices of Bill Gates Sr.'s white-shoe law firm in downtown Seattle, demanding that he send ISI a writ of holy war. A gentler missive was penned, and Kent and Bill were rehired by ISI to finish the job, in exchange for five thousand hours of computer time. They'd have until June 30, 1972, to use it.

By that time, Kent Evans would be dead.

IT'S TEMPTING TO suppose that the sudden passing of his closest friend had the same shattering impact on Bill that Leila Buffett's tantrums had on Warren: In each case, the boys' foundations were shaken, and they retreated into numbers, and logic, and systems, to shore themselves up. This isn't to suggest that Bill Gates and Warren Buffett are psychologically identical—they were not and are not—but to point out that they both reacted to trauma by sharpening their focus. For Bill, the cataclysm came in the midst of his and Kent Evans's next programming assignment, this one for their school. In 1971, Lakeside merged with St. Nicholas School, an all-girls' academy, and the coat-and-tie-wearing male students were flummoxed by the sudden influx of estrogen into the atmosphere. Hormones weren't the only thing ricocheting around: Most female students split their course load between Lakeside and the St. Nick's campus some ten miles off in Capitol Hill, and school administrators were tearing their hair out trying to assemble coherent class schedules. Stymied, they turned to Bill Gates.

Working with Kent, Bill set about building a scheduling program from scratch. Seemingly infinite variables had to be accounted for: How could software make sense of one kid requesting English lit, calculus, a biology lab, choir, and French—but, please, don't put three courses in a row—and another kid requesting the same course load, but with drum practice instead of choir, when, oy, you can't have drums upstairs and choir downstairs at the same time? Then add on the administrators' desire that class sizes be balanced, and all the girls commuting to and from St. Nick's . . . The two boys exhausted themselves working on the scheduling program. Sometimes they'd spend the night in the teachers' lounge or sleep in an unlocked classroom. It may have been too much for Kent.

While Bill would shoot straight down the slopes when skiing and could jump out of a trash can without touching the rim, this der-ring-do and athleticism set him apart from his best friend. Chubby Kent Evans was earthbound. But, spurred on perhaps by the arrival of girls at Lakeside, Kent was trying to get fit, and he'd enrolled in a mountaineering class. Bill was skeptical. "He didn't strike me as somebody who had any business up on the slopes," Bill later said.

Knowing his son was drained from his work with Bill, Kent's fa-ther pleaded with him to skip his class's upcoming hike on Mount Shuksan. On May 28, 1972, as the beginner mountaineers crossed a gentle but still-icy slope, Kent slipped, and wound up tumbling down the Curtis Glacier, hitting his head on jutting rocks as he fell. He died in the rescue helicopter.

Some observers blamed the pressures of the scheduling program for Kent's death. If that seems a reach, consider this: The teacher who'd first attempted to build the program expired mid-project, in a single-engine plane crash. Overwork and fatigue were cited as fac-tors in that tragedy, too.

Surely, Bill would have been forgiven for dropping the project. He was crushed. Kent Evans had been his constant companion. Asked to speak at the memorial service, he bowed out at the last minute, fearing he wouldn't be able to restrain his tears. "For two weeks I couldn't do anything at all," Bill later said. And then, sick of mourn-ing, he slogged on, calling on Paul Allen for aid. "And that," accord-ing to Bill, "sort of started a partnership that led to Microsoft."

Silver linings, as they say. Paul and Bill wrestled the scheduling program into submission, and then, with a thousand dollars' worth of computer time left before the ISI clock struck midnight, they wasted as much of it as they could writing a program that executed an endless loop. There must have been something Zen about watch-ing the circle retrace and retrace itself, drawing a black hole into which the two grieving young men could cast away their feelings. Years later, Paul Allen and Bill Gates funded a new building at Lakeside, named after Kent Evans. As of 1993, an updated version of their scheduling program was still in use.

BY THE TIME Warren Buffett and Bill Gates met, they'd spent a long time looking for each other. Though each man had claimed close working relationships over the years, this was a different kind of soul-connection, a friendship with no strings attached. And in the summer of 1991, both of them were in need of a friend: Bill was at the very start of the yearslong government investigations into Microsoft, and Warren was embarking on the beleaguering task of dragging the investment bank Salomon Brothers back from the brink. Each man was a lonely titan fixed in the public imagination as a personal brand—Bill the billionaire tech brat, Warren the Oracle of Omaha—with less power over the course of events in their business and private lives than the public gave them credit for. They had something else in common, too: Both Warren and Bill owed some measure of their success to Harvard. Bill, because he got in, and then quit; Warren because he hadn't gotten in in the first place.

When Bill returned to Seattle after that first-ever meeting and talkathon with Warren, one of the first things he did was to reach out to his brand-new bosom pal with a question: What did Warren consider to be the very best book about business? Warren responded by mailing him a copy of John Brooks's *Business Adventures*, a compilation of Brooks's *New Yorker* pieces detailing the triumphs and failures of executives at Fortune 500 companies like Xerox and Ford. "He loaned me his copy and we had a lot of fun talking about what we had learned from it," Bill said many years later, writing on his blog *Gates Notes* in 2014. The book was out of print at the time, but Bill still recalled it so fondly, he'd gone to the trouble of asking Brooks's family to let him print an excerpt online—a chapter on Xerox's triumphs and travails that proved so popular, *Business Adventures* was rushed back into print.

Warren, for his part, cemented the friendship by purchasing one

hundred shares of Microsoft. In Buffett terms, that's akin to someone throwing a penny in a wishing well; the act has symbolic, rather
than financial, meaning. Those hundred shares were Warren's way
of carving out mental space for the brilliant young man he'd just
met—he'd see the MSFT symbol float by on the ticker and recall that
he owned a tiny piece of the thing Bill so well understood: the future. "I wish I'd bought more," Warren later joked.

2

GETTING THERE

One of the young Warren Buffett's favorite texts was Dale Carnegie's *How to Win Friends and Influence People*, which he'd discovered in the back bedroom of his grandfather's house. Though it took some years for the lessons to settle, that book taught Warren that there are time-tested strategies for getting along with folks. Rule one: "Don't criticize, condemn or complain." Another: "If you are wrong, admit it quickly and emphatically." There were thirty rules in all, ones that an introverted kid could rely on.

The Intelligent Investor was another favorite book. Authored by Benjamin Graham, it was a user-friendly guide to "value investing," an approach to picking stocks that rubbished Wall Street smoke and mirrors and replaced it with mathematical analysis. Graham counseled that you could tell when a stock was underpriced by measuring the cost of a share of a company against the value of that company's assets. If the share price was less than what you'd get by selling the company for parts, well, congratulations: You'd just found yourself a great investment, with little downside risk. The thing of it was, you had to do your research.

Warren Buffett *loved* research. He read *The Intelligent Investor* shortly after it was published in 1949, and, as was his wont, reread it and read it again. And then as he waited for a response to his Harvard Business School application, Warren moved on to the academic tome from which *The Intelligent Investor* was derived, *Security Analysis*. Harvard rebuffed Warren, to his shock—after all, as a nineteen-year-old self-made businessman of some means, he'd figured his odds of getting in were very, very good. Alas. But *Security Analysis* co-authors Ben Graham and David Dodd both taught at Columbia Business School. Warren hastily submitted an application; a month before classes were to start, the application landed on the desk of the school's associate dean, David Dodd. Warren's fawning essay on their work *did the trick*. He was off to New York.

The fawning over Graham and Dodd was entirely sincere. Warren arrived at Columbia with the 725 pages of *Security Analysis* virtually memorized. It was his bible. And his admiration was repaid in kind: Dodd's class, Finance 111–112: Investment Management and Security Analysis, became a kind of pas de deux, with Warren and the professor going back and forth on matters such as the proper valuation of defaulted railroad bonds.

The next semester, Warren was enrolled in Benjamin Graham's marquee seminar. Considered the "dean of Wall Street," Ben Graham taught one class at Columbia, a "seminar on common stock valuation." The twenty students gathered around his table in January 1951 included working money managers auditing the course. They, like Warren, wanted to learn how the Graham-Newman Corporation was beating the stock market's overall performance by an average of 2.5 percent a year. Moreover, thanks to his unique value investing philosophy, Graham was posting these winning returns even as he minimized downside risk.

How had Ben Graham flipped Wall Street's "more risk = more reward" equation on its head?

Imagine, for a moment, that you—the reader—are a publicly traded company. Let's say you have assets worth $200,000, comprising your house, your car, the total resale value of all the stuff you've acquired over the years, and some savings. On the other side of the ledger, you carry $100,000 worth of debt: mortgage, credit card balances, et cetera. According to Graham, your *intrinsic value* is $100,000, or assets less debt. Now let's say you've divvied You Corp into one thousand shares of common stock, and each one trades for $100. In that case, the share price accurately reflects You Corp's intrinsic value. Ben Graham wouldn't buy a share of You Corp unless it was trading at a 50 percent discount on that value, or $50 per share. His belief—or, rather, his meticulous, market-tested theorem—was that it didn't matter whether You Corp stock had been heading up or down, because most of the time, eventually, the price of a stock and its intrinsic value would reach a rough parity. An investor could tune out the noise of market fluctuation, ignore the bearish or bullish forecasts of a company's earnings, and wait.

The other way that Graham minimized risk was by diversifying his portfolio. He bought tiny amounts of stock in lots of companies that met his 50 percent discount standard—"Cigar butts," as he referred to them, because the idea was to scoop up the stocks other investors had cast aside and drag out one final puff of profit. Some butts still smoldered; a few, inevitably, would turn out to be dead ends. Graham's insistence on a high discount on intrinsic value, and on spreading out his bets, created a "margin of safety." Even with a solid system, there had to be room for error.

If all of this sounds commonsensical, that's because Benjamin Graham and his business partner, Jerry Newman, and followers such as David Dodd and Warren Buffett made it so. Graham's thinking struck Warren with biblical force because, pre-Graham, stock-picking was a pastime a bit like surfing—paddle out and look for a wave. Many people, even now, surf the market that way. For Warren, Graham was an oceanographer mapping currents and breaks. He *understood* the waves.

If I hadn't read [The Intelligent Investor] in late 1949, I'd have had a different future. It instantly clicked with me, that what he was saying made sense. And then the chance to study with him, and under Dave Dodd . . . it shaped my professional life.

As Graham's star pupil, Warren had fixed his post-graduation hopes on a job at Graham-Newman. Uncharacteristically, he even offered to work for free. Graham may have been tempted, but he turned him down.

He just said, "Lookit, Warren. In Wall Street still, the 'white-shoe' firms, the big investment banks, they don't hire Jews. We only have the ability to hire a very few people here. And, therefore, we only hire Jews." . . . It was sort of like his version of affirmative action.

Warren was familiar with the anti-Semitism commonplace in early-to-midcentury America. His grandfather Ernest wasn't coy about his contempt for the Jewish owners of Sommers and Hinky Dinky, two of the grocery store chains cutting into his market. As a stockbroker, Warren's father rubbed elbows with Jewish money managers and bankers—witness the meeting with Sidney Weinberg, of Goldman Sachs, when Warren was ten—but Congressman Howard Buffett's isolationist foreign policy wasn't entirely extricable from a general antipathy in America to Jewish immigration, what with Hitler on the march and millions of Jewish refugees desperately seeking visas. And it didn't seem to bother him, or Leila Buffett, that their home in Washington, D.C., was in a "restricted" neighborhood that disallowed Jews from purchasing houses.

Fortunately, Warren Buffett had no anti-Semite impulses. Indeed, Ben Graham was his hero. Jumping ahead, he'd count numerous Jews as friends, among them Walter Schloss, Graham's sharp-minded employee, and Rabbi Myer Kripke, an early investor with Buffett who presided over the Beth El Synagogue in Omaha. Later, on behalf of Berkshire Hathaway, Buffett would invest in numerous companies founded and led by Jews. He deeply admired those proprietors, for they ran tight ships, as Buffett believes everyone should. Long story short, Warren Buffett has always been an intrinsic-value man, through and through.

And so, when it was explained why there was no job for him at Graham-Newman, Warren was disappointed, but he understood. He licked his wounds and headed back to Omaha, where another dream awaited him: Susan Thompson, the woman he was dead set on making his wife.

IT WAS SUMMERTIME when Warren met Susie. He was about to head off to Columbia; his younger sister, Bertie, was on her way to Northwestern, where she and Susie were set to live together. On an inspired whim, Bertie fixed her older brother and her future roommate up on a date. "I walked into their house, and he was sitting in this chair in the living room, and he made some sarcastic quip," Susie recalled years later. She quipped back at smart-aleck Warren, and wondered: *Who is this jerk?*

Susie Thompson was out of Warren Buffett's league: pretty, popular, confident, and worldly in ways that belied the fact that she hadn't yet strayed far from Omaha. It's easy to imagine the two of them suffering through their first date—say, at a local lunch counter, with soignée Susie casting side-eye glances at Warren's rumpled trousers, laughing politely at his rehearsed jokes, and draining her malted milkshake as he droned on about his favorite topic, stocks. Susie dazzled Warren, and she understood that, by rights, a congressman's son with the Midas touch was a catch. But she had no interest in being caught by him.

The thing was, Susie Thompson had already met the man she considered the love of her life: tall, handsome Milton Brown. Warren was the hand grenade Susie's father, William "Doc" Thompson, a psychology professor at the University of Nebraska, launched at his daughter in an effort to blow up this relationship. The problem was that Milton Brown was Jewish. Susie continued seeing him. Off in New York, Warren penned Susie letter after letter, even as he distracted himself with other entanglements, such as an oddball romance with Miss Nebraska 1949, Vanita Mae Brown.

Both Browns—Milton and Vanita Mae—wound up on the dustheap. Warren won over Susie by wooing her by proxy: He'd show up at the Thompson house, Susie would slip out the back to avoid him, and Warren would spend the evening "flirting" with her father.

Warren was smarter than you even know. My dad had a mandolin up in the attic, and Warren said, "Doc, get out your mandolin and I'll play with you, with my ukulele." So they played together. And my father fell in love with Warren, and he kept saying to me—you don't understand this boy, he has a heart of gold.

Warren figured that the only way he'd earn Susie's love was by vanquishing his social awkwardness once and for all. Thus, he signed up for a Dale Carnegie course in public speaking, and the week he proposed to Susie, he won the class's "pencil award"—a prize given to the student who'd best utilized their training. A framed Dale Carnegie certificate now hangs on the wall in Warren's office at Berkshire Hathaway, not far from a portrait of Howard. It is, Warren likes to say, the most important degree he has. But it wasn't Warren's budding self-confidence that won Susie over. Quite the opposite: Once she and Warren began dating in earnest, Susie glimpsed the vulnerable boy under Warren's cocky veneer. All his life, Warren had sought out women who could shore up the emptiness in him that his mother had carved out during her terrible rages. Now he'd found a woman who nourished herself by being a source of comfort to people in need. Susie Thompson wanted to take care of Warren. He wanted nothing more.

The more time Warren spent with Susie, the more she noted his declining desire to spend time with his mother. As a consequence, Susie never got to spend much time around the person she was replacing as the woman in Warren's life. In the few moments when they were all in one another's company, she started noticing that Warren could manage to say only a couple of words to his mother, and those through gritted teeth. Sometimes while turning his back. With Susie, it was a very different story; they couldn't keep their hands off each other. "They were so infatuated," complained one relative. "Kissing, sitting on each other's laps. It was awful." As for what Warren's mother thought of being abandoned for a woman she'd barely met—well, we can only imagine.

Warren and Susie were married on April 19, 1952. Warren packed up his aunt Alice's car for the honeymoon, drove it to the Dundee Presbyterian Church, and, before a crowd of hundreds that he couldn't see clearly because he'd decided not to wear his glasses, vowed to love and cherish Susan Thompson for richer or poorer, in sickness and in health, 'til death did them part. And the vow held—if not in quite the way either newlywed expected.

When Susie got into Aunt Alice's car after the ceremony, excited for her honeymoon road trip out West, she discovered that Warren had filled the back seat with business ledgers and copies of *Moody's Manual*.

The *Moody's Manual*s would become a familiar sight in the tiny apartment near downtown Omaha where the young couple settled. Warren was indifferent to the colorful furnishings Susie had bought with the lean $1,500 budget she'd been given; he wasn't fussed about the quality of his wife's cooking, so long as there was ice cream in the freezer and Pepsi in the fridge. As a practical matter, Susie Buffett's new husband mainly required that she monitor the light bulb in his reading lamp, for when he was home, reading was what Warren did. *Moody's Manual*, annual reports, the *Wall Street Journal*. Other wifely duties included "head rubs, cuddling, hugs, and assistance in dealing with people." She helped him get dressed in the morning. She even cut his hair.

"It was the same kind of unconditional love you would get from a parent," Warren recalls. "Susie was as big an influence on me as my dad, or bigger probably, in a different way."

Years later, Susie would say that Warren saw himself as a flower and her as a watering can. And because Susie loved to tend the human garden, how, she'd ask, could she not feel good about that?

Soon there was another flower in the Buffett patch. On July 30, 1953, Susan Alice Buffett was born—"Little Sooz," as the family called her. She was a delightful, easygoing baby, and by the spring of 1954, Warren and Susie's elder son, Howard, was on the way.

A rumor floated around that Little Sooz had to sleep in an unused dresser drawer because Warren refused to pay for a crib. That wasn't true, but Warren's reputation for tightfistedness was well earned: He relished thinking about all the work dollars could do—and, consequently, hated spending any of the small fortune he was amassing. Susie tolerated her husband's penny-pinching on the condition that every night when Warren returned from work, he'd put Little Sooz to bed. For a few minutes each evening, the *Moody's Manuals* were forgotten in favor of Warren's warbling rendition of "Over the Rainbow," Little Sooz's favorite lullaby.

Warren needed to be prodded to bond with people—even, in this case, his baby daughter. For Susie, though, bonding came naturally. She skipped the small talk, looked straight into folks' eyes, and asked them, sincerely, *How are you?* "When Susie said that," recalls one friend, "she meant: How are you doing in life? How is your soul?"

Yin to her husband's yang in so many ways, Susie did share with Warren a willingness to chart an independent course. Just as it required a certain subversive streak for a bright young trader in the 1950s to eschew Wall Street and go it alone, so Susie's extracurricular activities were, at a minimum, unorthodox. Most budding housewives in that *Leave It to Beaver* era were consumed with propriety;

they wanted to move into a big house in the best neighborhood and join the right clubs and make the right friends. Susie had additional concerns. The girl who'd once wanted to marry a Jewish boy against her father's wishes had become a woman alert to the burgeoning civil rights movement: *Brown v. Board of Education* was decided in 1954; the Montgomery bus boycott began in 1955. Though she had plenty to keep her busy with two young children at home, Susie-the-gardener began planting the seeds of a lifelong avocation, trying to play her small part to make the world a nicer, fairer place.

Neither Warren nor Susie minded that their lives ran on parallel tracks, as Susie would later put it. She cared for the children and cultivated her interests, while Warren, operating from an upstairs study, read until late at night, seeking fresh ways to invest the increasing amount of capital at his disposal. By October 1956, Warren was managing more than half a million dollars, including his own money, not to mention still doing all of his own filing and bookkeeping. The parallel tracks did converge occasionally, however: As the summer of 1957 faded from view, Susie discovered she was pregnant again.

BILL'S OWN YOUTHFUL dreams were written on a computer chip. The history of personal computing arguably begins in 1969, when Intel was approached to develop the programmable 4004 chip. The programmability was key—if software could be written onto that speck of silicon and wire, it would obviate the need for gargantuan mainframes. An apparatus like the ASR-33 could be fitted with chips that allowed it to process data; it could calculate the equation $2 + 2 = 4$ all by itself. That was the idea, anyway. The rub was that not much information could be stored on a 4004. Which is why, in the spring of 1972, Bill Gates and Paul Allen were so enamored of an article in *Electronics* magazine announcing Intel's release of the 8008, a chip with double the processing firepower. Paul figured that he and Bill could write a version of BASIC for the 8008. Which would be a monumental feat, Paul figured, because "ordinary people would be able to buy computers for their offices, even their homes."

And those computers would still be "dog-slow and pathetic," snapped Bill.

He did see one use for the 8008: Whereas a version of BASIC would gobble up most of the chip's memory, a car-counting program was less greedy. Paul agreed that this was a sound idea. Lakeside had paid $4,200 for the class-scheduling software; Bill and Paul used $360 of that to buy themselves a "computer on a chip," as Intel called the 8008. Their fingers trembled as they undid the foil wrapping to reveal a purple ceramic rectangle with a gold-plated metal lid, about an inch long, with nine tiny pins protruding from each side, like teeth. "For two guys who'd spent their formative years with massive mainframes, it was a moment of wonder," Paul recalled.

Bill named their new venture Traf-O-Data; the short-term aim was to develop a piece of hardware with the capacity to count passing cars. The long-term goal was total global domination of . . . something. Bill was about to set off for Harvard when with the help of Paul Gilbert, an engineering student at the University of Washington, they unveiled the first properly working Traf-O-Data box. The key thing was the simulator, a program mimicking a mainframe's operations that would support Bill's car-counting code. If you want an explanation of these technicalities, look elsewhere—Manes and Andrews's biography *Gates* goes into excruciating detail. For our purposes, suffice it to say that as a program that girds other programs, programs that *do* things for the end user, a simulator is a distant cousin of an operating system. Like Microsoft Windows, to cite the obvious example.

And so, Bill swashbuckled off to Cambridge, certain that his future as a traffic data magnate was secure.

The impression he made upon arrival was poor. Professor Thomas Cheatham, director of Harvard's historic Aiken Computation Laboratory, described 1973-era Bill thusly: "He's an obnoxious human being. . . . He'd put people down when it was not necessary, and just generally not be a pleasant fellow to have around the place." Bill's roommate recalls that he rarely bothered to use bedsheets, and no one remembers him going to parties or having a girlfriend. His social life seems to have revolved around weekly, all-night cram sessions for Math 55, a course so difficult, it made the brightest of Harvard's math prodigies sweat spinal fluid. Bill discovered to his horror that he was not among the brightest, at least where higher math was concerned. Home for winter break, he told Paul that his professor had gotten a PhD at sixteen. It hurt Bill, Paul later wrote, that he would never be "the smartest guy in that room."

Meeting math minds better than his stung. But Bill still had his computing pedigree to consult when his ego needed soothing. Comprehensive rejection by women, though—that *burned*.

Recall the panty raid sequence in *Revenge of the Nerds*, played for yuks in 1984 and horrendous to watch now: The trio of nerd heroes spy on sorority sisters showering, et cetera, and distribute nude shots of one of the women. Hilarious. At Harvard, Bill reports that as a freshman he skirted this type of hatefulness: instead poring over his sizable collection of *Playboy* and *Penthouse* magazines and, if rumors are true, making visits to Boston's so-called Combat Zone, known for its porno theaters and prostitutes. "I used to hang out in the Zone for a little while, just watching what was going on," Bill says. "Mostly I just sat at this pizza place and read books."

Make of that what you will.

Some guys start rock bands to meet women. Maybe Bill figured that the fortune he was sure to make from Traf-O-Data would do the trick. Alas, as biographers Stephen Manes and Paul Andrews put it, the company "continued to roll down the highway of commerce like a Mercedes with three flat tires." Bill concluded his first year at Harvard covered with bruises—emotional ones, at any rate.

Paul Allen, twenty-one and a college dropout, was urging Bill to drop out of school, too. In the summer of 1974, Paul accepted a job as a programmer at Honeywell, in Boston, and when Bill returned to Cambridge, the two visited frequently. The computer revolution was on the horizon, and Paul was worried they'd miss it. And what was Bill getting out of Harvard, anyway? His sophomore year was soon off to a bumpy start: Bill took up poker and was racking up thousands of dollars in losses.

The good news was that Bill Gates had just met Steve Ballmer. They lived in the same dorm and had befriended each other in a graduate-level economics class. On the surface, Steve was Bill's opposite—a big, socially hyperactive guy, very hail-fellow-well-met. They studied together, went to the movies, engaged in high-volume debates. In some ways, Steve was the second coming of Kent Evans, and Bill trusted him so much, he even let Steve drag him out to parties at the Fox Club, a social organization similar to a frat. "I was so antisocial I wouldn't have even known they existed," Bill later admitted, "but Steve Ballmer decided I needed some exposure to, I guess, drinking."

And Bill Gates might have kept on muddling along like that, had it not been for a magazine article.

Paul Allen recalls the afternoon he ran to Bill's Harvard dorm room with a hot-off-the-presses copy of the January 1975 issue of *Popular Electronics*, with a photo of the Altair minicomputer on its cover: "I burst in on him cramming for finals," Allen writes. "As Bill read the story, he began rocking back and forth in his chair, a sign that he was deep in concentration."

The Altair was a computer you could build yourself from a kit. An Albuquerque model-rocket-modules outfit called Micro Instrumentation and Telemetry Systems (MITS) was retailing the kits for $397, and according to Paul Allen, the base model came with just enough memory to program the box's lights to blink. There was no keyboard, no screen, no USB port; from the perspective of the twenty-first century, the Altair doesn't look like a computer at all. Bill, reading, saw the Altair as the beginning of the future, for, in his rocking, he'd cottoned on to the essential thing about the machine: You could add memory. And with more memory, that box could *do things*.

The personal computing revolution was officially underway.

Bill and Paul dropped everything, scrambling to write a version of BASIC that could run on the Altair's 8080 Intel chip, a recent upgrade from the holy 8008. What they didn't know was that the picture of the Altair on the *Popular Electronics* cover was basically a sham—a cardboard mock-up. The MITS founders were scrambling, too, trying to assemble working models of the Altair as kit orders flooded in from hobbyists nationwide. Paul and Bill didn't bother ordering an Altair of their own—they figured their leg up on the competition was the simulator Paul had built for the Traf-O-Data machine. All they had to do was find a computer they could work on as they updated Paul's simulator code for Intel's 8080 chip.

Harvard's Aiken Computation Laboratory had computers.

Bill and Paul more or less moved into the lab. Paul was still working at Honeywell, kind of, and Bill was still going to class, kind of, but they spent every night holed up in Aiken, coding furiously between catnaps. As a nonstudent, Paul wasn't even supposed to be there. But because they were usually the only people around, no one cared. At least not at first. Computer time at Aiken was free to Bill, as a student, but not free to the university, and Bill and Paul were gobbling up huge chunks of it. The goal was to write a program that consumed a little less than the 4K of memory promised by an enhanced Altair, and so as they worked, they competed to see who could execute subroutines—blocks of code—in the fewest bytes. Their work was stored, via the U.S. Defense Department's ARPANET, on a mainframe hundreds of miles away at Carnegie Mellon University.

Looking to get a jump on the (still-hypothetical) competition, Bill and Paul wrote to MITS on Traf-O-Data letterhead, saying they had a version of BASIC that worked with the 8080 chip, and were hoping to sell it to Altair hobbyists alongside the kits. When they received no reply, they phoned. MITS founder Ed Roberts picked up. He'd been getting plenty of this kind of call, he said; the first person who showed up in Albuquerque with a working version of BASIC would get the contract.

At the end of February 1975, Paul Allen flew to New Mexico with a punch tape printout of a 3.2K BASIC program. Roberts, a burly former air force engineer, picked him up from the airport and drove him to MITS headquarters in a down-at-the-heels strip mall. The next morning, after Roberts had located an Altair model with sufficient memory to run the program and hooked it up to a Teletype, Paul loaded in the code. That took ten excruciating minutes. The skepticism in the room was palpable. Paul had never tested the program on an actual Altair—he and Bill had only ever simulated the machine. "A single character out of place might halt the program cold when it ran on the real chip," Allen later recalled thinking.

But then, as Paul wrote in his memoir, the Teletype printer "clattered to life."

"I gawked at the upper-case characters," he says. "I couldn't believe it. But there it was: MEMORY SIZE?"

Roberts's colleague Bill Yates yelled out, "Hey, it printed something!" None of the other software hawkers had gotten that far. But the proof in the pudding would be getting the BASIC-installed Altair to execute a command. Allen typed:

PRINT 2 + 2

"Oh my god!" shouted Ed Roberts. "It printed '4'!"

Paul returned to Cambridge with a licensing agreement from MITS and a working Altair. Then the shit hit the fan: Harvard administrators had gotten the rental bill for those two months of "free" computer time in Aiken Lab, and they were irate that one of their students was abusing his access, and for commercial rather than academic purposes, at that. They were threatening Bill with disciplinary action. Bill scrambled to mount a defense, bowing and scraping before the disciplinary committee and agreeing to both steer clear of Aiken Lab and put a version of his BASIC in the public domain. (Note: Importantly, this wasn't the version of BASIC demoed in Albuquerque.) Bill spent the rest of the semester with his head down, working off the Altair in his dorm room. Following his sophomore year, he took a semester off, came back in 1976, then promptly dropped out, with two semesters left for graduation. Mentally he was already long gone, off to join the revolution.

ONE OF THE astonishments for Bill upon meeting Warren was the discovery that Warren didn't own a computer. He tried with all his might to convince Warren to buy one; Warren couldn't see the need. "I don't care how my stock portfolio is doing every five minutes," he told Bill. "And I can do my income taxes in my head." Bill offered to send the best-looking woman at Microsoft to Warren's home in Omaha to teach him how to use the machine.

"You've made me an offer I almost can't refuse," Warren replied. "But I will refuse it."

Bill was less stubborn. Before he boarded his helicopter to fly back to Seattle, Warren had coaxed a promise from his new friend to visit him in Omaha and take in a Cornhuskers game and play a few hands of bridge. Bill agreed on the condition that Warren return the favor. "Whenever," Warren said, because although he was a busy man, he kept his schedule open. Another astonishment: When Warren Buffett showed scheduled-to-the-minute Bill Gates his day planner, Bill saw that its pages were nearly empty. "How do I know what I want to think about when?" Warren explained.

This moment has come up again and again in interviews with Bill: In a 2017 appearance with Warren on the *Charlie Rose* show on PBS, for instance, Bill once more detailed the revelatory impact of realizing that there was real value—including financial value—in leaving himself time to let his mind, just . . . drift. "I had every minute packed, and I thought that was the only way you could do things,"

Bill told Rose. But Warren showed him that "you control your time, and that sitting and thinking may be of much higher priority . . . you feel like you need to go and see all these people[, but] it's not a proxy of your seriousness that you fill every minute in your schedule."

As Warren explained, more succinctly, to Bill: You can buy anything you want, basically, but you can't buy time. It was the first of many lessons these men would teach each other over the years.

3

BUSINESS ADVENTURES

On a Friday afternoon in late May 1998, Bill and Warren ambled into the University of Washington's Husky Union Building in Seattle. They were there to give a talk to 350 business school students, and because the talk would be filmed, a makeup artist powdered Bill's nose and trimmed Warren's eyebrows, much to the amusement of Melinda, Susie, and Kay Graham, who'd be watching the chat from the sidelines. Bill had just spent two days hosting several dozen prominent CEOs, including Warren, at Microsoft's annual summit meeting, and he'd spend the next two days hosting Graham and the Buffetts at his home, where a great deal of bridge-playing was on the agenda. (Teammates Bill and Warren with their silent gameplay, reading each other's clues, are tough to beat, as their opponents would regularly find out.)

A primary concern, heading into the talk, was that it would go on so long it would interfere with that evening's bridge game. A *Fortune* reporter, observing backstage, noted with some wonder that forty-two-year-old Bill was starting to look like a man rather than an overgrown boy, and that he treated Warren with "a warm hint of deference, quite a contrast to his usual debater's demeanor."

The first topic on the table was the obvious one: How had these two men both gotten "richer than God"?

Bill credited his luck in having been exposed to computers when both he and the tech industry were relatively young. He demurred on describing the myriad ways in which he had steered his and Paul's small company into a position of global dominance, midwifing in the process a digital age wherein barely a calculator could function without some debt to Microsoft software.

Warren, for his part, spoke at some length about "rationality"—more important than IQ, in his opinion—and the importance of good habits.

All this was not much of an explanation. If you really want to know how Warren Buffett became worth a cool $36 billion by mid-1998, and Bill Gates an even better $48 billion, here goes.

IT IS SIMULTANEOUSLY very easy and very difficult to explain how Warren Buffett became so fabulously wealthy. The difficulty is apparent if one merely cocks an eye at Berkshire Hathaway, the company he purchased in 1965, and specifically at its organizational chart: The company is a many-tentacled thing, and to understand—like, *really* understand—how each dollar of the Buffett fortune was made, you'd have to write a book thousands of pages long that digs into the singular details of every one of Warren's business deals. And yet, if you pan out, so you can see the forest for the trees, the secrets of Warren's success aren't so hard to discern. He worked like a dog, looked for bargains and drove harder ones, evolved his thinking as he went along, and surrounded himself with people who could be counted upon, like Charlie Munger, vice chairman of Berkshire Hathaway and Warren's right-hand man until Charlie's death in 2023. Warren also made money by, whenever possible, not spending any: Kay Graham liked to tell a story about once asking Warren for a dime so she could make a phone call, and Warren replying that he only had a quarter on him, so he'd have to make change. He was just as miserly with the managers of the many businesses that fed into Berkshire, scouring expense reports and scoffing at development schemes he considered too dear. A penny saved isn't just a penny earned, in Warren's accounting; a penny saved is *many* pennies earned, thanks to the magic of compounding.

Much has already been written about the magic trick Warren Buffett performed in turning the slender $105,000 invested in Buffett Associates, Ltd., founded May 1, 1956, into the behemoth Berkshire Hathaway, one Class A share of which trades for $544,050 as of September 26, 2023. Other great fortunes have been made in America, but only Warren Buffett has minted a treasure on par with the GDP of a medium-size nation simply by *investing*. He bought stock in companies, and then he began buying companies outright, always paying cash. That's it. Think about it: Warren Buffett didn't drill any oil wells, or invent anything, or build any skyscrapers, he just *made money*. Nothing much has changed in his approach to collecting money since he was a kid; he's still finding every which way he can to earn another dollar, just because he likes to watch fat stacks of cash pile up, then figure out how to turn those piles into more piles. Lots of boys have fathers who are stockbrokers and decide to go into the same business as their dads; only Warren, ailing at the hospital at age seven, scribbled a list of numbers signifying his future capital and seized on it as a reason to live.

Warren Buffett is a lovely man in so many ways, but can we all agree that this is *weird*?

Which is another thing about Warren worth pointing out: He's happy to be weird. Not alienating—the man likes to be liked—but an outlier, singing his own tune. The walls he threw up around himself to protect against his mother's scathing rebukes have provided cladding against peer pressure and groupthink; he seems to have taken deep to his heart the line of Emerson's his father used to recite: "The great man is he who in the midst of the crowd keeps with perfect sweetness the independence of solitude." Or, as Benjamin Graham wrote in *The Intelligent Investor*, "You are neither right nor wrong because the crowd disagrees with you." You're only right if you're *right*, and time will tell, in that case.

Time has told. Warren Buffett has been proven monumentally, epochally correct. And the first big bet he made was on himself: When he launched Buffett Associates, Ltd., he rejected the common practice of working as a broker-on-commission, a model that necessitated making trades for the sake of making trades, and instead structured his business as a partnership, taking half the upside on his investments above a 4 percent threshold but also assuming personal responsibility for a significant portion of the downside. "If I broke even, I lost money. And my obligation to pay back losses was not limited to my capital," Warren explained. "It was unlimited." He was thus incentivized to perform.

For the first five years of Warren Buffett's solo investment career, he performed by investing the Ben Graham way, hunting down "cigar butt" stocks. From Graham, he'd also learned the art of capital allocation, the practice of moving money around, ideally from less profitable businesses to ones with higher rates of return. Warren's partner/clients were pleased—he beat the market—and Warren set up several additional partnerships. But with the Dow Jones soaring 34 percent in 1958, cigar butt stocks were hard to find. Warren sniffed a bubble, and he wasn't alone: As Gilbert Burck wrote in a 1959 article in *Fortune*, "The market's sheer exuberance baffled almost everybody, including the professionals." Burck went on to argue, cautiously, that investors might be witnessing the birth of a new kind of stock market, wherein the laws of gravity that had prevailed in 1929 no longer applied, given the bullish outlook for American business as a whole.

Warren was dubious. He was still hunting companies like Dempster Mill Manufacturing, a Nebraska-based maker of windmills and irrigation systems that, when he started buying the stock, traded at a fourth of the price of its liquidation value. This kind of investing required patience and a certain grim determination to pry shares of a cheap stock out of the death grip of whoever was holding them. Warren excelled at this. But change was in the air, and it was augured by Charlie Munger.

The first Warren Buffett heard of Charlie Munger, it was at a meeting with two prospective investors. Dr. Edwin Davis and his wife, Dorothy, were Omaha locals given Warren's name by a prominent New York City money manager. Considering the investment of a significant sum, the Davises were a touch nonplussed by the rumpled whiz kid who turned up in their living room and made an improbable pitch: He'd require the couple to give him absolute control over their money, no questions asked and no information given, aside from an annual summary of the fund's performance. Dr. Davis seemed to tune out as Warren talked, but when Dorothy turned to him to ask what he wanted to do, he suggested they give Warren $100,000.

I said, "Dr. Davis, you know, I'm delighted to get this money. But you weren't really paying a lot of attention to me while I was talking. How come you're doing it?"

And he said, "Well, you remind me of Charlie Munger."

Two years later, Warren and Charlie met in person. It was a date with destiny. Munger came from a prominent family in Omaha—in fact, he'd briefly worked Saturday shifts at Warren's grandfather's grocery store—but he'd left for California years earlier. Returning in the summer of 1959 to settle his father's estate, Munger joined Warren and two other men for lunch at the tony Omaha Club. "A book with legs," according to his children, Munger had talked his way into Harvard Law School despite never completing his undergraduate degree. Which is to say, Dr. Davis was on to something when he noted the similarity between him and Warren Buffett, who'd talked himself into Columbia Business School at the last second.

Six years Warren's senior, Charlie boasted a thriving Los Angeles-area law practice. But he was bored. Listening to Warren talk about money management—and listening was something Charlie Munger didn't do much, since he liked to talk—he wondered whether he could dabble in some money managing of his own. Warren didn't see why not, and when Charlie returned to the West Coast, he and Warren got into the habit of speaking daily on the phone. At first, Warren was the teacher and Charlie very much the student, where investing was concerned. Over time, however, Charlie would prod Warren to think beyond the hunt for cigar butts.

Warren had encountered his future Berkshire Hathaway business partner just as his money management practice was set to take off in earnest. By 1960, Warren was no longer scouting for new clients; they came to him, and he was selective. That year, Buffett's several partnerships outperformed the market by an astounding 29 percent. He was still handling all the bookkeeping and filing and check mailing himself.

On January 1, 1962, Warren dissolved the eleven partnerships he'd set up into one consolidated fund: Buffett Partnership, Ltd. BPL, as the entity was known, launched with $7.2 million in net assets. It was time to get a proper office.

The space he rented at Kiewit Plaza (now Blackstone Plaza) made for a short commute, a mere twenty blocks from his house on Farnam Street. Warren likes to say that he would "tap-dance to work"; back then, when he was young and spry, he perhaps literally could. He shared the space with his father, and for the last years of Howard Buffett's life, he and his son worked within shouting distance of each other.

Warren's big break was a stock market slide. He'd been waiting, waiting, waiting for the bubble to burst—for it was, indeed, a bubble—and when it did, he pounced, scooping up underpriced stocks like so many "show" and "place" tickets at the racetrack. Panic-selling brokers must have been infuriated when they turned on their TVs to see crew-cut young Warren, utterly sanguine, explaining why the market tumble had been all too predictable. "For some time, stocks have been rising at rather rapid rates," he explained. But neither corporate earnings nor dividends had increased in tandem, he went on to note, and so, Warren pointed out, it was "not to be unexpected that perhaps a correction of some of those, uh, unusual factors on the upside might occur on the downside." At this, young Warren Buffett couldn't keep a little smile—maybe even a smirk—from crossing his face.

Warren went on a buying spree. But he wasn't only hunting down cigar butts: Charlie Munger encouraged him to get his nose out of balance sheets and consider a company's "intangibles." Munger was especially interested in the concept of *competitive advantage*. As he saw it, and as he'd come to convince Warren, if a company has a sustainable edge in its niche, it will rebuff competitors and continue to thrive. To cite a simple example of the principle: Customers who have already purchased a Gillette razor are much more likely than not to continuously buy the Gillette blades that fit that razor, rather than start over by switching to another brand. In industry parlance, this type of competitive advantage is called a "moat," because it protects a company's leadership position in the marketplace. A drug patent constitutes a moat; so do the economies of scale enjoyed by behemoth retailers such as Walmart, and the enduring fandom of the *Star Wars* brand.

A trusted brand can also make for a moat—as Warren proved when he tested out Munger's competitive advantage theory with his legendary investment in American Express. Which is a story of distress: personal distress, civic distress, a distressed stock.

The prologue to the story goes like this: A commodity trader had decided to corner the global soybean oil market. He was warehousing vast quantities of the stuff in tanks belonging to an obscure American Express subsidiary, and, as he borrowed against the value of the oil in said tanks, he filled them with seawater so it appeared he owned much more inventory than he did. American Express had guaranteed the quantity of oil. When the ruse was discovered, lenders to the swindler called on AmEx to recoup their losses, which were in the $150–$175 million range. American Express stock nosedived.

Two days later, President John F. Kennedy was assassinated.

Like everyone else in America, Warren was stunned. But he did not lose his focus. Buried in the back pages of papers filled with news of the shooting there were a few items about American Express's travails. Investors were racing for the exits—in short order, AmEx's share price fell by about 40 percent—and it seemed that one of the nation's blue-chip financial firms was about to go belly-up.

As was his wont, Warren decided to do a little digging. He figured what American Express sold was *trust*, and he wanted to find out whether the scandal had shaken Main Street consumers' confidence in the brand. Were people still whipping out their AmEx cards and purchasing American Express Travelers Cheques? Turned out, they were.

By this point, American Express was considered a distressed stock—cheap, but to the naked eye, high risk. While Warren mulled whether to purchase shares, his own father lay dying. He'd sit at Howard's bedside and run the Buffett version of Hamlet's soliloquy in his head: "To invest, or not to invest?"

Warren chose to invest, working solidly through his grief. He did it bit by bit, not wanting to make a big move and so drive up the price. Still, in short order he sank $3 million into the stock. He would spend his days at the office, come home briefly to change, and then head straight out again to sit with his father in the hospital. But one day, his children saw him arrive home, more miserable than ever, and announce that he was going to his mother's house instead of to the hospital. They asked him why. "Grandpa died today," he said, and then left. Those were his last words on the matter; he sat through his father's funeral in silence. His slow, steady purchase of AmEx stock— the biggest investment in Warren's career so far—continued without a hitch. Over the next three years, his investment would quadruple.

As a father, Howard Buffett was adored and adoring, yet remote. When Warren was a kid, he'd camped out at his father's office, watching him work, and campaigned with him on his long-shot but ultimately successful run for Congress. Fiercely Republican—a friend described his politics as "to the right of God"—Howard was likely to be found with his nose in a book or a newspaper, emerging now and then to inveigh against President Franklin Delano Roosevelt and his free-spending New Deal initiatives. He'd work himself up into a real lather, cursing fiat currency and preaching the nobility of the gold standard. Warren wound up scrapping his dad's ideology, but he never stopped looking up to him. This was a man who, when the bank employing him went bust in the wake of the great crash of 1929, stripping him of both job and savings, had the sangfroid to open a brokerage of his own. That it was soon profitable was due in no small part to Howard Buffett's willingness to buy when everyone else was yelling, "Sell, sell, sell!" To this day, a portrait of Howard Buffett hangs over Warren's desk, the paterfamilias a constant reminder of the principles of honesty, scrupulousness, and keeping an even keel. His death, Warren confessed to a friend many years later, was "like someone beating me."

IT'S HARD TO decide where to start the story of Warren Buffett and Berkshire Hathaway. You could start it way back on December 12, 1962, when Warren called his broker in New York and told him to buy two thousand shares of Berkshire for $7.50 a share—a classic cigar butt, trading well below liquidation value. Or you could commence on May 10, 1965, the date Warren finally seized control of the corporation, a takeover launched out of sheer pique. But the most entertaining way to begin this story is with Hetty Green, the notorious "Witch of Wall Street."

Green was one of the original investors in the textile mill business that later became known as Berkshire Hathaway. A value investor *avant la lettre*, Henrietta Green sold her trousseau to buy government bonds, turned her inheritance into a fortune worth more than $2 billion in today's dollars, and, thanks both to her financial chops and a parsimoniousness that would put Warren Buffett's to shame, died the richest woman in America in 1916. They called her the Witch of Wall Street because she went about in widow's weeds. And Green was just one in a pantheon of eccentrics who played starring roles in Berkshire Hathaway's odd history. The eccentric who Warren found himself tangling with in the 1960s was Seabury Stanton, grandson of the founder of the New Bedford, Massachusetts–based firm.

When Warren Buffett put in that first order for two thousand Berkshire shares, New England's textile industry was already on its last legs, but Seabury Stanton reigned defiant. Labor was cheaper down South, where the cotton came from, but Stanton was convinced he could save the company by pulling a switcheroo and dedicating most of the Berkshire Hathaway product line to rayon. This was delusional. Stanton took to drinking, and to fighting pitched battles with his brother, Otis, who was ready to get out of the fabric business while the getting was still relatively good. Warren had noticed that Seabury Stanton often made tender offers for Berkshire shares, and he assumed that his small investment would pay off when Stanton wanted to buy the stock back.

When the call came, Berkshire Hathaway stock was selling for, as Warren recalls, "$9 or $10 a share." Warren told Stanton he'd sell at $11.50. Stanton assented. Soon, though, a letter arrived offering owners of Berkshire Hathaway stock $11³/₈ a share, 12¹/₂¢ less than agreed.

"It really burned me up," Warren told his biographer Alice Schroeder. "This guy was trying to chisel an eighth of a point from having, in effect, shaken my hand saying this was the deal."

Warren went ballistic. As Schroeder writes, "He vowed that he would have Berkshire; he would buy it all." At last, after chasing down share after share, he had his way. At which point he realized to his horror that he was now in charge of an expensive-to-run company on its very last legs. Irrational! Yet, in what may have been the masterstroke of his whole career, he found a way to use Berkshire Hathaway's foundering fortunes to his own advantage.

Seabury Stanton had been wrong, extremely wrong, in his belief that he could single-handedly resuscitate the New England textile trade. Forget the low wages down South—automation was on the rise, and, just over the horizon, efficiencies in global transportation would make it possible to produce goods for the domestic market ultra-cheaply overseas. In other words, there was no point in reinvesting Berkshire Hathaway's capital back into the business. But there was also no point in letting the capital sit there—it had to compound. It had to do something.

Warren decided that Berkshire Hathaway ought to buy a "pinball machine."

The machine he chose was a tiny insurance company called National Indemnity. Headquartered a few blocks from Warren's office at Kiewit Plaza, National Indemnity had carved out a profitable niche for itself writing oddball policies, insuring, say, lion tamers, or burlesque performers' body parts. (Its owner, Jack Ringwalt, was something of an oddball himself, given to lugging hundreds of stock certificates around in his gym bag.) Warren had been casing the National Indemnity joint for a while, and by the time he got word that Ringwalt might be ready to sell, he wanted the company so badly, he agreed to pay $50 a share, $15 more than Warren figured it was worth.

What Warren did in buying National Indemnity was graft a small moneymaking apparatus onto the ailing body of Berkshire Hathaway. It was a move a bit like splicing cheetah DNA into a manatee, and in so doing, breeding a voracious new animal. Warren could pull capital out of Berkshire and give it to its profitable subsidiary, allowing it to expand; meanwhile, that subsidiary threw off tons of "float" from its insurance policies that could in turn be used to buy other profitable firms. Warren would repeat this trick again and again. And again.

So, for instance, Warren decided it was high time Berkshire got into the business of selling candies. See's Candies, to be precise. Initially, he purchased the confectioner on behalf of Blue Chip Stamps, a stock in the Berkshire Hathaway portfolio—but before long, he realized that Blue Chip Stamps was destined for the graveyard, and See's Candies was the real moneymaker. He had Berkshire buy the company outright and turned it into a serious luxury brand. As he wrote in a letter to See's CEO Chuck Huggins, the candies "should be very hard to get, available only periodically, and then (to the consumer) apparently only in limited quantities." The strategy paid off: As Bloomberg reported in 2015, diplomats at the U.S. State Department had spent at least $330,000 on boxes of See's Candies in the previous five years. Faced with the delicate task of finding a gift for foreign dignitaries that read simultaneously as all-American and a luxurious but not overly expensive treat, officials turned, as if by rote, to See's. Whitman's or Russell Stover simply would not do.

The next landmark acquisition was GEICO. The insurer was the first stock Warren really liked; back in his Columbia days, he'd sunk three-quarters of his assets into it. By the 1970s, though, the firm was in trouble—$190 million in the red, and seemingly on the brink of collapse. But Warren still liked GEICO; he thought the business remained sound. Its stock had once been trading at $61; now, Warren bought $4 million in GEICO at $2 a share. His instincts were right: The company is still one of Berkshire's major assets today. After that, the training wheels were off: Berkshire started buying up chunks of the world's best-loved brands in quick succession: Dairy Queen, Fruit of the Loom, ABC News, Coca-Cola . . .

This is just a sliver of Warren's portfolio. Many of Berkshire Hathaway's holdings, today, are insurance companies whose float money subsidizes other acquisitions. As of this writing, Berkshire Hathaway wholly owns more than sixty-five companies. These assets do *not* include any New England textile mills.

BY 1985, WHEN *Forbes* included him, for the third consecutive year, in its famous list of the 400 Richest Americans, Warren Buffett was a billionaire. He'd made his investors very, very wealthy, too: $1,000 invested with Warren in 1964 was worth more than $1,000,000 two decades later. As Rabbi Myer Kripke of Omaha's Beth El Synagogue put it, the money "mushroomed like an atomic bomb."

And the explosion was only going to get bigger.

After doing deals together for years, Charlie Munger and Warren had officially joined forces in 1978, with Charlie, from his perch in Southern California, becoming vice chairman of Berkshire Hathaway. At this point, the company was sitting on billions in capital— which meant that Warren found himself in the unusual position, in the highly leveraged 1980s, of doing business in cash while everyone else was loading up on debt. The trendy thing in that era of junk bonds and hostile takeovers was the leveraged buyout, wherein "corporate raiders" like Carl Icahn and T. Boone Pickens financed acquisitions by borrowing against their quarries' cash flow. Warren hated everything about those deals. For one thing, they stripped capital from productive companies and put it in the pockets of flashy Wall Street barons eyeing yachts and Hamptons estates. For another thing, these deals were too damn risky. Warren retained just enough of the old Ben Graham pessimism to smell a rat. And he wasn't shy about saying so: The Berkshire Hathaway annual reports were for a time transformed into broadsheets excoriating leveraged buyouts, junk bonds, and the whole gaudy, speculative spectacle of '80s-era dealmaking in general.

In one way, and one way only, Warren followed the zeitgeist, buying himself that must-have CEO accessory: a private plane, albeit a secondhand one. Writing to the Berkshire shareholders in 1986, Warren extemporized.

Your Chairman, unfortunately, has in the past made a number of rather intemperate remarks about corporate jets. Accordingly, prior to our purchase, I was forced into my Galileo mode. I promptly experienced the necessary "counter-revelation" and

*travel is now considerably easier—and considerably costlier—
than in the past. Whether Berkshire will get its money's worth
from the plane is an open question, but I will work at achieving
some business triumph that I can (no matter how dubiously) attribute to it.*

Warren used the plane to fly to D.C. for a state dinner at the Reagan White House. He flew to the Academy Awards, where he mingled with Dolly Parton; he flew to Palm Springs to golf with Reagan,
and he flew back to Omaha to host Berkshire Hathaway's annual
shareholder meeting, which, with about four hundred people in
attendance, was taking on something of a convention atmosphere.
And one day in 1987, he flew the plane to New York, to make the
biggest, least Warren Buffett–like, most treacherous deal of his life.

Ben Graham liked to think of the securities market as a character,
"Mr. Market." In his 1987 letter to Berkshire shareholders, Warren
explained Graham's thinking this way:

*Ben Graham, my friend and teacher, long ago described the
mental attitude toward market fluctuations that I believe to
be the most conducive to investment success. He said that you
should imagine market quotations [e.g., the price of a stock] as
coming from a remarkably accommodating fellow named Mr.
Market . . . Without fail, Mr. Market appears daily and names
a price at which he will either buy your interest [in a business]
or sell you his.*

*. . . Sad to say, the poor fellow has incurable emotional prob-
lems. At times he feels euphoric and can see only the favorable
factors affecting the business. When in that mood, he names a
very high buy-sell price . . . At other times he is depressed and
can see nothing but trouble ahead . . .*

*Mr. Market has another endearing characteristic: He doesn't
mind being ignored. If his quotation is uninteresting to you to-*

day, he will be back with a new one tomorrow. Transactions are
strictly at your option.

But, Warren added of moody Mr. Market, it was only worth playing ball with him if you bore two provisos in mind. First, Mr. Market
was there "to serve you, not to guide you." In other words, don't look
to either a rising or falling market for cues, because Mr. Market's
mood might not accurately reflect business fundamentals. Which
led to proviso number two: "If you aren't certain that you understand and can value your business far better than Mr. Market, you
don't belong in the game."

In the 1980s, a lot of people were treating Mr. Market as a sage,
and some of the most notable Wall Streeters leaving tributes at his
altar worked for Salomon Brothers. CEO John Gutfreund had transformed the firm from a boutique trader of bonds—the Street's stuffi-
est business, once upon a time—into a swashbuckling bank dealing
in foreign currency and equities, underwriting mergers and acquisitions and IPOs, and, most significantly, revolutionizing the bond
market by innovating products such as the mortgage-backed security. Crowned "the King of Wall Street" by *Business Week* in 1985,
Gutfreund came off as the polar opposite of the Oracle of Omaha:
As immortalized in Michael Lewis's memoir *Liar's Poker*, the work
environment Gutfreund cultivated at Salomon was dog-eat-dog and
rewarded employees who brought in big returns, whether or not
they played by the rules. As former Salomon bond trader Tom Bernard put it, Gutfreund "liked to throw a piece of meat in a cage and
see who got it." (Bernard, for what it's worth, was described in *Liar's
Poker* as "a human piranha.") Gutfreund's second wife, Susan, was
one of the poster girls of go-go 1980s extravagance, famously redec-
orating the couple's duplex on Fifth Avenue in a style evocative of
Versailles (why not?) and refusing to skimp on amenities such as the
bathroom refrigerator she used to keep her perfume cool.

Still, Warren liked the guy. They'd done successful deals together in the past—Gutfreund had helped save GEICO back in 1976. So, he was prepared to hear Gutfreund out when he phoned in a panic: Salomon's stock price had been slipping and slipping, and Gutfreund needed an infusion of cash to keep the bank from falling into the clutches of Ron Perelman, the corporate raider whose junk-bond-financed acquisition of Revlon made him the biggest bogeyman on Wall Street.

Warren proffered an offer that might have caused Gutfreund to think twice about his desperate request: He told Gutfreund that Berkshire Hathaway would drop $700 million in the bank's kitty, but only with a guaranteed minimum profit of 15 percent. That was the kind of return a lucky investor might get from high-risk junk bonds, but the deal sweetener for Gutfreund was that he'd keep his job. The two men shook hands, and as of that moment, Warren, who had railed against "casino-type markets" in his shareholder letters, found himself with his own little Las Vegas. "In effect," wrote Lewis later in the *New Republic*, "the moralist had sold his reputation, without pausing to measure the man willing to pay such a price for it."

Warren Buffett was a man who adhered to certain codes. Ben Graham's arm's-length approach to "Mr. Market" was one code; another was the principle that you don't invest outside your "circle of competence." Simply put, this means that if you're going to put money into a company, you had better know what it does, how it does it, whom it does that thing for, and whether the people running the shop knew what they were doing whenever they did what they did. The size of one's circle of competence doesn't matter much, Warren has repeated over and over again; what's vital is that you don't breach the perimeter. The "circle of competence" theory explains both Warren's longtime disinclination to invest in tech, and his affection for companies like Coca-Cola, which he purchased 14 million shares of in 1988, and then another 9 million the following year: Warren didn't own a computer and didn't want one, but he was an inveterate soda drinker. Staying within the circle of competence, that was the vital thing.

Warren understood that with the Salomon deal, he was straying to the boundary of his circle, and possibly over it. But the 15 percent guarantee on his investment gave him his margin of safety—another key code. His miscalculation was in not realizing he'd exited his circle of competence when it came to judging *people*. Warren put great store by his business relationships, as he wrote to his shareholders:

Working with people who cause your stomach to churn seems much like marrying for money—probably a bad idea under any circumstances, but absolute madness if you are already rich.

John Gutfreund would make Warren's stomach churn. As Lewis pointed out, Warren had sunk more than money into Salomon; he'd invested his sterling reputation, too. By the late 1980s, "Warren Buffett" had become something like a Good Housekeeping Seal of Approval on a business: If he was buying, surely it was safe for others to buy, too. This was profitable for Warren—his ability to move markets meant that when he went in on a stock, it was likely to rise. But playing this role, of imprimatur, was also dangerous, because so much was staked on his personal brand that it couldn't withstand any big hits. "His whole credibility as an investor is at stake," wrote Carol Loomis in the pages of *Fortune* in early 1988.

By 1991, Salomon Brothers had devolved into something like a failed state, governed by factional heads who exercised baronial control over the bank's divisions. From his seat on the board, Warren had seen some of these fiefdoms go rogue—notably, the bond arbitrage fiefdom, where a guerrilla squad of PhDs digitally modeling risk forecasts staged a mini-revolt. Just as that mole got whacked, a toothier one cropped up in the stodgy government bond department.

On Monday, August 12, 1991, the *Wall Street Journal* ran a story on a brewing scandal, which involved a rogue trader at Salomon illegally manipulating the U.S. Treasury bond market. Gutfreund, when made aware of the fraud, kinda just forgot to mention it to either the Treasury or the Fed during his regular get-togethers. The *Journal* piece listed off such alleged misdeeds as "market manipulation, violations of the antifraud provisions of securities law, misrepresentations to federal authorities," and, the cherry on top, "wire and mail fraud" that might carry criminal charges.

Just earlier that year, when asked why he'd ridden into Salomon Brothers to play white knight, Warren had told the *Los Angeles Times* that John Gutfreund was "an outstanding, honorable man of integrity." Now Gutfreund's head was on the chopping block, and Warren held the ax. In what would turn out to be a trailer for the full-length feature *The Last Days of Lehman Brothers*, released in 2009, lenders to Salomon began a run on the bank, and the Treasury secretary and the chair of the Federal Reserve were "trying to figure out who the hell [they were] going to get to come in and run the firm." Salomon stock stopped trading. News was imminent.

And Warren was in the air, flying to the rescue in his Falcon jet. On Friday, August 16, 1991, he was named the interim chair of Salomon Brothers. "Somebody had to take this job," he said.

Most of Warren's time in late 1991 and early 1992 was dedicated to the task of making Salomon Brothers boring. His strategy: "Full disclosure, cooperation with investigators, apologies to customers, regulators and politicians and a wholesale housecleaning of miscreants," as one reporter put it at the time. Mainly, what Warren had to do was *talk*. According to the *Los Angeles Times*, he "jawboned" Treasury Secretary Nicholas Brady into letting Salomon resume trading government bonds. He gave lengthy press conferences. He testified before both houses of Congress, dropping an indelible one-liner explaining his management approach: "Lose money for the firm, and I will be understanding; lose a shred of reputation for the firm, and I will be ruthless." The crisis elevated Warren to a new echelon of celebrity, as did the unprecedented publicity stunt he pulled in October 1991, writing a letter to Salomon shareholders that he published as a two-page ad in the *Wall Street Journal*, the *New York Times*, and London's *Financial Times*.

"In the end, we must have people to match our principles," Warren wrote, as he assailed Salomon's old regime, and invited a staff exodus by announcing that he was cutting bonus payments for the year. "He is so rigid and doctrinaire, with no humanity or compassion," fumed one employee. Others confessed, sotto voce, that they planned to ditch Warren's ethical safeguards as soon as the crisis blew over. Onlookers were more impressed: "Buffett has set a new standard for managements' response to fraud," commented Samuel Hayes, a professor of investment banking at Harvard Business School. "The squeaky-clean operating procedures he set in place defused and disarmed the people who were going to throw the book at Salomon. His actions will be studied chapter and verse in future scandals."

With the world turning on Salomon Brothers, viewing them as total crooks, wanting them to go down and stay down, Warren stepped in to run the place, at least until he got his money back. By the time he returned to Omaha, he'd gotten back every penny. Warren was setting a pattern here. Eventually, he'd be putting his reputation on the line again—not just for one measly firm, but for the entire U.S. economy.

4

NATURAL MONOPOLY

Just as Warren's "Oracle of Omaha" brand was getting a spit and polish, Bill's reputation as techie boy wonder was taking a beating. After founding Microsoft with Paul Allen on April 4, 1975, he'd built the company into the tech industry's standard-bearer. For the next fifteen years, Bill had been treated as a media darling, making appearances on the *Today* show and the cover of *Time*, being lauded by *Esquire* as among the "best of the new generation," and showing up on the *Good Housekeeping* list of America's most eligible bachelors. This sunshine-and-candy-hearts era came to a screeching end with the publication of the final issue of *Business Month* magazine in November 1990. Bill was on the cover; or, more precisely, his head was on the cover, photoshopped onto the body of a posing muscleman. The headline read: "The Silicon Bully: How Long Can Bill Gates Kick Sand in the Face of the Computer Industry?" In the article, an anonymous IBM employee stated that he'd like to drive an ice pick into Bill Gates's head. And that pretty much set the tone for press coverage of Bill for the rest of the 1990s. His days as a media darling were kaput.

Honestly, it's a little surprising that Bill ever *was* such a darling. Warren may have liked him a ton, soon after their first meeting

making him his date to University of Nebraska football games, vacationing with Bill and the extended Gates clan in Palm Springs, and
playing seemingly endless hands of bridge together whenever they
found themselves in the same place, but by most other accounts,
Bill Gates as a young man was, well, difficult. Indeed, in the earliest
days of Microsoft, he and Paul Allen seem to have had a good cop/
bad cop thing going, with Paul the genial "idea man," as he saw himself, and Bill the guy who worked over MITS on deal points. The key
deal point, for Bill, set out precisely how and how much he and Paul
would be compensated for their BASIC; he wanted to be paid for every copy of BASIC sold, rather than receive a flat fee for allowing the
software to be packaged with Altair kits. Bill wasn't in this just for
the money, but if the money was there, he damn well wanted a share
commensurate with his key role in generating it.

Not everyone had their eye on dollar bills. Early participants in
Silicon Valley's Homebrew Computer Club viewed the computer not
as a toy, not as a business opportunity, but as a vehicle for personal
liberation, and they'd managed to get ahold of Bill and Paul's BASIC
code. Members began giving out copies to Homebrew compadres,
and the deal was that anyone who took a bootleg BASIC had to cir-
culate two fresh copies of their own.

Bill was blissfully unaware that his BASIC was emerging as the
go-to among Silicon Valley hobbyists until the first end-of-year roy-
alty check arrived from MITS: $16,005 was a ludicrously low number
given that Altair kits were selling like hotcakes, and the computer
was virtually impossible to use unless you anted up for a copy of BA-
SIC. A little digging supplied the explanation: Homebrew bootlegs.
One club member alone had punched out fifty copies of the program.
"This just isn't right," Bill complained. "We've worked so hard on this
thing, and people are just ripping us off." The first time the larger
public heard of Bill Gates, it was via the byline of his "Open Letter to
Hobbyists" in the February 1976 issue of *Computer Notes*. Writing
on MITS letterhead, as "General Partner, Micro-Soft," Bill lamented:

Hardware must be paid for, but software is something to share....

Is this fair?... One thing you do [by stealing software] is prevent good software from being written. Who can afford to do professional work for nothing?... Most directly, the thing you do is theft.

Ed Roberts was furious that Bill had used MITS letterhead without permission. The Southern California Computer Society was so furious about Bill's characterization of software sharing as "theft," they threatened a class action defamation suit. The editor of a hobbyist newsletter responded to Bill's letter by writing of "rumors" that he'd stolen computer time from Harvard, and wondered in his column whether it was even legal to commercialize a product developed on computers paid for in part with government funds. Even readers who might have been sympathetic to Bill's argument were put off by his snide tone. These were the people driving computing into the mainstream, creating a market for hardware and software alike—and their first impression of Bill Gates was that he was a, well, whiny jerk.

Bill might have held his tongue, because, before long, the money started rolling in. The personal computer boom had well and truly begun, and in 1976, Bill and Allen were locking in deals for Micro-Soft's BASIC about as fast as contracts could be written. Corporations he licensed the software to, on a flat-fee basis, included Data Technology Corporation, Citibank, and General Electric. The strategy was to price the product so low that a business would be dissuaded from trying to develop software in-house. Bill quickly realized, however, that *low* didn't have to mean *superlow*—after cutting a $50,000 deal with GE, he decided to raise the price to $175,000 when National Cash Register came knocking. Even splitting the proceeds with MITS, that was enough money for Micro-Soft—or Micro-soft, as they'd registered the business with the Office of the Secretary of State of New Mexico—to hire its first employees and expand its product offering. By the end of 1976, Microsoft had moved out of its headquarters in Bill and Paul's living room and rented a proper office. As Paul writes, the company was "ready to rock 'n' roll."

Other companies were ready, too. Three rival PCs with attached keyboards and either built-in or add-on monitors were released in 1977: Tandy's TRS-80, Commodore's PET, and the luxurious Apple II. Here, at last, were computers for non-nerds. And they'd all need software to match.

Microsoft was off to the races. And Bill Gates drove his new employees as hard as he drove his Porsche, jibing coders who'd worked eighty hours straight to deliver a product on deadline for expecting to take the following day off. Bill didn't take days off. He'd drive to the office in the morning at ninety miles per hour, making sure he was the first to arrive, then keep an eye on the parking lot to see how long it took for his underlings to show up. Sometimes, he didn't leave the office at all, going on a coding binge and then crashing out on his office floor. Once, he was out so cold, that his secretary worried that something worse might have happened. That must have been a peaceful morning at Microsoft. Because when Bill was awake, he was often to be found having pitched battles with his programmers, rocking back and forth and yelling, "That's the stupidest fucking thing I've ever heard!"

Still, the résumés kept coming. Every bright comp-sci grad wanted to work for Microsoft, the company whose BASIC had become the default programming language—no little thanks to the bootleggers who had popularized the software. Microsoft was the best of the best, and the people they hired had to be the smartest of the smartest.

Anyway, it wasn't like it was all cookies and baby talk at the other firms spearheading the digital revolution. Apple co-founder Steve Jobs might have dressed like a hippie, but he was known for calling his co-workers "dumb shits." Bill lacked Jobs's visionary aura—a sore point for him—but he earned his employees' respect in other ways. He really understood code, for one thing, and he'd happily roll up his sleeves and jam alongside his programmers when deadlines loomed. For another thing, Bill wasn't just venting spleen when he argued—he was debating, and he wanted the young talents he hired to push back. "He wanted be viewed as tough but fair," wrote Allen in his memoir. Sometimes he pushed people too hard and didn't realize it, but when Bill locked horns with colleagues or employees, "it was never merely for effect." The give-and-take bred loyalty. When Microsoft left Albuquerque for Bellevue, Washington, in 1979, virtually all of the company's employees packed up their lives and headed north.

Still, Bill could be alienating. He burned Paul Allen, making him agree to a reduced stake in the company; as Allen later wrote, the nickel-and-diming made him see that his partner "was out to grab as much of the pie as possible." He screwed Seattle developer Tim Paterson by offering him a paltry $50,000 for the QDOS (Quick and Dirty Operating System) code that Microsoft would use as the basis for MS-DOS (Microsoft Disk Operating System), as used on the IBM PC—the deal that would launch Microsoft into the ranks of the Fortune 500. And he pissed off IBM, refusing to sell the firm the operating system outright, and insisting on Microsoft's right to license versions of the OS to other manufacturers.

Bill could afford to be disliked: From coast to coast, American companies were investing in desktop computers for their employees, and IBM was the natural go-to. More than 2.5 million IBM PCs were sold between the product's launch in August 1981 and Microsoft's IPO in March 1986, part of an incomparable wave of corporate investment globally in a single technology. Nor has any innovation since the PC done quite so much to change the nature of work. But this was Bill's victory, not IBM's. As he'd surmised when he struck his deal with computing's eight-hundred-pound gorilla, users would habituate themselves to the PC interface, not the hardware cladding it.

Which opened the field to a litter of PC clones. So long as manufacturers such as Dell and Compaq licensed the interface—Microsoft's MS-DOS—users would be satisfied.

"Before DOS," Allen says, "Microsoft was an important software company. After DOS, it was the essential one."

Paul and Bill handled the pressure of rapid growth very differently. Paul invited musicians to his house on Lake Sammamish for all-night jams. According to Paul, Bill got so many speeding tickets, he had to hire the best traffic attorney in Washington to defend him. Paul retreated into his office, performing his duties as Microsoft's head of research and new product development by daydreaming about the future of technology. Bill stepped forward as the Microsoft front man, giving an interview to the charter issue of *PC Magazine*, appearing on the cover of *Money*, and preaching the gospel of global operating system uniformity at public forums. To wit, using language he'd come to regret:

> *Why do we need standards? It's only through volume that you can offer reasonable software at a low price.... I really shouldn't say this, but in some ways it leads ... to a natural monopoly.*

Steve Jobs was not prepared to concede this fight. As he saw it, Apple was a renegade force battling PC hegemony, and he believed consumers would happily throw off the brutal regime of the MS-DOS and its torturous C:\> prompts if offered an interface that was more pleasant to look at and easier to use. (Look no further than Apple's famous "1984" ad for evidence that Jobs really did see the computer revolution in these Orwellian terms.) Jobs's weapon in the fight was GUI, short for graphical user interface.

Innovated at Palo Alto's legendary R & D lab Xerox PARC, the earliest versions of GUI featured on-screen icons that represented programs and a mouse that allowed computer users to navigate a desktop via the now-familiar point-and-click. Paul Allen was as dazzled by GUI as Jobs, but Jobs was the techie throwing body and soul into the interface, intending to make it the signature feature of his new Macintosh. To achieve that, he insisted that Mac hardware and software had to fit together, hand in glove.

But even Steve Jobs couldn't escape the fact that, software-wise, Microsoft was making the weather. Apple's in-house team simply lacked the bandwidth to supply all of the programs the Mac required. And so, warily, Jobs invited Bill and Paul to Cupertino to get a sneak preview of the company's magic machine, and sent them back to Bellevue with a prototype Mac—a bunch of circuit boards in a carrying case—and an offer to produce a few applications, including a spreadsheet program that would come to be called Excel.

The Microsoft programmers were enamored of their Mac. Bill was impressed, too—more impressed than he was with the man behind it. He looked askance at Steve Jobs's tendency to be "either in the mode of saying you were shit or trying to seduce you," recalls Andy Hertzfeld, an Apple programming dynamo who collaborated with Microsoft during the Mac's development. But as Walter Isaacson notes in his mammoth biography of Jobs, Bill was also envious of the Apple impresario's "mesmerizing effect on people." And he himself wasn't entirely immune.

One of the weirder artifacts to emerge from the early days of personal computing is a video from the Apple sales conference in 1983. Psyching up his battalion of pitchmen, Jobs staged a coup de théâtre called *The Macintosh Software Dating Game.* YouTube clips show Bill and two other software company founders shuffling onstage in their khakis, and then, as they slouch down in their seats, fidgeting and gazing imploringly at Jobs, the prince they're all trying to win over. From his perch behind the podium, Jobs lobs a question at Bill: "Will Macintosh be the third industry standard?"

"Well, to create a new standard, it takes something that's not just a little bit different," Bill replies, his heart in his mouth. "It takes something that's really new, and really captures people's imagination, and the Macintosh, of all the machines I've ever seen, is the only one that meets that standard."

Bill meant what he said. He thought the Mac's GUI was so good, in fact, he wanted to make his own.

On November 10, 1983—two months *before* the launch of the Mac—Microsoft announced plans for Windows at a splashy event at the Helmsley Palace Hotel in New York. Some of the biggest names in hardware, including Compaq, Radio Shack, and Hewlett-Packard, were on board, the company revealed. Bill told *PC Week* that Microsoft's goal was for its GUI operating system to be pre-installed on 80 percent of PCs.

In reality, Windows—which would come to dominate the world's PC market by the following decade, with an over 90 percent market share—was then but a mirage: Microsoft still had to build the damn thing. But Bill was becoming renowned, among tech insiders, for this kind of rug-cutting—there were rumors of times Microsoft heard pitches for an application, and shortly thereafter, announced they'd be launching similar software of their own. These rumors persist today in the widespread perception of Steve Jobs as a once-in-a-generation innovator and Bill Gates as a power-mad rip-off artist. The fact that the earliest editions of Windows were kludgy clones of the Macintosh OS is given as prima facie evidence for this. But the truth is more complicated. Steve Jobs didn't invent GUI. And Bill Gates was hip to Xerox PARC's version, and knew right when he saw it that "GUI was the future," as then-Microsoft employee and Xerox PARC alum Charles Simonyi told *Wired* in 1997.

But perception matters. And by 1991, the rumors had caught up with Bill. He'd spent the better part of the previous year on Microsoft's $2 million "Seeing Is Believing" rollout of Windows 3.0—or Win 3, as this breakthrough product was affectionately known at headquarters—and celebrating Microsoft's fifteenth anniversary by becoming the first personal computer software firm to exceed $1 billion in revenue in a single year. Then the mocking *Business*

Month cover arrived, and after it, the revelation, in March 1991, that the FTC was investigating Microsoft for anticompetitive practices, a probe aimed at putting flesh on the bones of the tech industry's yearslong whisper campaign against the company. Press coverage continued to sour: Nearly a decade earlier, Bill had been mobbed by attentive young women after giving the keynote address at COM-DEX, the industry's premier event, and, that night, at a party at Caesars Palace, where, a few drinks to the good, he let down his guard enough to shout over the music to a journalist the classic young man's cri de coeur: "I want to get laid!" Now here he was, attempting to quash publication of Robert X. Cringely's deliciously tart 1992 bestseller *Accidental Empires: How the Boys of Silicon Valley Make Their Millions, Battle Foreign Competition, and Still Can't Get a Date*, in which Bill is, among other insults, described as evolving from being the youngest self-made billionaire to "the self-made billionaire who acts the youngest." Cringely also has great fun with the redoubtable Mary Gates, the first woman president of United Way, who, he reports, helped "run her son's life through yellow Post-it notes left throughout his home."

"Like a younger Hugh Hefner, or perhaps like an emperor of China trapped within the Forbidden City, Gates is not even held responsible for his own personal appearance," Cringely writes, intent on taking down a peg the man who a few years prior had made his debut on the *Forbes* billionaire list. "When Chairman Bill appears in public with unwashed hair and unkempt clothing, his keepers in Microsoft corporate PR know that they, not Bill, will soon be getting a complaining call from the ever-watchful Mary Gates."

Still, bad press could be brushed aside, or parried, as when Bill's new pal Warren Buffett—a national hero for having saved Salomon Brothers—told *Fortune* magazine in 1992 that he regarded his friend's business acumen as "extraordinary." "If Bill had started a hot dog stand, he would have become the hot dog king of the world. He will win in any game."

But the government was a more formidable foe than the odd snarky journalist—particularly once the Justice Department decided to follow up on the FTC's investigation into claims that Microsoft engaged in monopolistic practices. Cringely might have gotten a few jabs in, but it soon became clear that the Justice Department was set on simply smashing Bill's empire apart.

MONOPOLY IS NO joke: In theory, if the government finds that a company has created a monopoly in its marketplace, it can break that company up. Perhaps the tech industry as a whole would have been more forgiving if Microsoft was perceived as an innovator, but it wasn't. A joke floating around the scene, back in those days, went as follows:

> QUESTION: *How many Microsoft programmers does it take to change a light bulb?*
> ANSWER: *None—the company just changes the standard to darkness.*

BY THE TIME Warren joined Bill onstage to give their talk at the University of Washington in 1998, he'd gotten pretty adept at his own brand management, and he was ready and willing to come to the defense of Bill's now troubled brand as well. To play Butch Cassidy, if you will, to Bill's Sundance Kid.

Warren summoned all that midwestern mystique as the night's one loaded question was posed. The question was about the appropriate role of antitrust legislation in American business. And it was loaded because just days prior, the Department of Justice and attorneys general of twenty states had filed antitrust charges against Microsoft.

"I am no antitrust scholar," began Warren, whose presence, the *Fortune* reporter had noted, "seemed to calm" Bill. "I met Bill eight years ago, and he's a terrific teacher. He spent about six or seven hours explaining Microsoft to me," Warren continued. "Here I am the world's biggest dummy on technology, and he explained it to me pretty darn well. When he got through with it, I bought a hundred shares of stock so I could keep track of it. That shows two things," he concluded. "One is that I've got an IQ of about fifty, and the second is that I didn't think he had any monopoly."

That is not an argument that would stand up in court.

IN 1994, BILL must have thought he was in the clear. Microsoft seemingly concluded its wrangling with the Justice Department by entering into a consent decree pretty much everyone in tech considered toothless. This was only the first skirmish in what would go on to become a pretty nasty war of attrition—but for now, the gist of the agreement was that Microsoft couldn't bundle extra software with copies of the Windows OS that it sold to computer makers. However, it *could* add "features" to the operating system itself. The tech world turned on how the courts chose to interpret the slippery distinction between extra software that was bundled and new, integrated features.

For Netscape's attorney, Gary Reback, it looked as though the DOJ was happy to let Microsoft continue to exert a "suffocating dominance." Developers were scared off from innovating new software products, having seen Microsoft crush WordPerfect and Lotus 1-2-3 with their competing Microsoft Word and Excel; conventional wisdom in the Valley was that venture capitalists wouldn't even consider funding an idea that Microsoft seemed likely to copy, because Microsoft had such a gigantic head start in getting its products to consumers. By the mid-1990s, Windows was in use on 90 percent of PCs, and Microsoft Office, its suite of business-related software, ran on virtually all workplace desktops.

"If somebody controls [a] technology standard, they will choke you and choke you and choke you," Reback warned in *Wired*. "If you let a company seize control of multiple standards, they'll choke you to death."

An obscure antitrust law—the Tunney Act—requires judicial review of any consent decree the government enters into with a private business. Usually, Tunney reviews amount to a rubber stamp, but Microsoft's case happened to land in the courtroom of federal judge Stanley Sporkin, a former director of enforcement for the Securities and Exchange Commission, and, as *Fortune* noted at the time, Sporkin had "left his rubber stamp at home." He put out a call for briefs.

Reback, who was representing Netscape, happily complied. Unnamed tech firms—rumored to include Apple—underwrote a hundred-page brief detailing a raft of complaints about Microsoft's aggressive marketing schemes and efforts to muscle in on every damn thing connected to computing. As computing was touching more and more aspects of everyone's lives—witness "tbone," aka Warren Buffett, playing bridge online—the question of whether Microsoft was rigging the marketplace took on an ever-increasing urgency. By the time Reback filed this memo, Microsoft had announced a deal to acquire Intuit, maker of the personal finance program Quicken; revealed its agreement with Visa to develop software for online credit card transactions; and a few months later—most notably—released plans for Windows 95 that included automatic access to the internet for any user with a modem.

The internet was the elephant in the room. Netscape, the pioneering web browser, had launched on December 15, 1994, providing an on-ramp to the information superhighway. This was, by Bill Gates's own reckoning, the biggest thing to happen in tech since the launch of the IBM PC. It had the potential to disrupt the whole industry, Microsoft along with it.

Steve Lohr, a technology reporter at the *New York Times*, recalls that Netscape co-founder Marc Andreessen wanted to "reduce Windows to a buggy set of device drivers underneath the browser, which would be the new top player that people would see and interact with," noting, "Microsoft wasn't thrilled about that."

No, Microsoft was not. In the first months of 1995, Chairman Bill found himself fighting on two fronts: After a fractious final Tunney hearing, Judge Sporkin struck down the DOJ consent decree, a ruling that Microsoft immediately appealed; now, with the company's lawyers back in court, Bill had to rally his troops for the Battle of the Internet, wherein Netscape's guerrilla army had already seized an immense territorial advantage.

As you read the following excerpts from Bill's May 1995 email memo, "The Internet Tidal Wave," it may be fruitful to imagine him as Shakespeare's Henry V, delivering the Saint Crispin's Day speech to his soldiers at Agincourt.

Perhaps you have already seen memos from me or others here about the importance of the Internet. I have gone through several stages of increasing my views of its importance. Now I assign the Internet the highest level of importance. . . .

A new competitor "born" on the Internet is Netscape. Their browser is dominant, with 70% usage share, allowing them to determine which network extensions will catch on. They are pursuing a multi-platform strategy where they move the key API into the client to commoditize the underlying operating system. . . .

We enter this new era with some considerable strengths. Among them are our people and the broad acceptance of Windows and Office. . . .

The next few years are going to be very exciting as we tackle these challenges and opportunities. The Internet is a tidal wave. It changes the rules.

Cue applause.

Needless to say, the folks at Netscape weren't clapping. In August 1995, the same month the company went public and spurred the dot-com bubble, Microsoft released Internet Explorer. Based on a predecessor of the Netscape browser that Andreessen had worked on as a student, Internet Explorer was, like many original versions of Microsoft software, kludgy. But as founding Netscape engineer Jon Mittelhauser notes in an oral history published at *The Ringer*, that didn't mean the program wasn't a threat.

"Microsoft's whole modus operandi at that point was the first version was bad, the second version was OK, and the third and fourth version started to pass the other folks," he explains. "That's what happened with the word processor and the spreadsheet. Microsoft had billions of dollars and hundreds of developers. They could throw a lot of effort into problems."

So far, so capitalism. But this is where the system-rigging Reback had railed against kicked in. Andrew Gavil, an antitrust professor at Howard University, points out that Microsoft had hardly been chastened by its legal battles; rather, the company went to extravagant lengths to ensure that Internet Explorer would be the default web browser on any computer running Windows.

"They sort of spread the [Internet] Explorer code throughout the Windows code, so that if you tried to remove it, you would actually mess up all of Windows," explains Gavil. "There was no technical or business justification for writing it that way. The main reason to write it that way was to make it not removable."

As Gavil also noted, Microsoft also impeded manufacturers' freedom to offer alternative browser software with their computers. "Essentially," he says, "they couldn't choose the best browser on the market." They had to choose Microsoft's Explorer. Which meant it wasn't a choice.

And then Microsoft just started giving Internet Explorer away.

Pause the story here for one second. Do we *care* about any of this? "We" as in the hoi polloi, as opposed to tech industry insiders, I mean. If people are perfectly happy with their Excel spreadsheets and so on, and if Microsoft hands them gratis web browsers, isn't the consumer winning out? But stop for a moment and ask yourself: When was the last time your computer did something glitchy and you lost half a day's work, then spent the other half banging your head against the wall? What if there was a product out there that didn't glitch like that but you'd never know about it because the "industry standard" product you and everyone else you know uses made it impossible for anything better to get a foothold in the marketplace? It's useful to think of Microsoft's complaining competitors as canaries in the coal mine. The harms they suffer, jostling for business against a would-be monopolist, will radiate out and touch everyone, eventually. He who holds the keys to the kingdom makes all of us his subjects. Today Facebook is a keyholder. When Mark Zuckerberg was asked, before the Senate, to name Facebook's biggest competitors, he uh, um, could only mention the various categories in which other companies "overlap" with Facebook's premier offerings. Consumers are locked into the service. Even if you don't have a Facebook account, it's nigh-on impossible to avoid interacting with the platform somehow, whether you use one of the services it has acquired, like Instagram or WhatsApp, or because your idiot cousin took an online quiz and unwittingly handed Mark Z.–and by extension, Cambridge Analytica–all your browsing data. (How? No idea.) Facebook's role as the world's primary news curator has simultaneously jerked the rug out from under traditional outlets, forced them to optimize their content for the Facebook algorithm, and diminished the public's trust in journalism by providing access to its platform to purveyors of *dezinformatsiya*. But if you want eyeballs, you've got to deal with Facebook. That's what keyholding is. As Gary Reback and his co-authors put it years ago, speaking about Microsoft's foray into "information services": "It is difficult to imagine that in an open society such as this one, with multiple information sources, a single company could seize sufficient control of information transmission so as to constitute a threat to the underpinnings of a free society. But such a scenario is a realistic (and perhaps probable) outcome."

Long story short, there was a great deal at stake in how the government chose to address Microsoft's efforts to consolidate power. Its answer to the question of whether the company was engaging in illegal monopolistic practices rested on regulators' ability to adapt their interpretations of the law to a business environment far different from that of the Rockefeller era. Gary Reback was pressing them to think ahead.

And now he had a new client: Netscape.

Reback had gotten a call from Jim Clark, Netscape's co-founder, who described a visit the company had just received from Microsoft reps, who suggested—in the way Mafia dons suggest things—that Netscape ought to let Microsoft take over the browser market and agree not to compete with Microsoft in other areas, in exchange for which concessions Microsoft would invest in Netscape, and take a seat on its board.

"They basically said, OK, we have this nice shit sandwich for you," recalled Mike Homer, a Netscape exec who was at the meeting. "You can put a little mustard on it if you want. You can put a little ketchup on it. But you're going to eat the fucking thing or we're going to put you out of business."

Reback phoned Joel Klein, a high-ranking lawyer in the Department of Justice's antitrust division, telling him that the word around town was that Microsoft planned to "cut off Netscape's air supply"—for instance, by threatening to cancel Compaq's Windows license if it tried to replace Internet Explorer with the Netscape browser. And Reback decided to take his case to the public, too: He was going to write a white paper.

With his law firm colleague Susan Creighton, a former clerk for Justice Sandra Day O'Connor, Reback produced a 222-page tome detailing Microsoft's rise to power and explaining how, in scheming to crush Netscape, it had "engaged in a variety of anticompetitive acts that surpass its previous illegal conduct." To wit, recall this stirring line, from Bill's "Internet Tidal Wave" memo:

*They are pursuing a multi-platform strategy where they move
the key API into the client to commoditize the underlying operating system.*

Creighton and Reback saw this as the key to the puzzle. Bill's jar-
gon loosely translates as: Holy shit, if everyone's primary interaction
with their computer is going to be with their browser, the "underlying operating system"—that is, Windows—won't really matter to
people anymore; it will become a fungible commodity. Creighton
and Reback argued that, in giving the Netscape browser no quarter,
Microsoft was engaged in illegal "monopoly maintenance," stifling
innovation that threatened to render its most dominant and profitable business moot.

"The only thing J. D. Rockefeller did that Bill Gates hasn't done,"
Reback would say, "is use dynamite against his competitors!"

Reback and Creighton's "White Paper Regarding the Recent Anticompetitive Conduct of the Microsoft Corporation" landed on Netscape CEO Jim Barksdale's desk with a thud. Once the situation was
spelled out, in all its gory detail, it made the young company's pre-
dicament plain: It couldn't survive without government intervention. Netscape had gone public the previous year—what would all
those investors do if they read the report, and then the government
continued sitting on its hands? Publication was out of the question,
but Reback quietly sent copies to the DOJ and other government
bodies, and runoffs of the white paper made the Silicon Valley
rounds like samizdat. One copy landed on the desk of Mark Tobey,
Texas's assistant attorney general. Tobey was both reform-minded
and eager to protect his state's native tech industry—Texas was home
to key Microsoft clients Compaq and Dell—and he began lobbying
other state attorneys general to take an interest in the case. Meanwhile, Netscape was bleeding market share.

Bill, for his part, was busy jamming Microsoft's fingers into as
many pies as he could. In early 1995, Microsoft got into gaming when

it announced a joint venture with DreamWorks, the Hollywood studio co-founded by Steven Spielberg; the following year, Microsoft launched the online magazine *Slate* and partnered with NBC to bring the twenty-four-hour news network MSNBC to the airwaves. "If any media mavens still think Bill Gates isn't after their lunch, they had better wake up," noted *Forbes* in a piece with the provocative title "He Wants Your Eyeballs."

In 1997, the Justice Department slapped Microsoft with a fine of $1 million a day for violating its 1995 consent decree. That was for requiring manufacturers to add Internet Explorer to their computers if they wanted a Windows 95 license, and the fees began adding up on October 20, 1997. ("These people have no idea who they're dealing with," stated a close friend who had spent the day, on which the action was announced, with Bill.) A few months after that, while visiting Belgium, Bill got hit in the face by a cream pie. And two months before his appearance with Warren at the University of Washington, Bill was called before the Senate Judiciary Committee to answer the charge that he was a monopolist the likes of which hadn't been seen since the Standard Oil days.

Gary Reback and Susan Creighton's white paper was having its intended effect. Its distribution to various agencies—and Mark Tobey's efforts to recruit state AGs—had galvanized a pressure campaign to get the Department of Justice to take action. Joel Klein, head of the antitrust division, wearily gave in. He wasn't a born crusader, but then, Microsoft kept pushing its luck. For instance, in December 1997, federal judge Thomas Penfield Jackson had issued an injunction forcing Microsoft to offer computer manufacturers a browser-free version of Windows; the company complied by giving its customers a choice between an old Windows operating system and a current version that didn't function. It was impossible, they said, to extract the Internet Explorer code from the latest Windows. "Usually the phrase 'contempt of court' is metaphoric," Klein groused. "In this case, it was literal."

Judge Jackson was likewise chagrined. And skeptical. He directed his clerks to do some hacking, and then informed a packed courtroom that Explorer could be harmlessly uninstalled from Windows in "less than ninety seconds."

Ill winds were blowing in Microsoft's direction.

Bill spiraled. He complained to friends that he hated his job, hated his life. He railed about a "witch hunt." He decried the injustice of a government that, instead of thanking him for planting the seeds of the New Economy, was painting him as a villain, and aiming cannonballs at his company. "His own government, suing him, that's not chocolate sundae!" Bill Sr. told *Newsweek*. At one meeting with his directors, Bill launched into a feverish tirade, the gist of which was that ne'er before had anyone, ever, been treated so unfairly as he, William H. Gates III. "The whole thing is crashing in on me," he concluded, eyes reddening. "It's all crashing in." And then he began to cry.

Bill's pessimism was well founded. On May 18, 1998, the DOJ and twenty states filed their joint suit against Microsoft. U.S. Attorney General Janet Reno held a splashy press conference, telling reporters that Justice had "charged Microsoft with engaging in anticompetitive and exclusionary practices designed to maintain its monopoly in personal computer operating systems and to extend that monopoly to internet browser software."

"This is a step backwards for America," Bill proclaimed. "How ironic that in the United States, where freedom and innovation are core values, these regulators are trying to punish an American company that has worked hard and successfully to deliver on these values."

It was war. A browser war.

BILL *HAD* SECURED one major victory by this time: Warren Buffett had bought a computer. "You've got to get a computer to do your income tax," Bill urged on one of his now semi-regular visits to Omaha. "I don't have income," Warren replied. "Berkshire doesn't pay a dividend." "You can keep track of stocks," pressed Bill. "I only have one stock," retorted Warren. It was bridge that changed his mind, in the end. He picked up his new bridge tutor, Sharon Osberg, on the Falcon and flew her to Omaha so she could help him pick out a PC. "Just write down the things I need to know to get in to play bridge," he told her. "Don't try to explain to me what this thing is doing." Logging on as "tbone," he'd play bridge online with Osberg and other partners four or five nights a week. Once, he was so engrossed by a game that he didn't even notice when a bat got into the house and was flapping around the room in which he was playing.

Bill had taken up the pastime with a vengeance, too. He'd learned the game from his parents, but it didn't become an obsession until he began playing with Warren. Bill had even taken on Osberg as his tutor, on Warren's recommendation. They'd play the classic, four-person game, divvied into two teams, exhausting their opponents as they dealt new hands late into the night. They could go on for hours.

And they played other games, too. Warren once showed Bill a pair of "tricky dice," nontransitive dice that come in a set of three and that force players to calculate maddening probabilities in seeking out the highest score—unless they cotton on to the trick of the game, which is to avoid being the person picking out which die to roll first. A hard game to explain to someone who isn't math-minded, but Bill "immediately caught on, of course," much to Warren's delight.

They teased each other about who was richer, Bill claiming *Forbes*'s top spot among the wealthiest Americans in 1992, and Warren overtaking him a year later. They had serious conversations about what to do with all their money; Bill was mooting the launch of a small family foundation, which his father would run, and Warren suggested he dedicate some of its resources to international family planning. And Warren inducted Bill into his inner circle: It's a testament to precisely how much Bill impressed Warren, upon their very first meeting, that he invited him to the next conclave of the Buffett Group, composed of Ben Grahamites who numbered among

Warren's closest business confidants and friends. A typical Buffett
Group session might find the members reviewing the most valuable
companies of the previous five decades—a fleshed-out iteration of
the analytical exercise Warren had introduced to Bill at Hood Canal. When talk turned to a tech company—say, IBM—Warren nodded
at Bill and said, "I think we've got somebody here who can add a
little something."

And Bill invited Warren into his inner circle, too. For he didn't
attend those Buffett Group sessions solo: He brought along his girlfriend, Melinda French.

5

PARTNERS

Bill Gates and Melinda French spent Easter weekend of 1993 at his parents' vacation home in Palm Springs. Bill and Melinda had been dating for a while, off and on and then more seriously, but Bill was slippery when it came to making plans for a future together. His heart seemed to belong to Microsoft. Melinda's heart was in the company, too; as well as being Bill's girlfriend, she was a Microsoft employee, hired in 1987. She was used to playing second fiddle to business: In one notable incident, Bill and Melinda took his private seaplane to Vancouver for a Buffett Group meeting that Melinda might have assumed would be a quick social call, but after being warmly welcomed by Warren, she found herself watching as he and Bill spent the day glued together, talking about what the new digital camera technology would do to Kodak's share price.

So, it's hard to know what was going through Melinda's head when she got off the plane back from Palm Springs. For one thing, they were not—as she'd expected—in Seattle. Bill had given his pilot secret instructions to fly to Omaha, where Warren Buffett was awaiting him and Melinda on the airport tarmac with a trumpet in hand. "Surprise!" Warren cried, probably, as Melinda stepped off the plane. For once, Warren wasn't there to talk business with Bill; he was there for her. He drove Bill and Melinda to Borsheims, a local fine jewelry store that Berkshire Hathaway owns, and invited Bill to pick out a ring. Melinda was flabbergasted. Warren reported that when he'd gotten engaged in the 1950s, he'd spent 6 percent of his net worth on the ring. "I don't know how much you love Melinda," Warren told Bill. "But 6 percent is the yardstick in Omaha." Given that Bill Gates was worth around $6.2 billion at the time, Melinda would have needed to pick out a ring worth $372 million to satisfy Warren. The one Bill bought cost far less, but it was still weighty enough to prove distracting. After the engagement, when a rep from Meca Software met with Melinda about a product she was developing, he described the diamond on her ring as extending "from one knuckle to another." She rolled the stone to the underside of her finger to stop the guy from staring.

The description "famously private" has never been more aptly applied than in regard to Melinda Gates. It's not just that her craving for privacy is well known, or that it's a signature aspect of her persona—it's that her privacy is so very, very public. As a co-founder of the Gates Foundation, she bestrides the world like a colossus, zipping from one country to another as she tackles sticky problems of endemic poverty, gender inequality, lack of access to education, and, to put it plainly, death. Who is this woman so intent on righting the ship of Planet Earth? We have yet to fully crack the veneer.

In 2019, Melinda published her first book, *The Moment of Lift*, a memoir-cum-manifesto on women's rights. In the main, *The Moment of Lift* comprises moving accounts of interactions Melinda's had with women in impoverished villages in, say, India or Niger, anecdotes intended to illustrate the vital necessity of the work the Gates Foundation is doing to promote women's equality worldwide. Melinda is keen to foreground these stories—to show the world what she's seen in the course of her travels on the foundation's behalf. But every so often, like grout between tiles, a little of Melinda's own story appears. She writes, without going into much detail, about her family in Texas and her education—unlike Bill, she completed college, graduating in 1986 with a degree in computer science and economics from Duke and then sticking around an extra year for an MBA. She describes a meeting with an IBM manager shortly before she graduated college. Melinda confessed that she was also planning to interview with a small outfit in Seattle called Microsoft. IBM's great, the manager told her, but if someone with your talent really wants to go places, choose Microsoft. "If I were you and they made me an offer, I would take it." Elsewhere in the book, Melinda talks about what it was like to date Bill Gates. In one particular passage early on, she strikes an odd note.

Or perhaps it only seems odd if you've immersed yourself in others' writing about Bill Gates and the nascent era of Microsoft. Recalling what drew her to Bill when they met in 1987, Melinda lists their shared enthusiasm for puzzles, games, and F. Scott Fitzgerald, and an untrendy taste in music: Bill's collection mainly consisted of albums by Frank Sinatra and Dionne Warwick. Then Melinda states, pleasantly enough, that she and Bill also shared "a belief in the power and importance of software."

"We knew that writing software for personal computers would give individuals the computing power that institutions had," Melinda writes, "and democratizing computing would change the world. That's why we were so excited to be at Microsoft every day."

Democratizing computers. Huh?

Listen, Melinda Gates knows her (now ex-) husband better than anyone else. Better than his biographers. Better than Walter Isaacson, who has interviewed Bill numerous times and given accounts of his work ethos in books such as *Steve Jobs* and *The Innovators.* Better than Paul Allen, who was, in a way, also married to Bill, and who knew him long before Melinda entered the frame. But it is notable that none of these keen observers-of-Bill ever mentions this profound desire to democratize computing, not as a motivating factor in his grand ambitions for Microsoft, nor in his interest in software, full stop. Is Melinda putting us on? Was this a bit of wifely spin, a way of saying that the civic-mindedness of Bill Gates circa 2020 was always at work in the man?

Here's another possibility: Maybe it's true. Maybe Melinda and Bill *were* passionately interested in democratizing computing, and talked about it a lot, and maybe that's because Bill only began thinking in those terms because Melinda, his girlfriend, did. Pre-Melinda, it was all about mastering challenges—writing the code, making the deal, beating competing products to market, hitting earnings benchmarks, and raising them again. Then Melinda changed the way Bill thought about his work by asking him to consider what it *meant*.

She wasn't his first serious girlfriend. Jill Bennett, who dated Bill for a year when he was in his late twenties, was a tall, gregarious blonde who recalled Bill, years later, as alternately flaky and focused. These were flip sides of the same coin: Bill's refusal to think about anything other than Microsoft led him to disconnect his car radio, eschew owning a TV, and take baths instead of showers, so he could use the time to read; it also led him to leave clothes in hotel rooms and lose his credit card so frequently that it got to be a running joke. He washed his hair only when screamingly necessary, and his sleeping patterns were, at best, irregular. He'd have "a real hard time sleeping at night," Bennett said in one interview, "and then during the day he could sleep instantly. He'd crawl under a desk. He'd crawl under chairs at the airport and fall asleep. People would lose him."

Bill met Bennett around the same time in 1983 that he was making goo-goo eyes at Steve Jobs onstage. He pursued his romance with work much more ardently; Bennett broke up with Bill because she couldn't take his insistence on a seven-hour turnaround time between going home for the day and returning to the office.

Then came Ann Winblad, the woman most of Bill's friends assumed he would wed. A software entrepreneur and self-made millionaire, having sold for $15.5 million the firm she'd co-founded in the mid-1970s with $500, Winblad was more than a match for Bill, whom she crossed paths with at various industry meet and greets. At some point, they crossed paths enough for the petite ex-cheerleader from Minnesota to be introduced to folks as Bill's girlfriend. They didn't see that much of each other during the three years they dated—Winblad lived in San Francisco, and the two would sometimes go on that era's version of "virtual dates," seeing the same movie at the same time in different cities, and then talking about the film afterward, on their car phones. When they did get together, the forceful Winblad was intent on upgrading her beau, who, nearing thirty, seemed to her like a kludgy 1.0 program with solid source code. A vegetarian, she made Bill stop living off burgers and Coke. She bought him a monitor and a VCR, because—for God's sake. She tried to improve his wardrobe but ultimately gave up. "It never works," Winblad, by then an ex but still close to Bill, told writer John Seabrook in 1993, referring to the many efforts made by the women in Bill's life, starting with his mother, to get him to shape up his look.

Winblad had more success enticing Bill to take time off from Microsoft. The two vacationed together, sometimes with humorous results. One time, Winblad recalls, she and Bill went to Cabo San Lucas in Mexico on a whim, and Bill "sublet" the car she'd rented to a pair of teenagers visiting for spring break.

Why Bill felt the need to rent out their beat-up Volkswagen for five bucks a day isn't entirely clear, given that around the time he was dating Ann Winblad, he had much larger dollar amounts swimming around in his head. "Ann, I think I can get this company to half a billion dollars in sales," he told her. "I think. And everyone's counting on me to do that. Now, in my mind, if I really stretch my mind, I can get the company to half a billion dollars in sales. Then everybody will expect more, and I don't have a clue how we'll ever get past half a billion dollars in sales."

In public, Bill never expressed any such qualms. When he started dating Winblad, Microsoft was gearing up for its IPO, and as Bill hit the road to meet with potential investors, he was telling them he expected Microsoft to smash the half-billion-dollar-a-year mark by the end of the decade. Meanwhile, he was also telling the PC clone manufacturers who'd signed up for Windows 1.0 that the program was nearly done, when it was not. Its release would be delayed and delayed, until the sweet words spoken at the product launch were but a fading memory.

Ann Winblad went on to have a storied career as a venture capitalist. She'll also go down in history as the coiner of the word "vaporware," which refers to software advertised for sale even if nary a line has been coded.

Bill stayed close friends with Winblad after their break-up—so much so that he sought her approval before he proposed to Melinda. ("I said she'd be a good match for him because she had intellectual stamina," Winblad recalled.) Even after he and Melinda were married, he'd vacation annually with Winblad, spending platonic weekends with her on North Carolina's Outer Banks, dune-buggying and talking about biotech, a blossoming interest of Bill's that Winblad had galvanized.

Melinda and Bill met not long after he and Winblad split. This is how Melinda describes their first encounter in *The Moment of Lift*: "I was on a trip to New York for Microsoft, and my roommate (we doubled up back then to save money) told me to come to a dinner I hadn't known about. I showed up late, and all the tables were filled except one, which still had two empty chairs side by side. I sat in one of them. A few minutes later, Bill arrived and sat in the other."

She goes on to say that she and Bill "talked over dinner that evening" and that she "sensed that he was interested." Elsewhere, she's said that she found Bill "funnier" than she expected; Bill, for his part, has volunteered that it was her "looks" that sparked an attraction. Twenty-three-year-old Melinda had recently arrived in Redmond (where Microsoft had moved its headquarters from Bellevue in

1986), the sole woman in a class of ten new managerial-level recruits. This was her first serious job; Melinda had just graduated Duke University, double-majoring in computer science and economics as part of a special program that allowed her to finish school in five years with an MBA. Melinda, too, was "focused"—as a student at Dallas's Ursuline Academy, she'd set daily goals for herself ("run a mile, learn a new word, that sort of thing") on top of her regular rondelle of high school athletics, volunteer activities, and keeping the accounts on her family's clutch of rental homes, a business that bolstered her father's slender income as an aerospace engineer. (He worked on the Apollo project.) Her first year at Ursuline, she researched the college admissions of recent grads, and discovered that only a handful had gotten into elite schools. "I realized that the only way to get into a good college was to be valedictorian or salutatorian," says Melinda. So, she became valedictorian.

The Bill 'n' Melinda love story continues thus: "One Saturday afternoon we ran into each other in the company parking lot," Melinda writes. "He struck up a conversation and asked me out for two weeks from Friday. I laughed and said, 'That's not spontaneous enough for me. Ask me out closer to the date,' and I gave him my number. Two hours later, he called me at home and invited me out for that evening. 'Is this spontaneous enough for you?' he asked."

Well, Bill Gates likes a challenge. Maybe he went into his relationship with Melinda assuming that this woman—so much younger and less pedigreed than tough cookie Ann Winblad—would be a soft touch. What he discovered was that she was a person who responded to his recommendation to read *The Great Gatsby* with a roll of her eyes, replying that she'd already read it twice, and who could beat him at math games, and best him at Clue. And she didn't play hard to get—she *was* hard to get. Elaine French warned her daughter that it wasn't a good idea to date the CEO. Melinda agreed in theory, but it appears she was trying to thread a very fine needle—going out with Bill, yes, but insisting they keep the relationship under wraps and drawing "this line in the sand that [she] would never, ever, ever go to him on anything related to work."

Here are some things we *don't* know about Melinda's tenure at Microsoft. We don't know what it was like for her to button her blouse, slip on her sensible pumps, and set her jaw in advance of her first day at the office, where she'd been slotted into a position as a marketing manager for a predecessor of Microsoft Word. We don't know how it felt, as a young, attractive woman, to wander around the Microsoft campus in Redmond and meet the gazes of the mostly male coders, who toiled in an atmosphere Ann Winblad once described as "bachelor heaven"–a tone set at the top, given that Bill was fond of inviting strippers back to his house to join in pool parties. (The soirees were legendary in the halls of Microsoft, with members of the boys' club praising them as evoking "the decline of Roman civilization," and outsiders citing them as an example of the company's "frat-house sexism.") We do know that Melinda found the Microsoft staffers "idiosyncratic" and "smart" and that she thought they were "changing the world." And also that she found the company culture "acerbic," and that, soon after she arrived at Microsoft, she considered leaving.

There's one more thing we don't really know about Melinda's first interactions with Bill–and it would turn out to matter later: Did he ever make her uncomfortable? For such is what other women who worked for Microsoft or, later, the Gates Foundation, perhaps felt when Bill (by then married to Melinda) made fumbling attempts at flirtation. Reading the recent *New York Times* report on Bill's pattern of picking up–or, at any rate, trying to pick up–women who answered to him in some capacity, it's difficult not to see Bill and Melinda's meeting at that Microsoft dinner in a different, rather dimmer light: "Standing with her at a cocktail party," the *Times* reports of Bill's interaction with an unnamed Gates Foundation employee circa 2007, he "lowered his voice and said: 'I want to see you. Will you have dinner with me?'" In reply to which, the woman "laughed to avoid responding." Years earlier, Melinda laughed at Bill, too–

because, she's said, she found him so funny. Perhaps the two circumstances are entirely incomparable, inasmuch as one involves a long-married man insinuating the possibility of a dalliance, and the other a bachelor making the acquaintance of the woman who would become his wife.

And here is what we *do* know about Melinda French at that time, and about the sensibility she brought to her relationship with Bill Gates. In her valedictory address at Ursuline Academy, she spoke to the school's motto—"Serviam" ("I will serve")—by exhorting her classmates to think of their own success as bought on credit, and thus, a bill to be paid. "If you are successful, it is because somewhere, sometime, someone gave you a life or an idea that started you in the right direction," she noted. "Remember also that are you indebted to life until you help some less fortunate person, just as you were helped." It's not unreasonable to believe that it was Bill's wife who brought Bill around to thinking this way—it would be another trait he shared with the wife-schooled Warren Buffett.

INSTEAD OF ASKING who was the woman in Warren Buffett's life, it may be more apt to ask who were the women.

Warren's first wife, Susie, was first among equals—but even she recognized she was part of a wider female coterie, as she saw it. "Someone for everything," she once put it years later, taking stock of the women in Warren's life. Sharon Osberg was his bridge coach and sometime traveling companion. Kay Graham was his dear friend, entrée to high society, and consigliere in the halls of power; she and Warren took trips together, as well. Carol Loomis, *Fortune* editor, helped him craft his lengthy and discursive annual letters to shareholders. Gladys Kaiser was the secretary who guarded the door to Warren's office at Kiewit Plaza—her successors, Debbie Bosanek and Deb Ray, once had to shoo away a lady who'd flown all the way from Japan to get his autograph, and prostrated herself on the floor. ("I *like* being worshipped," Warren complained after they hustled the supplicant out the door.) And then, later, there was Astrid Menks, who would become his second wife.

But Susie was the woman who changed the way Warren saw the world.

If you've read any profile of Warren Buffett recently, the writer is sure to have restated one fact: Warren Buffett has lived in the same humble Omaha home for more than sixty years. The home referenced is on Farnam Street, and it didn't seem so humble when Warren plunked down $31,500 for it in 1958. For one thing, it was the largest house on the block. For another, the cost of spending $31,500 on *anything* was mind-boggling to the compounding maestro—if you thought about what those dollars could turn into in a dozen years, as Warren did, then the cozy two-story house with its charming "eyebrow window" had just cost him a million buckaroos. He called it "Buffett's Folly."

And that was before he saw the decorating bill.

Hooray for Susie! Chrome-and-leather furniture—*très* Charles and Ray Eames. Splashy modern paintings on the walls. She made a nice little joke, too, covering Warren's study off the primary bedroom in cash-print wallpaper. Susie was determined to give her new home as convivial an atmosphere as that of the one she'd grown up in—which was now in walking distance. Doc and Dorothy Thompson became regular fixtures at the Buffetts', and Susie often ambled over with the grandkids: docile Little Sooz, wild Howie, baby Peter. Dorothy was a dream grandma, playing games and organizing Easter egg hunts and sighing lovingly at Howie when he ran amok.

Howard and Leila Buffett lived nearby, too. But emotionally, they were distant. Leila continued to be a thorn in Warren's side, and it's easy to imagine that his resentment of her had only sharpened as he watched his wife lavish love and attention on their children. A breach had begun to open between Howard and Warren, as well: Warren would always revere his father, but he watched with dismay as Howard lurched ever further to the political right, cheering on the McCarthy hearings and joining the newly formed John Birch Society. Here, too, Susie's influence on Warren was keen: For all his seeming aloofness to her concerns, Warren was taking in Susie's progressivism. She was his watering can; he was her blossoming flower. The boy who'd once tagged along with Howard Buffett on campaign jaunts now had to tell his ailing father that he was no longer a Republican. Out of respect, he wouldn't change his voter registration so long as Howard was alive, but he'd never again cast a ballot for the party, and the reason, he said, was civil rights.

THE HOUSE ON Farnam Street became ground zero in Susie's campaign against intolerance. Regular visitors included her best friend, Bella Eisenberg, an Auschwitz survivor; Rabbi Myer Kripke and his wife, Dorothy, who were the Buffetts' yearly Thanksgiving guests (Susie made sure to provide kosher food); and Black baseball pitcher Bob Gibson and his wife, Charline. This come one, come all ethos was then highly unusual among Omaha's WASP elite. And Susie's activism didn't end at home: The poor housing conditions in Omaha's Black neighborhoods were of particular concern to her, and she was often to be found at committee meetings in the neighborhood.

"Honey, your mother is going to get killed," Doc Thompson warned Little Sooz. "You're going to get kidnapped."

Susie's work to end segregated housing increasingly consumed her during the 1960s, and it took on new urgency as Omaha, like other American cities, flared with riots that brought the Black community and the police into direct confrontation in the streets. On a few occasions, Susie acted as a front for Black families trying to move into white neighborhoods, buying homes on their behalf. Warren, too, involved himself in the cause, testifying in the state capitol about the importance of integration. But it wasn't until autumn of 1967 that—in investment terms—Warren put a proper value on the civil rights struggle.

That October, Susie and Warren attended a convocation at Grinnell College, a liberal arts school about a three-hour drive from
Omaha. Speakers included author Ralph Ellison, media theorist
Marshall McLuhan, and artist Robert Rauschenberg, and the keynote address was one for the ages, given by Martin Luther King Jr.,
three years off his Nobel Peace Prize win and one day away from beginning his nineteenth jail sentence in the very prison where, four
years before, he'd written his famous "Letter from Birmingham Jail."
Warren listened, rapt, as King preached on the theme of "Remaining
Awake Through a Revolution," stirred by one line in particular: "It
may be true that the law can't change the heart, but it can restrain
the heartless." This insight struck Warren to his core. He left Grinnell with a new commitment to politics.

"That was one of the most inspiring speeches I've ever heard,"
Warren later recalled. "Took me right out of my seat."

In modern parlance, we might say that King's speech prompted
Warren to "check his privilege." Midcentury man to the core, he had
the freedom to believe in himself—to say, accounting for his own
success, as his peer John Updike had, "I was just made to feel that
I could do things." It suddenly struck him that not all people got to
feel this way. Depending on your race, your gender, your class, you
might start life with a jet pack strapped to your back or else dragging
a ball and chain. This was wrong, on its face, as Warren saw it—but
entrenched inequality also offended his belief in fair competition.
What measure of success was it, really, to rack up win after win if
you were playing with a stacked deck? Now, looking around, he saw
deck-stacking everywhere. Business deals were done on the links
of country clubs that didn't allow Jews to become members. Black
children in segregated housing were funneled into low-performing
schools. For goodness' sake, deck-stacking had been established as
the highest law of the land.

Said Warren: "You know, in 1776, Thomas Jefferson wrote 'All men
are created equal,' and then when they wrote the Constitution, they

all of a sudden decided: No, it was just three-fifths of a person if you were Black."

Warren wanted to join the fight for civil rights in earnest, using his wealth and social position in the best ways he could. He joined the Grinnell board, sitting on its investment committee. He began to involve himself with fundraising for Democratic candidates. Together with Charlie Munger, he underwrote a suit to liberalize abortion laws in California. And, deploying a bit of jiujitsu, he took it upon himself to get his Jewish friends inducted into the lily-white Omaha Club.

With Susie cheering him on, Warren decided to sponsor his pal Herman Goldstein for membership. Knowing that the excuse the country club offered to maintain its restrictive policy was that "they," meaning Jews, "have their own clubs that don't admit us," Warren asked another pal, Nick Newman, to sponsor him for membership at the all-Jewish Highland Country Club. There were hesitations.

"It created this big rhubarb," he told the Jewish Telegraphic Agency in 2006. "All of the rabbis appeared on my behalf, the ADL [Anti-Defamation League] guy appeared on my behalf. Finally, they voted to let me in."

Highland membership in hand, Warren returned to the Omaha Club and pushed for a vote on Goldstein. He was allowed to join, becoming the Omaha Club's first Jewish member.

As their sense of society's inequities evolved, Susie did not retire her taste for the finer things. And Warren had long found ways to indulge his wife; when she accompanied him on business trips to New York City, for instance, he'd send her to Bergdorf Goodman to buy designer clothes and furs. She drove a gold Cadillac. Susie's essence was her big heart, but that didn't mean she was above asking for, say, a holiday home in Laguna Beach.

The Buffetts often vacationed in California, and Susie was increasingly drawn to the state. She liked its color and its cultural variety. Plus, now that her children had all reached their teenage years, she had a little more time to focus on herself—and she felt she'd earned the right to her own space. Warren was as consumed with work as ever, and though Susie wasn't much for confiding in friends, she did let slip to one that she thought of her husband as an "iceberg." But she knew how to push his buttons: "If we were rich," she told him, apropos his hesitation at buying the Laguna oceanfront home she wanted, "you would just go up to that house, and ask the owner how much she wants for it, and pay however much she asked. But I know we're not rich."

In 1971, Warren bought her the house.

"Mom spent a lot of time supporting Dad so he could do his thing," Susie Jr. told Roger Lowenstein, author of the 1995 biography *Buffett: The Making of an American Capitalist*. Peter Buffett had a sharper description of his parent's marriage, telling Lowenstein that Susie "suffered for living for other people," Warren very much included.

Did Susie Buffett love her husband? Yes. Did he frustrate and astound her in equal measure? Yes. After twenty years of marriage, were the seeds of despair she'd unwittingly been watering springing to bloom? Yes, yes, yes. Warren was complex, and so was Susie's love for him. She'd learned to find fulfillment outside her home. Doing volunteer work. Playing nurse and therapist for family and friends. Susie forged other connections, too—she'd reunited with her high school sweetheart, Milt Brown, after running into him at the Chicago airport, and they'd stayed in touch, occasionally indulging in questions of "what if?" There was also the genial crowd at the Dewey Park tennis courts, including John McCabe, a handsome coach. Susie was playing a lot of tennis in those days. She was also starting to sing.

As Warren began to travel more frequently on business, Susie turned the house on Farnam Street into an ad hoc rehearsal space, playing chanteuse over jazz guitar tracks provided by her nephew Billy. Eventually, she worked up the confidence to perform in front of friends in Laguna Beach, with Warren cheering her on. In early

1975, she made her professional debut, prodded by a pal who'd found her an agent. Susie was so nervous about her gig, at a small nightclub on the Omaha outskirts, she begged Warren not to attend. Then she proceeded to wow the audience with smoky renditions of Aretha Franklin's "Call Me" and Roberta Flack's "The First Time Ever I Saw Your Face."

Was it at that moment, basking in applause, that it began to dawn on Susie that she'd be better off on her own?

In 1977, after twenty-five years of marriage, Susie moved to San Francisco. Like all cataclysms, this one had been in the works for a long time—and then happened all at once. Warren ought to have known Susie was eyeing the door. She spent more and more time in Laguna Beach, and on her singing career. She went to Kiewit Plaza and poured her heart out to Warren's mentee Dan Grossman, as Warren read *Moody's* in the office next door. She even roped Warren into taking a weekend workshop meant to help them "get in touch with yourself."

Or Warren could have read between the lines of a profile of Susie published in the spring of 1977 by the *Omaha World-Herald*. Titled "What Makes Susie Sing?," the piece dug into the backstory of the millionaire's wife with a local reputation as a secular saint, who was all of a sudden very interested in "the care and feeding of Susan Buffett."

"I said, I'm not leaving you, because I'll be wherever you want me when you want me," Susie later recalled of the day she told Warren she was moving to San Francisco.

He was gobsmacked. Again and again, Susie reassured him that nothing was really changing—she was still his wife, she'd be by his side for all the key events, and, after all, hadn't they been leading separate lives for many years? The days of sitting down to nightly meat-and-potatoes dinners with the kids were long past. As a matter of quantitative analysis, he knew Susie was correct; nothing was really changing. Looked at qualitatively, however—she was *gone*. He thought that the care and feeding of Warren Buffett was what his wife thrived on, and it turned out, he was wrong.

Who was going to take care of him now?

One of the places in Omaha where Susie liked to perform was the French Café. Between cabaret sets at the nightspot, she developed a warm relationship with the maître d', Astrid Menks. As diners tucked into entrees such as "le surf and turf," Susie sussed out the witty young blonde's hardscrabble history. Born to Latvian parents who had fled the country after World War II, Astrid arrived in America when she was five, living on a farm with no indoor plumbing or electricity. After her mother died of breast cancer, she passed through a succession of foster homes, fought her way into the University of Nebraska, and then dropped out when she ran out of funds. Running with a bohemian crowd—bohemian for Omaha—Astrid supported herself with a variety of menial jobs before finding an unsteady footing in the restaurant industry. Like Warren, she had simple tastes. Unlike Warren, with his $72 million net worth in 1977, Astrid Menks was poor.

Susie called Astrid from San Francisco, asking her to "look in on" Warren.

Someone had to. Warren was "empty and sad," says Peter Buffett. He called Susie every day, weeping, pleading with her to come back. Meanwhile, Susie was reveling in her new life in San Francisco: Several of her closest friends from Omaha had moved to the city before her, and now, as she decorated her apartment in a riot of colors, she was helping to find a place in town for her tennis coach, John McCabe. "Astrid, *please*," Susie badgered. At last, Astrid betook herself to Farnam Street, bearing soup.

A year later, she moved in.

BILL MADE A special video for Warren's sixty-third birthday in 1993. In it, he informs Melinda via pay phone that Warren has overtaken him on the just-published *Forbes* list and is now the nation's richest man. The line goes dead. "Melinda? Melinda?" says Bill. "You still there . . . ?"

The joke, of course, is that Melinda is only marrying Bill for his money. Yuks aside, this is something Melinda has emphatically denied: As she told *Fortune* in 2008, when she started dating her future husband, "It was like, Okay, Bill has money. Big deal." Really? She wasn't dazzled by his wealth? Intimidated? Awed by the thought of what all that money could do? Did she speak to Bill about the theme of her valedictory address at Ursuline—the idea that success was a social debt?

We do know that Bill markedly changed around this time. The *Seattle Times* dedicated a whole paragraph in an article, written as Bill celebrated his thirty-eighth birthday, spotlighting the improvements in "Bill Gates, Version 38.0." The piece noted his upgraded grooming and widening range of interests, and credited Melinda, at least in part, for the alteration. In some cases, her influence was clear. In 1988, Bill had commenced building his dream house, a 42,000-square-foot, high-tech mansion to be nestled near-invisibly in the hillside overlooking Lake Washington; the domicile was still unfinished when Bill and Melinda got engaged, and Melinda set about revising the blueprints. One room they decorated together: Bill's library, its ceiling inscribed with a line from the final page of *The Great Gatsby*. "He had come a long way to this blue lawn," the line goes, "and his dream must have seemed so close that he could hardly fail to grasp it." It was a tribute to Melinda, for when they were dating, Bill could see her window from his office, and she'd turn on her green-shaded lamp on nights when she wanted him to swing by. "It was like the light at the end of Daisy's dock," Bill explains. They picked the quotation "just for each other."

In other instances, Melinda's influence would make itself felt only years hence. For it was she who, in a life-changing act, planted the seeds of the Gates Foundation on a pre-wedding trip with Bill to East

Africa. Little did either know the far-reaching, life-changing significance that this little romantic getaway would have on both of them,
and eventually, the world at large.

This was to be Bill's longest-ever vacation from Microsoft, and
Melinda's first travel experience outside North America and Europe. The couple was looking forward to seeing the wildlife. Melinda
found herself awestruck by the vastness of the savanna sky—and
troubled by the extreme poverty she and Bill encountered in the
countries they visited. "It was both eye-opening and heartbreaking,"
she recalled.

*I have vivid memories of watching women walking down the
street, babies on their backs, and wondering what their lives
were like. What did they hope for and worry about? What were
the barriers keeping them trapped in poverty?*

At the conclusion of the trip, Melinda and Bill went for a long
stroll on a beach in Zanzibar. They ruminated on all they'd seen.
And wondered what they, with Bill's immeasurable wealth, could do
about any of it.

Not long after returning to Seattle, Melinda and Bill hosted a dinner for Nan Keohane, then the president of Duke University. Talk
turned to the Africa trip, and a researcher attending the dinner told
Bill and Melinda about "the huge number of children in poor countries who were dying from diarrhea and how oral rehydration salts
could save their lives."

Following that dinner, Melinda writes, she and Bill dug into the
latest development report published by the World Bank, and it
"showed that a huge number of deaths could be prevented with low-
cost interventions, but the interventions weren't getting to people."
The problem, as Melinda understood it, was that no one considered
delivery of these treatments "their assignment."

Did that mean it was Bill and Melinda's job?

Bill dove into the data. Naively, he'd assumed that by the time he retired and set about giving his money away, all the big problems would be solved, and he'd "have to struggle to find something really impactful." But what Bill discovered as he researched was precisely the opposite. It seemed as though people had given up on the big problems. Like 11 million kids unnecessarily dying every year. "It was mind-blowing to me that these preventable diseases—pneumonia, diarrhea, malaria and some other infections that infants get—had such a huge impact," Bill says.

That was the first time it dawned on me that it's not hundreds of different diseases causing most of the problem—it's a pretty finite number. And I was surprised by the huge disparity between poor countries, where 20 percent of children were dying before the age of five, and rich countries where that number is more like half a percent.

You can picture the wheels spinning in Bill's head. Hundreds of diseases are hundreds of separate problems. A handful of diseases—now *that's* a puzzle you can solve, if you're smart like Bill Gates is smart, and super-rich, and highly motivated. This attitude would prove to be somewhat naïve, too.

ON NEW YEAR'S Day 1994, Bill Gates wed Melinda French in a lavish ceremony in Maui. Extreme precautions were taken to keep the event private—Bill booked all the rooms at the Manele Bay Hotel, where the wedding was held, and rented every helicopter in the area so no snoopers could snap shots from above. Any reporters who violated the "Trespass Warning" notices were told that they could be arrested. To this day, not much is known about the event, aside from the fact that Willie Nelson played at the rehearsal dinner, and Melinda paid less than $20,000 for her dress and reception ensemble—peanuts, by society bride standards—and burst out laughing as she realized that Bill was doing math in his head when he cut the cake, in an effort to give every guest a slice of precisely identical size. (Melinda tweeted out a video of the cake-cutting moment on their twenty-fifth anniversary.)

Naturally, Warren was one of the lucky few to get an invite to the nuptials. He had to debate attending; Charlie Munger's seventieth birthday party was on the same day. In the end, he sent Susie to Los Angeles to serenade Munger in his stead and brought Katharine Graham to the wedding as his date. A coterie can come in handy.

WARREN'S CLOSE CONNECTION with Katharine Graham—Kay—dated back to the period of reflection following his attendance at the convocation where Martin Luther King Jr. spoke. In 1969, he realized a dream he'd been quietly nursing, buying the *Omaha Sun*, something of a muckraking weekly newspaper. But the *Sun* was profitable, if only just; Warren assumed that returns on the paper would be 8 percent a year, about the same as a safe bond, but far less than he earned when he bought into a business or invested in a stock. Had Warren decided to renounce profit and become a full-time newspaperman? Er, *no*. The *Sun* appears to have been a kind of midlife present to himself, a happy reminder of boyhood days delivering the paper, lobbing them onto porches. But the purchase whet his appetite for the media business, and Warren soon began buying up as many shares of the *Washington Post* as he could.

The Post had won the battle over the publication of the *Pentagon Papers* and was deep in its coverage of the Watergate affair when Warren first sat down for lunch with Kay. It was almost a parody of Warren's first date with Susie, only this time, in place of the rumpled recent college grad who loved to talk about stocks, there was a rumpled multimillionaire . . . who loved to talk about stocks. But while Susie was a sophisticate merely by Omaha standards, Kay was the cosmopolitan daughter of *Washington Post* publisher Eugene Meyer, and she counted the likes of Jackie Onassis and Henry Kissinger as friends. If ever Warren felt like a rube, it was in her drawing room. And yet, repeating Susie's reversal, Kay came to adore and rely on Warren. The two became so close, rumors of an affair swirled. What had changed?

Over lunch with Kay and others in 1973, Warren sought to assuage her concerns that he was mounting a takeover bid. Sure, sure, he'd spent $10,627,605 to buy *Post* stock amounting to 12 percent of the company. But it was all "Class B" stock, which limited his rights, and anyway, "the amortization of intangibles" made media companies hard to value, and therefore, hard to buy. Kay nodded, repeating the phrase "amortization of intangibles." Thrown into the role of publisher after her husband, Phil Graham, committed suicide, she'd gotten good at bluffing when seated across the table from powerful men. As Warren went on to clarify, deducing her unease, "amortization of intangibles" refers to the price put on assets like a company's "brand." See's Candies is a useful example: Its tangible assets, when Warren acquired the company in 1972, had a value of $8 million. These are the assets that Ben Graham considered important—the stuff you could auction off in a fire sale, if necessary. Warren was just as interested in the intangible assets belonging to See's: its reputation for making fine chocolate, the customer loyalty it had earned thanks to that reputation, the mystique that had grown up around the brand. How do you value all that? As Warren saw it, and as he was trying to explain to Kay, a newspaper's worth was mostly vested in intangibles, and it was subject to the vagaries of how the public responded to its work. The citizenry *might* appreciate a paper that helped drive a president's impeachment, or it might not. It just depended. From an investor's perspective, the only reason it made sense to put money into a paper like the *Washington Post* was because you liked what it stood for. Warren liked what the *Post* stood for so much, he told Kay, he intended to hold his stake in it "permanently."

The same logic applied to Kay's decision to make Warren Buffett her friend. Once she got to know him, she liked what he stood for.

Kay Graham inducted Warren into a whole new world. That first time he came to visit her in D.C., she threw a black-tie dinner for him and Susie at her Georgetown mansion, home to legendary soirees. Warren didn't exactly travel with a tuxedo in his suitcase, but arrangements were made, and soon enough, he and a glammed-up Susie were being ushered out of their taxi and into Kay's lavish living room. A Renoir hung on one wall. Washington's elite mingled until the dinner bell was rung, whereupon Warren, for whom a classy supper consisted of a T-bone at Omaha's Gorat's steak house, was introduced to *service à la russe*, a first course followed by a fish course followed by a main, all served off silver trays by uniformed waiters. Barbara Bush, wife of one future president and mother of another, was seated beside him. Warren fumbled with his fish fork, pretended to enjoy the food he didn't like, and warily ogled the handsy senator seated beside Susie. This was a whole new world for Warren, and he wasn't sure he liked it. But it intrigued him.

Soon, Kay and Warren were chatting on the phone with clockwork frequency. He'd tutor her in the finer points of business, walking her through deal points, and fly off at a moment's notice to lend her support—for example, jetting to New York to help her prep her speech to the New York Society of Security Analysts. What did Susie make of seeing Warren step into the role of watering can? Who knows?

But you can guess.

In the years leading up to Susie's departure for San Francisco, Warren was increasingly consumed by his business relationship and burgeoning friendship with Kay Graham. She invited him to join the *Washington Post* board. He stayed at her house when he came to D.C. for the monthly meetings, keeping a spare set of clothes in the guest room. Rolling her eyes at his perpetually unkempt appearance, she set about introducing Warren to the city's power brokers. Warren, in turn, invited Kay to a meeting of *his* informal board—that annual gathering of Ben Grahamites, plus Charlie Munger, unofficially known as the Buffett Group. Warren and Kay had grown so close, in fact, that the doyenne of D.C. society deigned to drop in on the Buffett family when they were vacationing in Laguna Beach, prompting Warren to do something unprecedented: Keen to show off, he waded into the waves that lapped below the cliffside home. Warren's wife and children burst into laughter at the improbable sight of Warren swimming.

"Only for Kay," Warren later said. "Only for Kay."

Warren hadn't exactly been the most attentive father. He took after his own dad, loving his children but usually to be found with his nose in a book, or a copy of *Moody's* or the *Wall Street Journal*. Dinner was often delayed because he was yakking on the phone to Charlie Munger. ("Oh-oh, Dad's talking to Charlie" was a common refrain, according to Little Sooz.) When he and Munger took their kids to Disneyland, they sat on a bench dissecting the park's financials as the children scurried off to enjoy the rides. And when Susie got the flu once when the kids were small, Warren mainly provided comic relief.

"I lay down in the bed and I say to Warren, will you get me a pan or something from the kitchen? I may not get to the bathroom I feel so sick," Susie recalled, years later. "So, he travels down to the kitchen and I hear this bang, biff, boom, bang, like a five-course meal was being fixed. And he comes up, and he puts down a *colander*." When Susie pointed out that, what with its holes, the colander wasn't quite suited to the purpose, Warren dutifully returned to the kitchen. "All this banging, and he comes up," said Susie, "and he puts the colander on a cookie sheet!"

Susie reproved Warren for his aloofness with his kids, telling him that he couldn't just be a father, he had to be a "daddy," too. In this, she was singing the same tune as Charlie Munger, who had urged Warren beyond the quantitative thinking entailed in hunting "cigar butts," and got him to consider investments qualitatively. American Express was a qualitative investment. So, too, See's Candies. But

Warren's learning curve was less steep at home than it was at work. Friends joked with Warren, "Those are your children—you recognize them, don't you?" One friend later described Susie as "sort of a single mother." The main way Warren seems to have made his presence felt on Farnam Street, where the beneficiaries of Susie's charity wandered in and out at random, often encountering rambunctious teenage Howie in a gorilla suit, was in his insistence that his kids not be entitled brats. He kept them on a short leash, money-wise—and made it clear they shouldn't expect to inherit his fortune when he died. The plan was, Warren would make as many dollars as possible while he lived, letting the savings compound and compound and compound, and then, on his passing, hand a vast sum over to Susie to donate as she liked. Susie was *good*. She'd know what to do with the money.

By the time Little Sooz tied the knot in 1976, Warren might have been reconsidering his parental regime of benign neglect. The nuptials were a lavish affair, with hundreds of guests flying in to Newport Beach to celebrate a marriage they were pretty sure was not going to last. Seemingly the most responsible of Warren's three kids, Sooz had hooked up with a good-looking surfer, dropped out of UC Irvine a semester short of graduation, and frittered away the money she inherited from her grandfather on a Porsche. *C'est la vie.* Maybe it struck Warren, somewhere in the back of his mind, that his daughter might be making up for a childhood of many denied luxuries. Maybe not. Also in attendance: Howie Buffett, the family tumbleweed, who'd recently started an excavating business, and Peter Buffett, the quiet, artsy one, who at least was on his way to Stanford. Kay Graham was there, too, no doubt arching an eyebrow at the psychedelic rock band that played at the reception.

WHEN BILL AND Melinda wed on Maui in 1994, the only cloud on the horizon was Mary Gates's breast cancer. This redoubtable woman, former United Way chair, member of the University of Washington

Board of Regents, and doyenne of Seattle's charity scene, had looked after her son well into his adulthood, picking out his clothes and setting him up on his blind date with Warren. Now she was terminally ill and passing the torch to Melinda. Prior to the wedding, she sent her future daughter-in-law a letter that ended with the line "From those to whom much is given, much is expected." Melinda already knew that, but she took the words to heart.

Six months after watching her son walk down the aisle, Mary Gates was dead. Soon after, Bill and Melinda established the first iteration of the Gates Foundation.

6

TO HAVE AND HAVE NOT

There's a great scene in Robert X. Cringely's book *Accidental Empires*: It's 1990, and Bill Gates is standing in the checkout line at an all-night convenience store in Seattle. "It was about midnight," writes Cringely, setting the scene, "and he was holding a carton of butter pecan ice cream. The line inched forward, and eventually it was his turn to pay." Bill starts digging around in his pockets, looking for a 50-cents-off coupon he can't find. "The clerk waited, the ice cream softened, the other customers, standing in line with their root beer Slurpees and six-packs of beer, fumed as Gates searched in vain for the coupon." Finally, one customer slams two quarters down on the counter.

"'Pay me back when you earn your first million,' the 7-11 philanthropist called as Gates and his ice cream faded into the night."

At that point, on paper, Bill Gates was worth $3 billion.

Bill has disputed this story. Some version of it may or may not be true. One thing's for certain: Warren Buffett would have been cheering Bill on as he hunted for his coupon. We can assume this because when Bill and Warren went to China in 1995 and Warren offered to treat Bill to lunch during a stop in Hong Kong, not only did the legendary cheapskate take his newlywed friend to McDonald's, but as locals waited in line to order their burgers and fries, Warren fished around in his pants pockets, eventually pulling out a few coupons he'd brought with him from Omaha. There's a photo of Bill and Warren laughing as they hold up the coupons for—who knows?—two Big Macs for the price of one, or a free Coke. The two richest men on earth, yukking it up.

How *should* Bill Gates and Warren Buffett spend their money? That was the implied question at the meeting of the Buffett Group that immediately preceded the China trip. At the group's biennial conclave, this time held at the exclusive K Club in County Kildare, Ireland, Warren handed out copies of Andrew Carnegie's pamphlet *The Gospel of Wealth*. He wanted to debate Carnegie's premise that they who die rich die disgraced. More specifically, he wanted to test the validity of his own theory that the wisest course of action was to die as rich as possible and give back from the grave, when the absolute maximum amount of money had been made.

This theory was well known: Since 1980, Warren had made a habit of publishing essays about why it wasn't a good idea to leave a vast fortune to one's children, and he'd opine about the magic of compounding whenever Susie or one of his friends came to him to request money for a good cause. (He'd loosened his purse strings a little after the MLK speech.) Among the Buffett Groupies, the matter of giving money away rather than leaving it to one's kids wasn't really in dispute; most of Warren's confidants had come to side with him on this over the years, though their notions of what constituted an appropriate inheritance differed. (Kay, for one, thought Warren's plan to leave his kids with about zilch was completely insane.) The crux of the issue for Warren and his friends was *when* to give, and here Warren and Bill sharply differed. Bill had imagined he'd devote himself to philanthropy decades hence, after retiring from Microsoft. But then he went to Africa and saw the need for action *now*. Sparring with Warren, logician to logician, he argued that the total given in aid didn't matter as much as the measurable effectiveness of each dollar. And if you could save more lives by giving less money today, wouldn't that be better?

Warren pondered this. And then he kept pondering as he, Susie, Bill, and Melinda headed from Ireland to China for a seventeen-day journey. The Gateses had taken special care to ensure Warren's comfort on the cross-country trip, going so far as having the kitchen staff at Beijing's Palace Hotel learn to cook burgers and fries. When the tourists climbed to the top of the Great Wall, champagne awaited them—plus Cherry Coke for Warren. "Boy, I sure would have liked to have been the company that got the brick contract for this thing," Warren quipped between slurps. In the Forbidden City, they were shown ancient scrolls rolled and unrolled by silent women; Bill whispered to Warren, "There's a $2 fine if you return a scroll not rewound." They took a train to the northwest, where they rode camels and admired giant pandas. All along the route, the couples played bridge. Hours and hours of bridge. "We were playing bridge while everyone was looking at the scenery," Warren recalled. "We played on the bus while balancing cards on our knees."

On the tenth day of the trip, they visited the Three Gorges Dam project, after which they boarded a cruise ship they had all to themselves for sailing down the Yangtze; on it, Melinda organized nightly activities, such as karaoke singing in the ballroom. Reaching the first of the gorges, the Shennong Stream, Warren watched as men using ropes pulled their longboats through a tributary, dragging them against the current.

"There could have been another Bill Gates among those men pulling our boats," he mused at dinner that night.

They were born here, and they were destined to spend their lives tugging those boats the way they did ours. They didn't have a chance. It was pure luck that we had a shot at the brass ring.

For years afterward, Alice Schroeder writes, Warren thought about those men "ceaselessly dragging the longboats upstream," and what they implied about destiny and fate. What emerged from that thinking was a deeper appreciation of the concept of justice that he calls the "ovarian lottery."

The ovarian lottery is a thought experiment, which goes like this: Twenty-four hours before you are born, a genie appears and offers you the opportunity to set the rules of the society you are about to join. Rad! Except, there's a catch. You don't know if you'll be born rich or poor. You don't know which country you're about to be born into—could be one that's stable and prosperous, or one struggling up the lower rungs of economic development, or one beset by war and plague. You might be white or Black or brown. You could be a woman or a man or something in between. Genetics determining, you might emerge into the world with any number of physical challenges or be a future Olympic decathlete. Aspects of poor mental health, where they are inheritable, will be just the cards you're dealt. All you know when the genie appears is that, as Buffett says, "you're going to get one ball out of a barrel with, say, 5.8 billion balls in it."

You're going to participate in what I call the ovarian lottery. It's the most important thing that will happen to you in your life, but you have no control over it. It's going to determine far more than your grades at school or anything else that happens to you.

"Now," Buffett asks, "what rules do you want to have?"

Maybe you're feeling lucky. Or maybe, like Buffett, you're an ace calculator of odds, and you decide that, lucky folk being few and far between, society should be governed such that every person, anywhere on earth, gets "an equal shot." Warren Buffett likes to say that he won the ovarian lottery. His trip to China convinced him he had to better the odds for everyone else.

While Warren pondered, Bill Gates Sr. got to work setting up his son's foundation. Bill was happy to let his dad take the reins, and Melinda—who might well have still been musing on Mary's wedding-day letter—wasn't going to prevent her father-in-law from managing things for the time being. After all, the foundation had been his idea to begin with. When requests for charitable donations started piling up on Bill's desk, Bill Sr. was the one who told him to set up a "real foundation." He knew the ropes, too, having spent plenty of time working with local charities and the Greater Seattle Chamber of Commerce. The William H. Gates Foundation, as it was then known, ran "more like a mom-and-pop store" than a major charitable entity, according to one knowledgeable observer, and managed a few hundred million dollars. Bill's father ran the shop, as it were, out of his basement with the help of one assistant—Suzanne Cluett, an expert on issues relating to reproductive health—and sometimes, for some reason, received mail at a nearby Burger King. The organization's first major gift was a $750,000 grant to PATH, the Program for Appropriate Technology in Health, which was developing new ways to deliver medicines in remote places in Africa and Asia. The money came out of the blue, recalls Dr. Gordon Perkin, who headed the non-profit at the time. "We'd never had an invitation from someone who wanted to provide funds," says Perkin, who, a few years after the initial grant, began vetting family-planning-based grant proposals for the Gateses.

They would soon set up a second foundation, to be run by Patty Stonesifer, the former head of Microsoft's Interactive Media Division, and by all accounts one of the most creative and dynamic alumna of the company's executive team. The Gates Library Foundation was established to bring computers and internet access to libraries in low-income communities in the United States and Canada—a cause close to Bill's heart, inasmuch as, in the mid-'90s, he'd taken on a side hustle as a great proselytizer for the web, going on *The Late Show with David Letterman* to encourage Letterman to get online, and publishing a book, *The Road Ahead*, that made optimistic prognostications about our interconnected digital future. However worthy the library cause, it did prompt some quiet sniping from tech types, for it was right at this time that Microsoft was launching Windows 95, and Bill was gearing up for the biggest business battle of his life: the browser wars, a take-no-prisoners fight over internet access. From the very beginning of his giving, there were Gates naysayers.

Bill, for his part, explains his motives in terms strikingly similar to Warren's "ovarian lottery" thought experiment. "Warren and I share certain values," he wrote in the January–February 1996 issue of the *Harvard Business Review*. "He and I both feel lucky that we were born into an era in which our skills have turned out to be so remunerative. Had we been born at a different time, our skills might not have had much value. Since we don't plan on spending much of what we have accumulated, we can make sure our wealth benefits society. In a sense, we're both working for charity."

ANDREW CARNEGIE HAD written the philanthropy bible, as far as Warren Buffett was concerned. But Carnegie's *Gospel of Wealth* isn't only a manifesto in favor of philanthropy; it's also a defense of plutocracy. Writing in the midst of America's first Gilded Age, when income inequality was at least as profound as it is now, the great railroad and steel robber baron asserted that capitalists must be forgiven for doing everything in their power to increase their profits, because, well, that's how business works. "Under the law of competition," Carnegie writes, "the employer of thousands is forced into the strictest of economies, among which the rates paid to labor figure prominently." There's no avoiding that, say, a factory owner is going to push for low wages, just as there's no avoiding that, as Carnegie goes on to posit, inequality will widen because, as successful businesses grow, they tend to concentrate wealth "in the hands of a few."

The trade-off, though, according to Carnegie, is that a person who has amassed outsized wealth can't think of it as their own. Rather, it belongs to the society that has permitted them to slurp up as much money as they can, by whatever means necessary. In so doing, the plutocrat accrues a debt, which they must pay back. (A concept Warren would echo, calling these debts "claim checks," and that Melinda had propounded in her Ursuline Academy valedictory speech.) Carnegie believed the best way to settle this debt was by endowing institutions that benefit the public—libraries, concert halls, museums, universities, and so on.

"Thus is the problem of Rich and Poor to be solved," he wrote. "The laws of accumulation will be left free; the laws of distribution free. Individualism will continue, but the millionaire will be but a trustee for the poor, entrusted for a season with a great part of the increased wealth of the community, but administering it for the community far better than it could or would have done for itself."

To put that more plainly and piquantly, as critic of billionaire philanthropy Anand Giridharadas has, Carnegie is "using after-the-fact generosity to justify anything-goes taking."

In case anyone was in doubt about the "anything goes" part of the Carnegie equation, look no further than the Homestead strike. Three years after penning *The Gospel of Wealth*, Carnegie presented laborers at his steelworks outside Pittsburgh with a new contract stipulating pay cuts of up to 35 percent, and when the union rejected the contract, he allowed his second-in-command, Henry Clay Frick, to sic Pinkerton agents on the striking workers. As Carnegie golfed in Scotland, sixteen people were killed.

The other great exemplar of modern philanthropy was also less than admirable as a human being, at least where business was concerned. By general consensus, the modern era of philanthropy commences in part with John D. Rockefeller's attempt, circa 1909, to roll $100 million of his Standard Oil fortune into a general-purpose foundation with a mission to prevent and relieve suffering, advance knowledge, and promote "any and all of the elements of human progress." When Rockefeller and his advisor Frederick Gates (no relation) went to Congress to seek approval of a bill to incorporate the foundation, they were met with outcry. Among the mildest of such was former president Theodore Roosevelt's comment that "no amount of charities in spending such fortunes can compensate in any way for the misconduct in acquiring them." A nice riposte to Carnegie's *Gospel*, but for many critics of Rockefeller's bill, sidelong to the main problem, which was that his proposed foundation was inherently *antidemocratic*. They saw it as "an entity that would undermine political equality, convert private wealth into the donor's preferred public policies, could exist in perpetuity, and be unaccountable except to a handpicked assemblage of trustees," explains Rob Reich, co-director of the Stanford Center on Philanthropy and Civil Society, in his book *Just Giving*.

The Rockefeller legislation went through the usual rounds of congressional sausage making, emerging several years later as a proposal to incorporate the foundation, but with stern checks on its size, life span, and discretion. Notably, the Rockefeller Foundation would be subject to public oversight. The bill failed in the Senate. There's an interesting counterargument to be developed here: Given that the Rockefeller Foundation, which was ultimately chartered without such checks by New York State, has provided a template for virtually all foundations created since, what might contemporary philanthropy look like if the bill in Congress had passed, and public oversight had been baked in at the Rockefeller Foundation's formation? Might we be rid of the scourge of "dark money" in politics? Or—on the other hand—would charitable foundations be forbidden to carry out work that is politically unpopular, such as the sponsorship of transgressive art or delivery of aid to undocumented immigrants?

Thus, to all those who criticize mega-philanthropy, the rebuttal is that giving by the rich can be a boon to democracy itself in that it foments pluralism—money sluicing to eccentric visions and minority points of view that might otherwise starve of funding. Government priorities do not always address need. While much, perhaps too much, of this wealth goes to classical orchestras and art galleries—as survey after survey shows—everyone needs schools, well-funded universities, minority rights groups, medicines, clean water, vaccines, scientific research.

Andrew Carnegie's famous library program shows how private dollars can work to boost civic engagement and promote egalitarianism. The program began in earnest in 1899, and over the next two decades, Carnegie personally funded public libraries across the United States. The funding was in the form of a onetime grant, and he would approve grants only for towns with significant public buy-in: The municipality had to supply the land, and it was responsible for paying the staff and maintaining the building; local officials had to guarantee an annual operating budget equal to 10 percent of construction costs. The only string Carnegie attached to the working of his libraries was that they offer free service to all—a stipulation he got around in the segregated South by building dedicated libraries for African Americans. Carnegie didn't meddle with the hiring of librarians, and he didn't order that certain books be stocked. Once he'd built the library, it was the citizens to run.

The establishment of a Carnegie library in Greenville, Texas, demonstrates the ways the program drew upon, and enhanced, civic engagement. The local Women's Review Club—one of the many female-led organizations that sprang up after the Civil War—determined that the town needed a proper library. The ladies of the club wrote to Carnegie, who offered $15,000 if his aforementioned conditions were met. Margaret Graubard writes in her family memoir, "Because the municipality of Greenville lacked the resources to secure the grant, the business community and ladies clubs mounted an ambitious campaign to raise the needed money. All businesses were approached for donations, and requests went out for individual contributions. The eight member clubs of the Federation of Women's Clubs pledged $1,000 for maintenance, and the city council passed a resolution promising an additional $2,000 'if needed.'" In February 1903, less than a year after the initial outreach to Carnegie, the Greenville library opened in a magnificent building that served as both a lending library and a meeting space; its marble stairs led to a three-hundred-seat auditorium. A local young woman, Mrs. James Bruce Quigley, was hired as the first librarian.

"The vast new network of Carnegie libraries appeared at a time when support for publicly funded libraries was growing," explain Joel L. Fleishman, J. Scott Kohler, and Steven Schindler in a case study of the library program. "In the mid-nineteenth century, many States enacted laws enabling municipalities to raise funds to support public libraries, beginning with Massachusetts in 1848. By 1887, twenty states had public library enabling laws on the books." The authors go on to note that once Carnegie libraries were sufficiently widespread, members of the public came to expect that a public library was something every municipality ought to provide—a common good due every town, whether Andrew Carnegie supplied seed funding or not.

The Carnegie library program worked as a spur to the state: The popular will was behind the establishment of libraries, but government budgets were lagging behind. It was the model Bill and Melinda drew upon for their own library program: "You know, Carnegie was a pretty hard-core guy," Bill told the *New York Times*, adding, "I'd be happy if I could think that the role of the library was sustained and even enhanced in the age of the computer."

Julius Rosenwald's funding of rural schools for African Americans in the early 1900s offers a case study in how philanthropy may step into the breach when popular will lags behind the law, and thereby propagates injustice.

After earning a fortune in Chicago retail as part-owner of Sears, Rosenwald cemented a relationship with Booker T. Washington, the head of the Tuskegee Institute. In 1912, he gave Washington a $25,000 grant to create offshoot Tuskegee campuses; Washington found he had $2,100 left over following the expansion, and asked

Rosenwald's permission to use the money to build six small school-houses in rural Alabama. Rosenwald agreed, and soon ponied up another $30,000 for the Tuskegee Institute to establish a hundred more schools throughout the state. Buoyed by the success of the program, which he tracked with great avidity, Rosenwald decided to "scale up," in modern parlance: In 1920, his Julius Rosenwald Fund opened an office in Nashville and hired S. L. Smith, a former super-intendent of African American education in Tennessee, to oversee the creation of schoolhouses all over the South.

By the time of Rosenwald's death in 1932, his fund had facil-itated the construction of 4,977 rural schools, as well as 380 com-plementary homes and shops; in some areas, the Rosenwald schools surpassed local whites-only schools in quality. The last Rosenwald school built, in Warm Springs, Georgia, was constructed at the spe-cial request of then-president Franklin Delano Roosevelt. Historian George Brown Tindall called the schools program "one of the most effective stratagems to outflank the prejudice and apathy that hob-bled Negro education," and saw its larger impact as sparking public support for African American schools "while neutralizing the op-position of white taxpayers." In the end, the Julius Rosenwald Fund contributed only 15 percent of the total budget to construct and op-erate the rural schools; a combination of additional private dollars and government funding made up the difference.

It is impossible to argue that the Julius Rosenwald Fund's school-building program was antidemocratic. But this campaign wasn't getting around the law so much as taking the law at its word: Rosen-wald believed that the 14th Amendment of the Constitution guar-anteed equal rights to citizens Black or white—and that one right of all citizens was access to a good education. Working hand in glove with grassroots activists—Booker T. Washington and his Tuskegee Institute team—he launched what we'd today call a pilot program, and once his initial outlay of capital had borne fruit, Rosenwald expanded the program, and used it to rally public support behind spending on African American education that should have been present all along. His investment sparked a systemic redress in underfunding of African American schools, and to the degree that disparities in funding and quality of education remained, they were ultimately attacked at the source, as the Supreme Court upheld Rosenwald's first principle—fairness—in the 1954 *Brown v. Board of Education* decision that ruled racial segregation in public schools nationwide unconstitutional.

Alas, not all charity is quite so effective. The nonprofit sector has been used to funnel money to politicians and Astroturf groups, for instance, or create a tax dodge for the rich or get their kids into posh schools. It's also replete with organizations that spend more on overhead than they do on good works, a scourge attacked by, among others, the philosopher Peter Singer, whose theory of "effective altruism" has been incredibly influential—notably on Bill and Melinda.

"Effective altruism is based on a very simple idea: We should do the most good we can." Singer's words make a very difficult thing sound easy. First off, what does it mean to "do good"? Singer answers a question that has vexed moral philosophers from Aristotle onward by saying that goodness is not so much negatively constructed—avoiding all those "thou shalt nots"—as positively, revolving around proactive efforts to alleviate suffering. If it's moral to not murder someone, then logic dictates it's just as urgent a moral imperative to save a life. And if you'd dive into a lake to save a person from drowning, then oughtn't you also donate money to save a person in a distant country from dying of malaria? In her book *Strangers Drowning*, a set of profiles of supercommitted do-gooders, journalist Larissa MacFarquhar provides a useful précis of Singer's thinking. "If we spend two hundred dollars on clothes that could have bought lifesaving food or medicine, we're still responsible for a death," she explains. "And, by extension, if we don't give much of what we own and earn for the relief of suffering, then we're responsible for many deaths."

Singer's moral imperative extends to everyone living comfortably in the wealthy West, not just the best-off. But the math makes plain that the rich bear more responsibility for the lives of the poor than do others, because it's they who can afford to save the most lives, relieve the most poverty, expiate the most exploitation. Singer does not dwell on the causes of suffering, or its relationship to our global social and economic infrastructure, but rather urges all of us benefiting from that infrastructure to consider our privileges, and give over whatever is unnecessary to the maintenance of basic health and welfare to the alleviation of suffering in places where it's epidemic. That's part of the "most good we can" equation.

But there's another part, too. "Philanthropy is a very large industry," writes Singer. "In the United States alone there are almost one million charities, receiving a total of approximately $200 billion a year with an additional $100 billion donated to religious congregations. A small number of the charities are outright frauds, but a much bigger problem is that very few of them are sufficiently transparent to allow donors to judge whether they are really doing good." Effective altruism, Singer continues, "seeks to change that by providing incentives for charities to demonstrate their effectiveness." For Singer, this means being empirically minded, and making donations based on analyses of return on investment (ROI), as one would if considering whether to put money into a business. This can be done well, but it can also be done glibly, with "investors" demanding instant improvements to complex problems, or favoring short-term projects that can be represented on annual spreadsheets. Metrics are very useful to an organization that, say, distributes chickens to rural farmers in a country in the Global South: They demonstrate the success of the initiative by counting the farmers who got chickens. This charity could also commission a follow-up report determining what proportion of those farmers had a going egg concern a year later, and then another determining things like whether farmers failed to convert their chickens into egg businesses because X percentage of them didn't have henhouses. The *why* of not having a henhouse, or the *how* of getting one built, or broader issues pertaining to, for instance, farmers' understanding of the breeding and rearing of chickens, or labor and animal welfare conditions in the supply chain, or reliable access to a market for eggs, will not go on the spreadsheet. Whether an ideal such as gender equality is measurable is another matter entirely.

The age-old question of what the rich ought to do with their money will always be difficult to disentangle from the matter of whether there ought to be rich people at all, but, as previously stated, mingling the two questions tends to lead to a rhetorical dead end. Another dead end: juxtaposing the morality of *giving* with the morality of *getting and spending*. As Stanford's Rob Reich points out, "relative to consumption—going shopping and buying things—and relative to investment—seeking financial returns on one's assets—philanthropy will always come out looking good." So that begs the question of whether certain types of philanthropy are better than others, or how the act of philanthropic giving on a large scale may either complement or pervert the egalitarian aims of a democracy. To address the latter—what Reich refers to as the "public morality" of philanthropy—you must ignore the *intent* of the giver, and instead situate all acts of philanthropy in a broader context, placing greater emphasis on the *impact*.

This, too, is not so easy.

SUSIE BUFFETT'S PHILANTHROPIC models were not Andrew Carnegie and John D. Rockefeller. Susie operated in the original sense of the word "philanthropy": Etymologically, it comes from the Greek, which literally translates as "loving people." If Susie has a forebear, it might be Elizabeth of Hungary, who lived in the thirteenth century. She founded a hospital for the poor at Marburg in Thuringia, and distributed food and clothing; her devotion extended to washing the feet of the indigent. She was duly sainted.

If you think this comparison is an exaggeration, read on. After resettling in California, Susie soon stumbled onto a new cause. In Omaha, she'd thrown body and soul into the civil rights movement; in San Francisco, she tended to the ill, the depressed, and the dying. San Francisco was in the early years of the AIDS crisis and many of Susie's new friends in the city were gay men. Without skipping a beat, she went back into action as Susie-the-watering-can. Her apartment was transformed into an ad hoc hospice: As friends infected with AIDS neared the end of their lives, she invited them to stay with her. Her assistant, Kathleen Cole, a former nurse, would administer IV drips. Susie took a few of these friends on "dream trips," such as going to see the Dalai Lama in Dharamsala. Peter nicknamed her the "Dalai Mama." "I'm comfortable with the transition people are making," she later explained of her time ministering to terminal AIDS patients.

In some ways, Susie and Warren grew closer, living apart: Astrid Menks took care of Warren, and Susie, relieved of that burden, shifted into the role of key confidante and advisor. They'd gab on the phone daily, talking more than they'd ever managed to while they were under the same roof. It helped that Warren was trying harder to connect with his kids. And it helped, too, that with the benefit of distance, Warren could view Susie as a peer, a dynamic woman with forceful opinions, determined to make her own mark on the world. All of which put Astrid in the odd position of being on the inside, looking in.

How did Astrid feel about that? She's never said, not publicly anyway. But you can guess.

Meanwhile, Susie's own health began to falter. It became commonplace for Little Sooz to get a call from Cole saying her mother was in the hospital. She was particularly plagued by abdominal adhesions, and in 1993, she had a hysterectomy. But Susie wasn't about to let her body bog her down now that Warren's interest in philanthropy was finally ramping up. She'd convinced him to add to the Buffett

Foundation kitty, and with the help of Little Sooz, she was starting to flex her charitable muscles. The amount Warren allocated to the foundation remained relatively paltry, but Susie made do, content in the knowledge that she'd be able to make hay with his billions once he passed on. In the mid-1990s, Susie-directed money from the Buffett Foundation helped finance the development of the abortion pill RU-486.

Susie kept her giving well out of the public eye. She'd perfected a strategy for hiding in plain sight: She'd join Warren at the marquee events on his calendar and retreat back to the shadows immediately upon returning to San Francisco. In Seattle, Melinda was performing a similar trick. Prior to her wedding, she'd issued a code of *omertà* to everyone who knew her, even writing to former neighbors to request they not talk about her. One Microsoft pal refused to confirm or deny that she and Melinda sometimes went jogging. Another would only say, "That was part of her agreement with Bill—that she stays private." Melinda seemed determined to disappear. Melinda-the-person was replaced by Melinda-the-specter, aglow with hypotheticals. "[Melinda] has the capacity to become one of Seattle's great benefactors," wrote the *Seattle Times*, noting her prior involvement with local nonprofits. "Some predict that she will someday head up a Gates foundation."

That prediction came partly true following the birth of Bill and Melinda's first child, Jennifer, on April 26, 1996. Bill was shocked when Melinda informed him that she wouldn't be returning to work after the baby was born. "Then what *are* you going to do?" he asked. Philanthropy supplied an answer.

It began with the libraries. You'll recall that Bill's first major foray into philanthropy was a program to bring computers and internet access to America's public libraries, helmed by Patty Stonesifer. Stonesifer agreed to come on board because she was impressed with Bill's ambition; when she'd proposed to Bill that they buy computers for "all of the public libraries," he'd replied by asking, almost nonchalantly, "In the United States or around the world?" Stonesifer realized, then, that he meant business. But it ended up being Melinda who really threw herself into the project. After all, like Bill, Melinda had been a teenage computer whiz. She had fond memories of her high school math teacher, Mrs. Bauer, who "saw Apple II+ computers at a mathematics conference in Austin, returned to our school, and said, 'We need to get these for the girls.'" Access to computers had changed Melinda's life beyond measure—didn't everyone deserve the same chance?

Melinda started getting her hands dirty, working on the ground with multiple schools to help bring technology into the classroom. It was exhilarating, but before long the true scale of the issue became apparent. America's schools simply weren't working, and it would take a lot more than an injection of free computers to cure their ills.

"If there are miracle education drugs, they haven't emerged yet," notes Paul Hill, founder of the Center on Reinventing Public Education at the University of Washington. Later, Melinda would turn her attention once again to America's school system, and this time she would try to reform it from the ground up.

But in the meantime, what about actual drugs? When it came to health, Bill and Melinda's financial resources could make a real difference, pretty much instantly. Vaccines were literally just a matter of giving a shot, as Bill did when he traveled to India on the foundation's behalf to administer polio vaccines. The trip had a surprising genesis: In 1997, the World Health Organization's director of the Program for Vaccine Development had sent a letter requesting a meeting to Bill's dad, who picked up the missive, at some point; the letter might almost have gone in the trash, because Bill Sr. had no idea his son was devoutly interested in the problems of immunization. But as it turned out, he was. Maybe he could see how vaccines offered the simplest way of doing the most life-changing good in the world, or maybe they appealed to his existing interests—after all, isn't a vaccine just a software patch for your body? In any case, representatives of WHO were duly granted an audience. This chat about jabs would be the first of many, many to come. PATH followed up with a pitch stressing the "moral imperative" of investing in children's vaccines—shots for polio, rotavirus, and other common, needlessly deadly diseases—and arguing that the best way to do so was by artificially creating a market to stimulate production. In 1998, Bill and Melinda established a children's vaccine program at PATH, endowing it with a $100 million gift.

Maybe even Bill didn't yet realize what was happening. Back then, he might have seen his growing foundation as a sideline—after all, what's $100 million to someone like Bill Gates? A private project, his way of giving back. But very soon, these charity trips would start to change his life completely. Then they'd change the world.

7

BOOM!

Bill was trying. *Really* trying. He spent way more time than he wanted to, in 1998, trying to repair his public image. He sang "Twinkle, Twinkle Little Star" on TV as he gabbed to Barbara Walters about the pleasures of fatherhood. He donated over $100 million to charity—peanuts to him, sure, but more money than most of his critics could ever dream of. He got bespoke suits, a haircut, and sleek wire-rimmed glasses, and showed them off while promoting the rollout of Windows 98. He made fun of his golf game in an ad for Big Bertha clubs. Bill's ROI wasn't impressive. The *Baltimore Sun* convened a panel of fashion experts to make fun of his style ("He dresses like a geek from the audiovisual club in high school," jibed one.) The *Wall Street Journal* noted the Big Bertha campaign in an article about Bill's failing efforts to join the invitation-only Augusta National Golf Club. "He wants it too badly," the paper said. At the 1998 Macworld Expo, a small video-game developer launched *Microshaft Winblows 98*, in which you fed your pet Billagotchi by giving him money.

Bill took solace from his family, and from his visits with Warren. Throughout all Bill's troubles, their friendship had only deepened, and Warren's public support of Bill's character had proved that Warren wasn't one to turn his back on a friend in need.

By 2000, they'd settled into a rhythm of seeing each other at least four times a year, not including at pooh-bah gatherings like the annual Sun Valley Conference, and on those visits, there was golf to be played (Warren *was* a member at Augusta), and bridge hands to be dealt, and football to be watched. One of Bill's regular jokes was to stock rolls of University of Nebraska toilet paper in the guest bathroom whenever Warren came to stay.

Then word got out that a campy TV movie about Bill's rivalry with Steve Jobs was in the works. The chances it would flatter Bill were nil. But there was no way Hollywood could do worse portraying Bill on camera than he'd done himself, in his taped *U.S. v. Microsoft* deposition that same year.

Joel Klein, honcho at the Justice Department, had retained superlitigator David Boies to help him nail Microsoft to the cross. The government's intervention came too late for Netscape; by August 27, 1998, the date Bill sat to be deposed by Boies, the company was a dead man walking. But if the DOJ couldn't save Netscape, they could still take down Microsoft.

When attorney Gary Reback had submitted his anti-Microsoft materials, he had proposed breaking up the firm, perhaps by severing its application software and operating system businesses. But Microsoft's whole strategy for growth was based on integration: The OS contained the browser, which opened onto the MSN portal, which linked to a whole plethora of websites—such as the travel site Expedia—created to pump money back into Microsoft. This proprietary system had played a large part in making Bill so rich, and he wasn't about to see this scheme be destroyed.

Judge Thomas Penfield Jackson intended to make *U.S. v Microsoft* a short trial, limiting each side to twelve witnesses, and he put the case on an accelerated schedule, skipping the usual rondelle of preliminary hearings. The trial was set to start in mid-October.

It was preceded by a long, tense summer. Preoccupied by the case and wallowing in self-pity, Bill must have scowled hard when he received a letter in July from the liberal activist Ralph Nader—a critic of mega-philanthropy on the basis that (1) the rich have no business being so rich in the first place and (2) they are the last people to be trusted with giving their wealth away by dint of being chronically self-interested—asking him to "team up" with his "dear friend and fellow card player" Warren Buffett to "sponsor, plan and lead a conference of billionaires and multibillionaires on the subject of National and Global Wealth Disparities and What to Do About It." You can practically hear Bill yelling, *That's the stupidest thing I've ever heard!* Especially coming from Ralph Nader, one of Bill's public *bêtes noires*. Summoning a diplomatic tone, he replied to Nader, telling him that he intended to give away his fortune in due course, but in his opinion, "people should give because they want to give, and not because of pressure from a conference or anyone who claims they have all the answers in this area."

Nader, not one to be put off, replied to Bill's reply. "Mr. Gates kindly recounted his present and future philanthropic initiatives. My letter was not addressed to his philanthropy. It requested that he and Warren Buffett convene a conference of billionaires on the structural issues of wealth inequality in our country."

History does not record whether Bill replied to the reply to his reply.

History *did* record Bill's August 27 deposition. Literally. It's on videotape. No need to split hairs: For Bill, and for Microsoft, the deposition was an absolute disaster. Facing off against Boies, considered one of the most brilliant litigators in American history, Bill came off as rude and pedantic, and like a man whose temporary amnesia had caused him to forget everything he ever knew about his company. He professed ignorance of Microsoft's marketing strategies—even when Boies presented him with copies of emails he'd written outlining those strategies. Stephen Houck, who was the antitrust bureau chief at New York State's attorney general's office recalls an illustrative exchange. "Did you write this?" Boies asked, pointing at the billg@microsoft handle. Bill said he didn't know. "So where'd it come from?" Bill shrugged, rocked, and answered: "A computer."

Boies deposed Bill for three days. By the end of the ordeal, he'd produced a powerful weapon in the government's case—and now Bill and the Microsoft legal team were faced with a conundrum: If they let Bill take the stand at trial, he'd be called to account on all his obfuscations; if he didn't take the stand, Judge Jackson would allow the DOJ to play tapes of the deposition in open court. They chose the latter.

The trial commenced on October 19. Boies, laying out the government's case, cued up the badly lit footage of Bill sniping, fidgeting, saying "I don't know" about stuff he clearly knew, and quibbling about the meaning of basic words and phrases. At one point, Judge Jackson laughed.

"I gave totally truthful answers," Bill would later insist. "When [Boies] would ask imprecise questions, I would simply point out to him the imprecise nature of the question." Bill genuinely hadn't anticipated that his character would be on trial—and not just before Judge Jackson, but in the court of public opinion, as well. The government's PR tactics infuriated him. It helped a little that Melinda had acquired a custom-made pinball machine, with Joel Klein's face in the crosshairs.

And where was Warren as all this was going on? Buying Dairy Queen. Buying vast quantities of silver. Decrying the stupidity of people pumping tech stocks full of hot air. At the 1998 Berkshire Hathaway shareholders meeting, Warren asserted that hot internet stocks such as eBay and Amazon were totally impossible to value. "If I taught a class, on my final exam I would take an Internet company and ask, 'How much is this company worth?' Anyone who would answer I would flunk."

Meanwhile, Warren was very much Team Bill. As Microsoft's lawyers geared up for trial and the stock market melted down following Russia's devaluation of the ruble, Warren and Susie joined Bill and

Melinda for a two-week "Gold Rush" trip from Alaska to California. They helicoptered over ice fields and cruised through fjords, and all the while, Warren's head was in New York, where Goldman Sachs was putting together a bid for Berkshire to take over the hedge fund Long-Term Capital Management, an overleveraged victim of the "Russian Flu," as the short-lived financial crisis came to be known. As everyone else in the traveling party ogled grizzly bears at Alaska's Pack Creek, Warren was trying to make contact with Goldman head Jon Corzine. "The captain would point out, *Look, there's a bear. I was saying, To hell with the bear. Let's get back to where I can hear the satellite phone.*" The bid fell through. Warren was consoled by bridge: When a private train car Gates had rented picked up the party in Montana, Warren was delighted to find Sharon Osberg and Fred Gitelman, another bridge fanatic, seated inside. As the train chugged past the waterfalls of Wind River Canyon, Bill, Warren, Osberg, and Gitelman played hand after hand, a twelve-hour marathon.

In January 1999, with the government resting its case and Microsoft calling its first witness, Warren quietly began buying blocks of Microsoft on Berkshire Hathaway's behalf. Maybe he had evaluated P/E ratios and calculated MSFT's liquidation value. Maybe he was just being a pal.

For, as the trial wore on, things were not going Microsoft's way. Not at all. Intel vice president Steve McGeady—testifying against his bosses' wishes—dropped bomb after bomb on the defense. The most explosive was McGeady's testimony about an August 1995 memo he'd written about a meeting with top Microsoft execs. Titled "Sympathy for the Devil," it read, "Bill Gates told Intel CEO Andy Grove to shut down the Intel Architecture Labs. Gates didn't want IAL's 750 engineers interfering with his plans for dominating the PC industry." Bill's own emails backed up McGeady's claims. After one meeting with Grove, he wrote: "We are the software company here and we will not have any kind of equal relationship with Intel on software." Later, as Microsoft began producing friendly witnesses, David Boies eviscerated them one by one. The defense was flailing. So much so, in fact, that in mid-February Judge Jackson started a day's court session by stating to no one in particular, "The code of tribal wisdom says that when you discover you are riding a dead horse, the best strategy is to dismount." Bill needed a friend like Warren.

THE PURCHASE OF Microsoft shares wasn't Warren's only reversal around this time. (Side note: Warren was forced to disclose the purchase, which he'd kept hidden for quite a few months; it's not clear when he unloaded the stock, but he did at some point, and never bought any again.) He'd also gone back on his word about not handing millions of dollars to his children.

Howie, the family troublemaker, had taken a job as spokesman for the Illinois-based agricultural company Archer-Daniels-Midland. As it happens, ADM was knee-deep in a worldwide price-fixing scheme, which Howie knew nothing about. Then his colleague Mark Whitacre informed him (1) that ADM was engaged in crime related to the amino acid lysine, (2) that he, Whitacre, was a government mole, and (3) that FBI agents were on their way to Howie's house for an interview. (This story was later immortalized in the Steven Soderbergh film *The Informant!* with Matt Damon playing Whitacre.) Howie, freaked out, called his dad. Warren told him he could leave ADM or he could stay, but he had to make up his mind in the next twenty-four hours. The next day, Howie resigned.

With Howie suddenly out of a job, and Little Sooz's second marriage also unraveling, Susie went to bat to get Warren to loosen his purse strings. (Musical Peter, doing his own thing, was busy composing songs for the Demi Moore film *The Scarlet Letter.*) Thus began a tradition of Warren gifting each of his kids $1 million every five years, on their birthdays. He also put Howie on the Berkshire Hathaway board, saying that his son would eventually succeed him in the role of nonexecutive chairman, a person with power but no real say, like King Charles III. So much for not believing in "the divine right of the womb." Warren assuaged concerns about scattered Howie's ascension to the head of Berkshire's board by joking that, first of all, he had no plans to die, and even if he did, he'd keep working. "I've given the directors a Ouija board so they can keep in touch," he wise-cracked.

Investing in Microsoft. Bequeathing privilege. Another flip-flop: In 1998, Warren did the unthinkable—well, unthinkable to financial analysts—and diluted Berkshire Hathaway shares by buying insurance wholesaler General Re via a stock swap. The deal was hugely expensive—much, much bigger than any of Berkshire's previous largest-ever acquisitions—and it left observers scratching their heads. Even Charlie Munger seemed dismayed, saying Warren hadn't consulted him about the deal until the very last minute.

People were starting to question Warren's judgment. Not loudly or vociferously, by any means, but there were the odd whispered asides. Over the course of 1999, the doubters began to raise their voices; to wit, business magazine *Barron's* published a cover story asking whether the Oracle had lost his touch. The main question on the doubters' minds was why—for God's sake—Warren Buffett was continuing to sit out the tech boom. More than five hundred companies went public that year, half of them internet start-ups. But Warren steered clear.

In July 1999, Warren and the Buffett clan touched down in Idaho for the annual Sun Valley Conference. Hosted by Allen & Co., a boutique investment bank, Sun Valley is an ultra-private gathering of the ultra-wealthy and the ultra-powerful. Conspiracy theorists might say it's where the world's head honchos get together to plan the future, and in broad strokes, they wouldn't be wrong. The honchos also golf and fly-fish and whatnot. Warren had been making the pilgrimage to Sun Valley for several years, and on this occasion, he'd be delivering the conference's closing speech. This, too, was by and large an exception: Warren had a rule about speaking only at Berkshire conclaves.

He broke this rule in order to shove a pin in a balloon. With numerous newly minted tech millionaires seated in the audience, Warren delivered a sermon on how to value stocks, and how you could tell when the market was in the midst of a speculative frenzy. It was clear he believed that folks throwing their money at tech start-ups had a bad case of tulip fever. "It's wonderful to promote new industries, because they are very promotable," Warren said.

> *It's very hard to promote investment in a mundane product. It's much easier to promote an esoteric product, even particularly one with losses, because there's no quantitative guideline.*

By this, Warren meant, in essence, that there was no performance history to evaluate. He continued:

> *But people will keep coming back to invest, you know. It reminds me a little of that story of the oil prospector who died and went to heaven. And St. Peter said, "Well, I checked you out, and you meet all of the qualifications. But there's one problem. . . . We have some tough zoning laws up here, and we keep all the oil prospectors over in that pen. And as you can see, it is absolutely chock-full. There is no room for you."*
>
> *And the prospector said, "Do you mind if I just say four words?"*
>
> *St. Peter said, "No harm in that."*
>
> *So the prospector cupped his hands and yells out, "Oil discovered in hell!"*
>
> *And of course, the lock comes off the cage and all of the oil prospectors start heading right straight down.*
>
> *St. Peter said, "That's a pretty slick trick. So," he says, "go on in, make yourself at home. All the room in the world."*

The prospector paused for a minute, then said, "No, I think I'll go along with the rest of the boys. There might be some truth to that rumor after all."

As the techies' jaws clenched, Warren clicked to a slide illustrating the vast degree to which the market's current valuation surpassed the output of the economy as a whole. Eventually, the imbalance would right itself, he said—at which point, the market would stagnate. For years. The other option was that the market would crash.

Now the crowd gazed at him with stony eyes. "As my mentor Ben Graham always used to say, 'You can get in way more trouble with a good idea than a bad idea,'" Warren continued. "Because you forget that the good idea has limits."

It's not that Warren was the only person arching an eyebrow at the start-up-fueled boom. Experienced Silicon Valley hands knew perfectly well that many of the dot-coms they were funding would turn out to be flops.

Still, when word of Warren's speech leaked to the press, it caused a stir. This was the Oracle of Omaha, after all. But nothing changed. The market kept climbing.

DRIVING AROUND DOWNTOWN Seattle in early 1998, you saw Bill Gates everywhere. A guerrilla artist had drawn a demoniacal caricature of his face and plastered it all over town with the legend "Anti Trust Me." Bill was probably avoiding downtown. The Microsoft campus in Redmond was one refuge; the Lake Washington compound was another. As Microsoft's lawyers sat down with Joel Klein and his team to discuss a settlement in March 1999, the Gateses' second child, Rory, was on the way. He'd be born in May, after the settlement talks collapsed, but before artist Allan Sekula photographed himself swimming as near as he could to the shoreline outside the Gates manse. He exhibited these images in Rotterdam the following year alongside a photo of a typewritten letter he'd sent to Bill, which made reference to Bill's recent purchase of the Winslow Homer painting *Lost on the Grand Banks* for the stunning price of $30 million, the most paid for an American painting to that date.

"So why are you so interested in a picture of two poor lost dory fishermen, momentarily high on a swell, peering into a wall of fog?" asked Sekula. "They're about as high as they're ever going to be, unless the sea gets uglier. They are going to die you know, and it won't be a pretty death."

He added: "And as for you Bill, when you're on the Net, are you lost? Or found?"

Even when Bill was nestled in his home, he couldn't get away from the hate.

He must have wondered what he'd done to become such a pariah. And maybe he started thinking seriously about what he could do to change people's minds about that.

IN 1999, THE Gateses merged their two foundations into one, creating the Bill & Melinda Gates Foundation. The name itself signaled something new: Bill might have been the face of the foundation, but in those years it was very much Melinda's work that kept it running. That said, the money was Bill's, and there was a lot of it. Over the course of the year, Bill started increasing the foundation's endowment by $5 billion quarterly. Recent gifts included a pledge of $1 billion over twenty years for scholarships for minority students, to be administered by the United Negro College Fund, and a $50 million grant to fund research into a malaria vaccine, a gift that effectively doubled the worldwide spending on such research. Yet the haters kept hating.

To put it plainly, Bill Gates, one of the smartest men in the world, was confused. The nature of his confusion was spotted by Ralph Nader: As Nader had observed regarding Bill's response to his letter in the summer of '98, Mr. Gates had responded to a query regarding structural inequality by talking about philanthropy, and these were two very different things.

If Bill thought that giving his money away would make people more comfortable with the fact that he had consolidated an immense amount of wealth and power, he was wrong. At the end of the day, he was still a plutocrat holed up in his dream house, staring at yeomen tossed about on stormy seas. And he'd paid a heck of a lot for the painting.

Judge Thomas Penfield Jackson apparently wasn't crazy about the concentration of wealth and power either, and on November 5, 1999, he delivered Microsoft a stinging rebuke: "A blunt 412-paragraph j'accuse that nails Microsoft not only on the two most critical issues— that it has monopoly control over PC operating systems and that it wields power in ways that harm American consumers—but on virtually every count brought against it," as *Time* wrote when the judgment was handed down. This was actually the first half of the judgment, a "findings of fact." Before Judge Jackson got to the second part, he wanted Microsoft and the DOJ to sit down with a mediator. On November 19, he appointed the eminent U.S. Court of Appeals Judge Richard Posner to the role.

Everyone wanted a settlement. Even lonely Bill fans, like columnist Jim Seymour, urged Microsoft to come to terms with the government. "Bill, settle. Period," wrote Seymour in an open letter. "Stretch it out a little, make it look good, huff and puff, talk about the importance of innovation—the whole *oeuvre* you've developed over the past year and a half—but settle, damn it."

The alternative was "structural remedies." That's code for "breaking up Microsoft."

Eleven days after Posner's appointment, Seattle rioted. At least forty thousand protesters hit the streets to march against the World Trade Organization meeting set to commence at the city's convention center. As sundry black bloc anarchists stormed through downtown smashing shop windows, cops fired pepper spray, tear gas, and stun grenades at peaceful protesters in an effort to break up their blockade. At noon, the opening ceremony at the convention center was canceled. Delegates keen to discuss adjusting the levers of global finance were stuck in their hotels. Previously nonviolent protestors began lobbing bottles at the police, the police struck back, the black bloc continued to rampage. One imagines that Bill Gates, watching the coverage out in Redmond, might have liked to don a balaclava and go incognito to join the melee and smash up a federal building or two.

Instead, he had just approved another Bill & Melinda Gates Foundation grant. This one, for a healthy $750 million, would establish GAVI, the Global Alliance for Vaccines and Immunizations. The more Bill and Melinda immersed themselves in global health policy, the more they discovered that horrified them. For instance, as Melinda points out in *The Moment of Lift*, when a new vaccine is developed in a rich Western country, it can then take fifteen to twenty years before it finally reaches the poor children in the developing world who need it the most. Clearly, the system as it stood wasn't working, so Bill and Melinda decided to build a new one from scratch. This was what GAVI set out to achieve. Per Melinda's description, the organization "use[s] market mechanisms to help get vaccines to every child in the world." In other words, by funding the alliance, the foundation created a market for pharmaceutical companies to sell into, with the aim of sparking them to innovate new and better vaccines. But what GAVI also meant was that the upstart foundation was already working with some very big players—not just the UN and WHO, but national governments in both the developed and developing worlds. And Bill and Melinda were the ones setting the agenda. Here, at least, Bill was the one forging ahead, while the federal government followed meekly behind.

Or, in other, other words: While the Battle of Seattle protesters noisily demonstrated against a world that seemed to be run for the benefit of the ultrarich, Bill and Melinda Gates were quietly using philanthropy to prove that their vast personal fortune could be a force for good.

IT'S PLEASING TO imagine that among the stacks and stacks of docu-
ments sitting in Judge Richard Posner's chambers as mediation talks
between Microsoft and the Department of Justice commenced, there
was a clipping from *The Onion*. Dated July 23, 1996, and headlined
"Bill Gates to Get Half," the satirical news item begins, "In a move
designed to hasten the inevitable, billionaire Microsoft tycoon Bill
Gates announced yesterday that from now on, he will be getting
half." Half of everything. From everyone.

"It has not yet been decided if Gates' half will be taken straight
down the middle or by liquidating all assets and dividing up raw
capital," the article continues. "The question will be settled later this
week by a special session of Gates' half of the U.S. Congress."

The question before Posner and the *United States v. Microsoft
Corporation* litigants was precisely a matter of whether and how
to divvy things up. Team Bill was arguing feverishly that Microsoft shouldn't be broken in two, as the government was advocating;
Judge Posner, for his part, would spend the next four months trying
to craft a mutually agreeable consent decree that would keep Microsoft intact but significantly restrict its behavior. In March 2000, with
the deadline for Judge Thomas Penfield Jackson's final verdict loom-
ing, Posner got Bill to sign off on the fourteenth of his draft proposals, only to have Joel Klein, at the DOJ, reject it out of hand. Drafts
fifteen, sixteen, and seventeen likewise got binned. On March 29,
the DOJ submitted its eighteenth draft of a consent decree. Among
other things, it required Microsoft to allow PC makers to license the
Windows source code, which would allow them to modify the desktop and integrate rival software. Huddling with consiglieres such as
newly elevated Microsoft CEO Steve Ballmer and general counsel
Bill Neukom, Bill reviewed the offer, weighing it against the threat
of his company getting chopped into bits. In his heart of hearts,
he just didn't believe that Judge Jackson would pull the trigger on
a breakup. He passed. Neukom scribbled a rival proposal—draft
nineteen—and sent it off. The DOJ laughed.

On April 3, Judge Jackson delivered his final verdict, a sweeping denunciation of Microsoft that codified his earlier "findings of fact" as "conclusions of law." The DOJ followed up the ruling by asking the court to chop up Microsoft. The company's stock plummeted on the news, with Bill alone taking a one-day hit of at least $12 billion. As the share price kept falling, he went on the attack, going on TV to disparage the government's proposed remedy as "out of bounds," "unprecedented," "radical," and—throwing down the lightning bolt—the work of people ignorant of the software business. Judge Jackson was not pleased. On May 24, he told a packed courtroom he was prepared to go along with Justice's preferred remedy—the division of Microsoft into two companies, one focused on operating systems, the other on applications. "The matter is submitted," said the exhausted judge, and banged his gavel.

"This decree will stimulate innovation throughout the software industry in operating systems, applications and computing devices," crowed Joel Klein, Justice's field general in the Microsoft assault. "The American consumer will benefit enormously from this proposed remedy." Klein, ultimately, was proved correct. As you might have noticed if you've come across a Microsoft product in the present century, the company was never actually broken up: The legal directive was overturned on appeal. Still, it's now generally agreed that the government's harrying of Microsoft in the late 1990s set the stage for a new wave of tech innovation. "You can draw a pretty straight line from [*U.S. v. Microsoft*] to the growth of Google and Amazon and Apple, the explosion of Facebook and the introduction of start-ups like Uber, Airbnb, Pinterest and Slack," wrote Kara Swisher in a *New York Times* opinion column. Once the "apex predator of tech," as Swisher described Microsoft, the company had been tamed, and made to play nicely with the other kids—some of whom would turn out to be bullies in the Microsoft mold, shoving their would-be competitors, Microsoft included, into lockers.

Now the nerds are taking revenge on each other.

For his part, Bill seems to have come to a separate peace about his long-running legal squabbles. For all his fire-breathing in public, privately he was settling into a new role at Microsoft, as the company's "chief software architect," and trying to leave day-to-day operations to Steve Ballmer.

A touch wistfully, perhaps, he watched as Microsoft employees left Redmond in droves; the fifty or so folks resigning each week included not just lowly coders off to launch their own start-ups but also some pretty senior figures—up to and including the company's first chief technology officer. Bill had a choice: He could play the part of a latter-day Bourbon king, presiding over a crumbling monarchy, or he could copy his old hero from high school war games, Napoléon, and conquer new territory.

He chose the latter. With Melinda at his side, Bill set out to become the emperor of philanthropy, and here, again, Warren would play a massive part.

At a recent event hosted by venture capital firm Village Global, Bill emphasized how essential Warren's moral support was to him during this difficult time. "The toughest thing that I went through was this antitrust lawsuit, where it didn't seem very predictable," said Bill, going on to explain that Warren provided him "great counsel." "Getting somebody who is successful in another domain, but yet has a kind of a business-type mindset . . . that was a huge gift."

The gift would keep on giving.

PART II

8

ALL I WANT IS YOU

One of the last questions asked of Bill and Warren at the University of Washington that day they spoke to business students in 1998 was about philanthropy: "As two of the world's most successful business-people, what role do you see for yourselves in giving back to your communities? And how do you use your influence to get others to give back as well?"

Warren talked about the ovarian lottery—and his sheer luck at having been born with the right skills in the right place at the right time. "As Bill says, if I had been born some time ago, I would've been some animal's lunch," Warren noted. Bill himself mostly stayed quiet during this portion of the event, which is odd, since there was plenty he could have mentioned. Patty Stonesifer was scrivening away at her Gates Learning Foundation office above a pizza parlor. PATH's Gordon Perkin was hammering out the details of a $100 million children's vaccine initiative—work Bill had dived into right around the time of his and Warren's visit to the university. He could have pointed out that, at that very university, he'd paid for a law school building and funded the establishment of its Department of Molecular Biotechnology, whose superstar head, genomics pioneer Leroy Hood, he'd helped to recruit. But he did not take credit for all that. Why?

Unlike Warren, Bill was still mastering the art of personal brand-ing. He often complained he didn't recognize the supervillain Bill Gates of myth. "Yes, I'm intense. I'm energetic. I like to understand what our market position is. But then it gets turned into this—*the ul-tracompetitor*," he told one reporter. "It's somewhat dehumanizing. I read that and say, *I don't know that guy*." He couldn't figure out why, around Seattle, people griped that Bill Gates had spent more money on his ever-metastasizing compound on Lake Washington, with its twenty-car underground garage, spa, theater, and giant indoor trampoline, than he had donated to local charities. (That may not have been true, but anyway—people griped.) Nationally, Bill's tan-gles with the government made any do-gooder move seem suspect, and he must surely have begun to conclude that he'd never again be measured by his deeds alone when ulterior motives were insinuated into every act of generosity.

IN 2005, BILL and Melinda made the cover of *Time* for their chari-table work, but they weren't alone on the cover. Under the title "Per-sons of the Year," wedged tightly in between them, like a celebrity party crasher, stood Paul David Hewson, better known as Bono, de-scribed by the magazine's managing editor Jim Kelly as "the Irish rocker who has made debt reduction sexy."

In fact, Bono had by then been trying to crash the Gateses' philanthropy gig for years. As Bill ratcheted up his giving efforts in the first few years of the twenty-first century, Bono saw a potential partner-in-activism. The only problem was getting to him. Luckily, they had a mutual friend: Paul Allen. Bono started barraging Paul with emails. "Would you help me get to Bill Gates?" he asked. "Be-cause we really need to professionalize our operation, and we need funding, and I know that he's interested in the same things that we are, and Melinda, too." Paul did his best. But Bill, whose relation-ship to pop culture was incidental at best, brushed him off. Appar-ently, he'd confused him with the singer-songwriter Sonny Bono.

Eventually a bashful Paul Allen simply stopped replying to Bono's missives.

That changed in January 2002. In the wake of 9/11, in a display of solidarity with New York, the World Economic Forum held its first-ever get-together away from the snowy peaks of Davos, Switzerland. Instead, they relocated to the Waldorf Astoria hotel. And that was where Bono finally met Bill. It must have been a bit like the day, more than a decade previous, that Bill first spoke to Warren. You can imagine Bill pouting at first, still short-tempered. *I'm trying to wipe out global disease, and you want me to talk to* who? *Sonny Bono? Not interested. Not unless Cher is with him, of course.*

But then he and Bono talked, and kept talking, and the world—subtly, almost imperceptibly at first—looked like it might get help in a few much-needed areas.

Back in 1991, on that pebble beach on Puget Sound, Bill and Warren had talked about software. In 2002, in some jeweled corner of the Waldorf Astoria, Bono and Bill talk about AIDS, already a Gates Foundation priority.

Bono, the energetic front man of rock band U2 and a do-it-yourself Christian, was no newcomer to the world of activism. Growing up, he'd been moved by the protests against apartheid South Africa; later he'd been inspired to get involved in charity work after attending the benefit show *The Secret Policeman's Ball* for Amnesty International in 1979; in 1986, he'd helped organize Amnesty's A Conspiracy of Hope concert tour featuring Sting, Joan Baez, and other greats; he'd been involved in the Band Aid and Live Aid projects organized by Bob Geldof; he and his wife, Ali Hewson, volunteered at a relief camp in Ethiopia in 1985 at the invitation of World Vision; the following year he visited Nicaragua and El Salvador to draw attention to the ongoing conflicts and its effect on children; and emerged in the coming years as a leader in the fight against poverty and debt relief in Africa, lobbying leaders around the globe. The fight against AIDS was on the Irishman's radar, too.

Still, Bill was surprised at how much this rock star actually understood. "I was kind of amazed," he recalled a decade later, "that he actually knew what he was talking about and had a real commitment to making things happen. It was phenomenal. Ever since then we've been big partners in crime."

Things move fast in billionaire-land. A day or two after that first meeting, Bill and Bono were on stage together, alongside George W. Bush's Treasury secretary and a former president of Mexico. The Bill on that stage is an almost unrecognizable figure. He's not geekily excited by some new software feature, and he's not angrily defending his tech monopoly in front of a government commission. He's there purely to talk about the AIDS crisis. It's "solvable," he says, "with pretty modest resources." You know, a few billion here, a few billion there. And he's the man who's going to solve it. It's just a problem, like any other, with right ways and wrong ways to approach it. How do you do it right? You get the best minds, you listen, you run models, you activate resources, you act.

Here was the new Bill Gates. While a semi-obscure musician John Vanderslice might have released a single in 2000 called "Bill Gates Must Die," thinking the old Bill was still roaming at large, a slow-moving target, the new Bill, alongside Melinda and now Bono, set to work on the AIDS crisis. In truth, Bill Gates was still being widely vilified—still seen as a beige-colored man in a world of beige-colored keyboards—but the image was fast ceasing to be the primary representation of the man.

As the new millennium dawned, Bill shocked many who thought they knew him by stepping down as CEO of Microsoft, taking on the newly created role of "chief software architect." It seemed he was resetting his priorities: The world Melinda had seen before he saw it—the world of shocking need and disastrous preventable mortality—was now apparent to him, and it was now human lives, rescuable ones, not copies of Windows, that would increasingly draw his famed focus. A *Forbes* report suggested he would split all his new free time between his two pet projects. One: modeling the human brain. Two: "the charitable foundation that he runs with his wife, Melinda." Well, Bill never did achieve stardom as the man who modeled the human brain, but he and Melinda sure went to work with world-conquering zeal.

ON MARCH 10, 2000, the Nasdaq peaked at 5,048 points. On March 11, it began a long, steep slide. Over the next two and a half years, it would lose a whopping 78 percent of its value, and vaunted start-ups such as Pets.com and online grocery Webvan would collapse. The dot-com crash was underway. One man, at least, had predicted this: Warren's "I told you so" moment had arrived, its taste as creamy and sweet as a Dairy Queen Dilly Bar. But it was as cold as a Dilly Bar, too: Circa the turn of the millennium, Berkshire was itself taking hit after hit, some of them self-inflicted.

To wit, Warren's purchase of General Re—the one he orchestrated via an eyebrow-raising stock swap—was looking like an incredibly expensive mistake, with the insurer paying out massive claims on ill-considered policies. Elsewhere in the Berkshire portfolio, the good ship Coca-Cola seemingly could not be righted, even after Warren had forced through a CEO switcheroo. His fortress of capital was under attack, the market he continued to believe was overheated made it impossible to allocate Berkshire's savings into new investments that would generate big returns, and the internet—emerging into its modern form, as the world's greatest-ever platform for the circulation of invective and innuendo—had become a hotbed of accusations that the so-called Oracle of Omaha was going soft in the head. Then, in February, Berkshire's share price cratered on rumors that Warren was dying. No sooner had he managed to stamp out the rumors than Warren was rushed to the hospital with a kidney stone.

Yowling in pain, Warren might have wondered whether the rumors had been some kind of self-fulfilling prophecy. He *had* to get better, and fast: His convalescence occurred right on the eve of

Berkshire's annual shareholder conference, the signature Warren Buffett publicity event. Upon dragging himself away from his sickbed, Warren, still the worse for wear, convened an atypically grim meeting of the Berkshire Hathaway-ites: Omaha's Civic Auditorium was half empty, and many of the shareholders who had shown up for the usually boisterous affair came with (figurative) pitchforks in hand. One piqued shareholder had traveled all the way from Santa Barbara to inform Warren that after buying BRK in 1998, at nearly its highest price, he'd only managed to offset his losses on the stock thanks to gains in his tech portfolio. Acting on the widespread assumption that the Nasdaq's recent nosedive represented a temporary blip, he urged Warren to throw some of Berkshire's idle capital at tech stocks while they were low. "Isn't there enough left in your brain power to maybe pick a few?"

Then, in the summer of 2001, Kay Graham died.

Body blow. Punch in the solar plexus.

Warren's business woes were of a relative kind, part of the ebb and flow of a career that was, by any standard, a historic success. But eighty-four-year-old Katharine Graham falling on a sidewalk in Sun Valley while attending the eponymous conference and never waking up again—that was definitive.

Kay's death utterly rocked Warren. He self-flagellated the way mourning people do, replaying in his mind the scene of Kay in her room in the intensive care unit at St. Alphonsus in Boise, pallid and unconscious and hooked up to blinking monitors. He wondered if Kay would still be alive had he played bridge with her the night of her stroke and escorted her safely back to her room, and he castigated himself for declining to speak at her funeral. She wouldn't, and he couldn't—his Dale Carnegie training hadn't prepared him to give a eulogy at the Washington National Cathedral before thousands of attendees, a former U.S. president among them, paying tribute to a woman he had loved dearly, and now lost. Instead, he sat beside Bill and Melinda in the pew and listened to others declaim.

It so happens that Warren had recently found causes, ones starkly at odds with his own financial interests, and at odds also with the views of some of his golfing buddies: He'd spent some of the first half of 2001 championing campaign finance reform and inveighing against newly inaugurated president George W. Bush's plans to phase out the estate tax, which would allow the megarich to pass on nearly everything, tax-free, to their kids—kids who might lack their parents' talent to know what to do with the power they had inherited. "Without the estate tax," he said, "you in effect will have an aristocracy of wealth, which means you pass down the ability to command the resources of the nation." That, he continued, would be a mistake tantamount to "choosing the 2020 Olympic team by picking the eldest sons of the gold-medal winners in the 2000 Olympics."

"We would regard that as absolute folly in terms of athletic competition," he added, in case anyone had missed the point. Many had. In June 2001, President George W. Bush—not one to look askance at inherited privileges—signed the Economic Growth and Tax Relief Reconciliation Act into law. This was a package of tax rollbacks that not only set in motion a phaseout of the estate tax but also reduced taxes on capital gains and sharply cut rates on high earners.

And it wasn't just EGTRRA, as the bill was known in Washington. A few months prior, Bush and the Republican-led Congress had also seen fit to give down-on-their-luck Americans the back of the hand, passing legislation that made it harder for people to escape their credit card debt by declaring bankruptcy—a move that the Berkshire-owned *Buffalo News* decried as threatening "to afflict those who simply have suffered hard luck in the form of job loss, illness or divorce." Wealth inequality was now the law of the land.

Warren seethed. As he saw it, rich folks like him were making the poor and middle class pick up the tab for the running of society. The natural result would be that the government was underfunded, with low priority given to the needs of those millions of people who didn't have K Street lobbyists to whisper sweet nothings in the ears of politicians on their behalf. Neglect of these communities would leave "a residue of humanity."

"I don't like a tax system that goes in that direction," he said, putting it mildly. "I don't like an educational system that goes in that direction. I don't like anything where the bottom twenty percent keep getting a poorer and poorer deal."

The vast majority of Americans didn't like it either, and the government's simultaneous heaping of favor on tycoons and short-shrifting of the rest might have led to some kind of popular revolt, were it not for the fact that America's attention was soon refocused.

Warren was hosting a celebrity golf tournament in Omaha when planes crashed into the World Trade Center towers on September 11, 2001—a cataclysm he took no pleasure in having vaguely foreseen. As the owner of several reinsurance companies, Warren was alert to the risk of terrorism; in May 2001, he'd instructed General Re and Berkshire Re to cut back on insuring buildings exposed to the danger, citing the World Trade Center as an example. Five days after the planes hit, Warren took to *60 Minutes* alongside former Treasury secretary Robert Rubin to reassure the country that the U.S. economy was not going to collapse alongside the Twin Towers. The next day, as the New York Stock Exchange reopened after its longest recess since the Great Depression, the Dow fell 684 points, at the time its largest point decline in a single day.

For Warren, the drop meant that, at long last, it was time to *buy*.

Swallowing the blow to Berkshire Hathaway's cash reserves from approximately $2.3 billion in reinsurance claims—$1.7 billion down to bad apple General Re—Warren and Charlie Munger went to work, looking for places to put all the cash they'd been hoarding. There were deals everywhere, and even more of them to be had following that autumn's wave of business scandals: Enron, WorldCom, Tyco, Adelphia, ImClone. Berkshire's spending spree included the purchase of Fruit of the Loom ("We cover the asses of the masses," quipped Warren) and several energy-related investments, oil and gas pipelines among them; meanwhile, playing the odds, Berkshire insurance honcho Ajit Jain wrote out polices for terrorism-related risk, covering airlines, landmark skyscrapers, and the 2002 Winter Olympics in Salt Lake City.

It was almost as though Warren Buffett had heaved the whole of America onto his sloped shoulders and promised to carry it to safety.

THE UNITED STATES can only fight so many wars at once. As ground troops landed in Afghanistan, a war on the domestic front was finally put to bed. In November, following an appeal of Judge Jackson's ruling, Microsoft and the Department of Justice at last reached a settlement. The headline was that Microsoft would remain intact. Many observers, glossing the news, handed Bill a victory in the case—but, in fact, anyone who read deeper into the appellate court's decision would find that the justices backed the DOJ's efforts to radically constrain Microsoft's business practices. Henceforth, Microsoft would have to play nice with the other kids, even the ones trying to steal its lunch.

Gary Reback for one is absolutely convinced that had there been no government intervention, and no finding that Microsoft had violated the Sherman Anti-Trust Act, the company would have run Google down the same way it had Netscape.

"Internet Explorer was literally 98 percent of the market," says Reback. "The only way you could get to Google was through Microsoft. You had to go onto the Microsoft browser and type www.google.com. Now if you did that," he continues, "there's no reason Microsoft had to send you to Google. They could have just put up the big red warning screen, saying 'Don't click on this site. It's a bad site.'

"The reason they didn't do that," adds Reback, "was the threat of antitrust enforcement. Because of antitrust enforcement, that's why we have Google. There is no other reason."

So, remember, whatever qualms you may have about Google these days, the alternative was Bing.

Bill never quite got over his sense that he'd been wronged by the government's case. But this resentment wasn't top of mind. The attack on New York happened, which had some conspiracy zombies going after Bill once again, somehow implicating Microsoft Word fonts. (A gross irony came fourteen years later when, on the anniversary of the attack, Al-Qaeda placed Bill and Warren on their "kill list," their deaths meant to deal fresh blows to the global economy.)

Four months after the September 11, 2001, attacks, at the World Economic Forum, Bill stood beside Bono, Desmond Tutu, Hillary Clinton, and Rudy Giuliani to call for greater international cooperation, the eradication of poverty, and the promotion of security and cultural understanding.

For the first time in years, Bill was enjoying himself at work. He liked his new role as Microsoft's "grand geek," which allowed him to spend his time chatting with developers rather than dealing with company admin. He'd left off peering at the Microsoft parking lot to see when his minions arrived and departed and instead was savoring his increasingly precious family time: Bill and Melinda now had two small children, and, according to their plan to space her pregnancies three years apart, it was about time for a third. Phoebe Gates was born in September 2002—right on schedule.

Bill would now spend more of his time rubbing elbows at international conferences regarding the state of the world than at tech mixers. If he was hungry for a break, he'd fly with Melinda and the kids—Jennifer (into horses), Rory (computers), and Phoebe (ballet)—to Omaha and enjoy a bridge marathon with Warren. Bill was, in a word, changing. His own father, still co-chair of his son's foundation, observed a "softening" in him, but some of the old relentlessness remained: For example, Bill earmarked his time on flights for reading reports on global health. There was now more than $20 billion worth of his own personal Microsoft shares sitting in the Gates Foundation coffers, and he had to figure out how to spend it.

Luckily, he had help. Patty Stonesifer had embarked on a hiring spree, finding experts to consult with in agricultural development abroad, and in education, the foundation's primary home-front focus. There was also Richard Akeroyd, the director of the free-internet-access-to-libraries program, which boasted a team of 110 young techies spread across the United States.

It's hard to wrap your head around the range of the Gates Foundation's efforts, even in its infancy. For the sake of clarity, it's useful to consider the foundation as two entities: one international, the other domestic.

In its global orientation, the Gates Foundation circa 2001 was concerned with endemic poverty and all matters related to health. The majority of its health-related financing went to its campaign to facilitate the delivery of medicine and medical services in parts of the world that were very poor and badly underserved. Funding was typically routed through existing, on-the-ground organizations, with the emphasis put on distributing simple tools—vaccines, contraceptives, nutritional supplements, single-use syringes. And care was taken to assure that local health workers understood how and when to use them. For example, the following scene was described in the *New York Times Magazine* by the writer Jean Strouse, who tagged along on a 2000 foundation trip to Africa:

"At an immunization clinic on our first day in Ghana, Dr. Perkin recognized a small circle on the label of a polio vaccine vial—a warning sign devised by a nonprofit organization he helped found in Seattle . . . He was delighted when the nurse in charge was able to tell him that the darkening circle meant the vaccine was approaching its expiration date and had to be used right away. Even health workers who cannot read can dispense this medicine."

This was the Gates Foundation spadework. Its showier efforts centered on the development of new vaccines: In 1999, it began to fund research into a malaria vaccine for infants and young children, and it also wrote a giant check to IAVI, the International AIDS Vaccine Initiative, which fast-tracked research into promising vaccine candidates by giving pharmaceutical companies the money to do the studies. (In exchange, IAVI's Big Pharma partners had to agree to provide any working vaccine at low cost in developing countries; in the United States, they could charge whatever they liked—and, as an added sweetener, they owned and controlled the patents on the drugs, a matter close to Bill's intellectual-property-rights-loving heart.)

Bill's participation with the foundation could be described as "hands-off," but "eyes on." He, Melinda, Bill Sr., and Patty Stonesifer had to sign off on all expenditures of $1 million or more, and he'd review requests with the same avidity he had contracts with IBM, once upon a time.

"Bill writes questions and comments all over the lists—sometimes saying simply yes (to a request for $40 million) or no, 'tell me more about respiratory diseases,' or 'why this country?' or 'if this does well what's the next step?'" wrote Strouse in the *New York Times Magazine*. Melinda, who has been described as more of an "experiential" learner than her husband, was more involved with the nitty-gritty of running the foundation, hanging around the office, and was soon going on fact-finding missions to India and Africa.

"On one of my early trips for the foundation," Melinda recalls, "I went to Malawi and was deeply moved to see so many mothers standing in long lines in the heat to get shots for their kids. When I talked to the women, they'd tell me the long distances they'd walked. Many had come ten or fifteen miles."

Melinda was focused on children, Stonesifer told Strouse, whereas Bill was "very interested in medical interventions and new tools, in figuring out what is possible with new scientific technology. And they are both passionate about how those areas can work together."

In the international arena, a preferred Gates Foundation tactic was to identify promising initiatives and supply the leaders of those projects with funds that would allow them to scale up. It was a venture capital model of philanthropy, with the baked-in expectation that a sizable number of these projects would ultimately fail.

For an American looking at the foundation's efforts abroad, the idea of some percentage of failure could seem benign, because it was abstract: It wasn't entirely clear, to most domestic observers, what "failure" might mean in countries far off and, in the popular imagination, already wracked by plague, poverty, war, et cetera. *At least they're trying* seemed to be the mantra.

But when it came to the U.S.-based initiatives arena . . . well, things wouldn't prove quite so simple.

MELINDA WAS UP to her elbows in foundation work. She left the public-facing aspects of the job of giving away billions in aid to her husband—not just for her sake, she writes in *The Moment of Lift*, but also for the sake of her kids. "I wanted to give them as normal an upbringing as possible," she notes. "And I knew that if I gave up my own privacy, it would be harder to protect the children's privacy." Melinda's desire to instill a sense of normality in young Jenn, Rory, and Phoebe Gates went so far as her decision to enroll them in school under her maiden name, French—but their cover was blown as soon as Bill started driving Jenn to school a couple days a week. A few weeks after Bill began pitching in with the kindergarten commute, Melinda noticed that there were more dads dropping their kids off than usual; she asked one of the other mothers what was going on. Turned out, wives were telling their husbands, "Bill Gates is driving his child to school; you can, too."

Despite her innumerable advantages—housekeepers, childcare, the works—Melinda still felt the pinch that many mothers do, taking on the unpaid labor of childbearing and childrearing, and running a household, to boot. "It's a lot of work raising kids," she says. "Taking them to school, to the doctor, to sports practice and drama lessons; supervising homework; sharing meals; keeping the family connected to friends at birthday parties, weddings and graduations. It takes a lot of time." Melinda also found herself in the familiar motherly position of clearing up after dinner, as though her husband and kids believed she had nothing better to do than load the dishwasher. One night, she says, she put her foot down. "There's nothing about being a mom that means I have to clean up while others wander off," she said. Bill agreed to pick up the slack.

In the event that Bill hadn't been entirely convinced by Melinda's foot-stamping, she had backup for her argument. The issue of women's unpaid labor had been vexing feminists for decades: In 1972, left-wing feminists from Italy, the United Kingdom, and the United States convened a two-day conference to discuss the matter, and emerged with the "Statement of the International Feminist Collective," which made the point that whether it's paid labor on the factory floor or unpaid labor at home, either way, it's labor. "They say it is love," wrote influential Italian feminist activist Silvia Federici in her 1975 pamphlet *Wages Against Housework*. "We say it is unwaged work."

"Capital had to convince us that it is a natural, unavoidable and even fulfilling activity to make us accept our unwaged work," Federici asserted. "In its turn, the unwaged condition of housework has been the most powerful weapon in reinforcing the common assumption that *housework is not work*, thus preventing women from struggling against it, except in the privatized kitchen-bedroom quarrel that all society agrees to ridicule . . . We are seen as nagging bitches, not workers in a struggle."

Melinda does *not* cite Federici in *The Moment of Lift*, perhaps because Melinda herself is a vocal proponent of capitalism. She does cite the work of Marilyn Waring, whose studies of women's unpaid labor in the home made Federici's point in terms that liberal technocrats could embrace. Importantly, Waring tried to assign a value to all that work: In her book *If Women Counted: A New Feminist Economics*, published in 1988, she made the case that if you had to hire workers at market rate to substitute for women's unpaid domestic labor, you'd find yourself with the single-largest sector of the global economy on your hands. "And yet," as Melinda points out, "economists were not counting this as work."

"Men won't easily give up a system in which half the world's population works for next to nothing," Melinda quotes Waring as saying. "Precisely *because* that half works for so little, it may have no energy left to fight for anything else."

It's clear from *The Moment of Lift* that as Melinda began to travel more frequently and farther afield on behalf of the Gates Foundation, her perspective on issues of global health and endemic poverty started to rotate on a feminist axis. Indeed, the book as a whole can be considered a lengthy explanation of why a woman who hadn't really thought of herself as a feminist became a crusader for equal rights, intent on stamping out gender bias in all its forms and providing women with access to reproductive services and opportunities to earn their own livelihoods. While the book is light on the *when*s and *where*s of her travels, we have an article in the *Washington Post* about a September 2003 visit by Bill and Melinda to a hospital in Botswana working with the foundation on AIDS interventions, a trip that followed on the heels of their co-hosting of a forum on the disease in South Africa with Nelson Mandela. Another exception: a photo taken in 2004 that shows Melinda sitting with sex workers participating in an HIV-prevention project in Kolkata, India.

Another who was clocking up plenty of frequent-flier miles was Susie Buffett. Calling herself a "geriatric gypsy," she traveled for months at a time, bouncing between far-flung family commitments and vacation jags and aid work, either on behalf of her now-flourishing foundation or in her guise as Susie-the-watering-can, tending to the infirm among her crowd of intimates, a group now so large it could have filled a small concert hall. Such was her focus and commitment to global issues, such as birth control—increasingly with Susie Jr. at her side—that Warren remained comfortable in restating publicly his intention to leave 99 percent of his wealth to her foundation. Susie would do the right thing, as she always had. Susie would find ways to give, and give shrewdly, and generously, on his behalf. Her living example—that we have a civic duty to serve others, a maxim that the Gateses had also learned from their parents—left Warren free to amass, with a clear conscience, as much money as he could, for his shareholders now, but also for the foundation's grantees of the future. It is not possible to overstate the degree to which Susie's wisdom and gentle soothing and guiding spirit had stabilized him over the years. Warren had changed for Susie, for now at least. She had opened him up, worked at keeping him open, made him blossom.

Still, day-to-day, Susie was hard to pin down—even Warren had trouble fitting into her schedule. One date was firmly set: Warren was to travel with the family to Africa for Susie's seventieth birthday. Howie, who had recently embarked on a project to establish a cheetah reserve in South Africa, had been planning the excursion for more than a year. "It would have been the eighth wonder of the world to see my father in Africa," Howie wistfully told Warren's biographer Alice Schroeder.

The trip never happened. Susie was unwell. Shortly before the Buffett clan was set to embark on their journey, in the spring of 2002, Susie was back in the hospital, with a bowel obstruction. She was also diagnosed with anemia and an esophageal ulcer. A year and a half later, she was in fine enough fettle to accept an invitation to speak at *Fortune*'s Most Powerful Women Summit, alongside her daughter. Their conference performance went off without a hitch; behind the scenes, however, Big Susie was awaiting the results of a biopsy.

In the fall of 2003, Susie Buffett was diagnosed with stage 3 oral cancer.

She had her "moment of tears" upon hearing the news, as Schroeder puts it. "Then, characteristically . . . [she] started chicken-souping everybody but herself. She called Warren. He did not say much. She called Susie Jr. and told her, 'Call your dad. He's going to be a mess.'"

Oral cancer can be very deadly. It's so deadly because oral cancers grow fast, and tend to be diagnosed only when they have metastasized; Susie's had already spread to at least one lymph node. Like virtually all advanced cancers, Susie's would be difficult to treat— and the treatment might be more painful than the disease. "If it were up to me, I would go off to a villa in Italy in privacy and just die," Susie told her assistant, Kathleen Cole. She was going to need major surgery, potentially disfiguring, and her doctors advised her that she'd need to undergo a follow-up course of radiation, as well. Susie scheduled the surgery but refused to commit to the radiation. Even with it, there was only a 50 percent chance that she'd survive five more years.

The day before the surgery, Warren flew to San Francisco.

WARREN HAD ALWAYS assumed that Susie would outlive him. In classic Warren style, he'd done the math. She was two years younger than he was—and anyway, as he told *Fortune* magazine, "women usually live longer than men." This calculation was the thing that supported his whole master plan, which required her to handle his fortune and also to look after their kids, and also the possible third signatory on all their Christmas cards, Astrid.

But now, his plan, and his world, was collapsing.

Susie's doctor found cancer in two lymph nodes. The surgery would remove the lower floor of her mouth, the inside of her cheek, and about a third of her tongue. A disastrous excision for a songbird but, in life-and-death terms, it was good news. When Susie came out of surgery, Warren steeled himself before entering her room: He didn't want even a hint of a flinch to cross his face, lest Susie catch it and believe he found her appearance shocking. It *was* shocking—she was hooked up to a feeding tube, with her swollen tongue hanging out of her mouth. But she was alive.

Once Susie had recuperated enough to leave the hospital, Warren flew—with her encouragement; life must go on—to Atlanta to speak to students at Georgia Tech. The speech was mostly pro forma—the ovarian lottery, an homage to Ben Graham—but during the Q&A

session following, Warren sounded an unfamiliar note. Asked about his greatest success and greatest failure, Warren left off talking about business, and told the students, "When you get to my age, you'll really measure your success in life by how many of the people you want to have love you actually do love you."

> I know people who have a lot of money, and they get testimonial dinners and they get hospital wings named after them. But the truth is that nobody in the world loves them. If you get to my age in life and nobody thinks well of you, I don't care how big your bank account is, your life is a disaster.
>
> That's the ultimate test of how you have lived your life. The trouble with love is that you can't buy it. . . . It's very irritating if you have a lot of money. You'd like to think you could write a check: I'll buy a million dollars' worth of love. But it doesn't work that way. The more you give love away, the more you get.

Dieting became a form of solidarity: Susie, resting at home ahead of the six-week course of radiation she still hadn't agreed to, was on a liquid-only regimen; Warren suffered alongside her by cutting his daily intake to a thousand calories. While Susie choked down meal replacement units, Warren went about eating all the junk he normally ate, just much less of it. "The easiest step was to cut back on all the Cherry Coke," Schroeder notes, "replacing it with nothing and thereby dehydrating himself." It was the same crash diet he went on every year before the shareholder meeting, but this time it was different, because he was doing it for Susie. He'd cut back on sleep, too, but not by choice: Most nights, he was getting about two hours.

What worried Warren most of all was the chance that Susie would refuse the radiation. She was already in great pain, and she wasn't eager to sign up for more of it. Her oncologist had warned her that radiation was *bad*. "Why can't I just lie in bed the rest of my life," she told Susie Jr., "and the grandchildren can come out, and it will be fine."

Warren, Schroeder writes, thought that Susie "might accept death as a natural thing and not fight it as he would." Behind his desk at Kiewit Plaza, he'd sometimes collapse into tears—great gasping sobs that shook his frame. The situation seemed hopeless. But even though he didn't know it, he had an ally in this fight.

Once again, out of the wings, enter Bono.

Not long after wowing Bill at the Waldorf Astoria, Bono had set his sights on Warren. The two first met at a NetJets marketing event. and you learn a lot about the Bono charm offensive from Warren's recollections of their first, fifteen-minute chat: When Warren said something Bono approved of, he'd reply "That's a melody!" At the end of their meeting, he summed it up with a grin: "I can't believe it. Four melodies in fifteen minutes." Warren was intrigued by the fact that U2's members split their revenues equally. "But," he recalled to Alice Schroeder, "U2's music doesn't blow me away."

Well, that's Warren. Susie, a U2 fan, disagreed. The band had become part of her daily ritual: When she went to bed, she'd listen to their song "All I Want Is You," night after night, to soothe her to sleep.

It worked. Susie stopped saying she just wanted to lie in bed forever. She worried less about her mental state. And she agreed to the radiation.

IT WAS AROUND this time that Bill started to joke that his habit of making small talk about morbidity rates and dengue fever made him unpopular at cocktail parties. Fact-check: The richest man in the world is never unpopular at cocktail parties. And as it happened, he was about to get richer.

By 2004, Microsoft had stockpiled more than $50 billion in cash reserves and that July the company finally decided what to do with the money: pay its shareholders a onetime dividend totaling $32 billion, increase its quarterly dividend, and buy back a boatload of shares. The onetime payment netted Bill $3.35 billion while the quarterly dividend increased his income that year by about $180 million—

chump change he might have kept for himself as he pledged the
$3 billion–plus payout to the Gates Foundation endowment.

The foundation was sitting on a world-historic nest egg. Its investment managers, Bill and Melinda appointees, consistently beat the
market, compounding the wealth. And yet, Bill and Melinda fretted
that this money just wasn't enough. Their money was, as Bill would
say, "truly a rounding error" compared to what various government
entities did or could or should spend. Would the Botswana government keep up with AIDS interventions when Gates left town? Had
the foundation set up a reliable enough infrastructure for vaccine
delivery to rural precincts that India would continue to use it?

Because the foundation couldn't fund its initiatives in perpetuity,
it needed to "lever up," as a hedge funder might say. GAVI, the vaccine alliance, was an example of levering at work: Seeded by $750
million in Gates grants, GAVI would attract fifty-five donor governments, plus the European Union, into the funding fold, and bring
immunization rates among children in developing countries for
several diseases to an all-time high. Levering up required getting
people outside the Gates Foundation and its motley collection of
grantees on board with campaigns. Which meant yakking to other
billionaire philanthropists, foundation executives, and heads of
state. And *that* meant Bill and Melinda had to get out on the hustings and advocate in earnest for their work. Like building support
for tackling the "Grand Challenges in Global Health," fourteen obstacles to scientific progress that, if solved, would radically improve
the overall health of the world. Or prodding for grants to match the
Gateses' $168 million pledge toward a malaria vaccine, or getting
the Bush administration to kick in more funding for bed nets and
insecticide. Or cajoling other members of the Forbes 400 to step into
the Gates Foundation's cracks. "I always say to people with a lot of
money, 'Do you want a disease?'" Bill remarked in 2005. "We can
give you this whole disease, or a whole region or a country. Whatever
you want."

It meant, in short, that Bill and Melinda had to become co-presidents of the nation of Philanthropy, seizing the bully pulpit and bestriding the world stage the way elected presidents and prime ministers do. The Gates Foundation boasted assets that rivaled the annual GDP of many countries. It had, as journalist Michael Specter put it, "the power of a government without actually being bound by a nation's political or economic constraints." It was a maker and mover of markets, an investment firm, an enterprise employing thousands of people, directly or indirectly, all over the world, and it was led by two founders wise enough to understand that the money it had was not, could not ever be, enough.

RADIATION WAS BRUTAL. By the end of Susie's course of treatment, her mouth was so badly burnt, she couldn't eat or drink. The doctors put her back on a feeding tube. She was perpetually cold, perpetually tired, perpetually afraid of being alone. The only people she trusted to see her in this unhappy condition were her nurses; her assistant Kathleen; her former tennis coach, John McCabe; Susie Jr.; and Warren, on the weekends he came to visit. He'd sit by Susie watching old episodes of *Frasier*, waiting impatiently for Susie's treatments to end and her doctors to determine whether they had, in fact, obliterated all remaining cancer cells.

The MRI came back clean. Susie told Warren this meant that her odds of a recurrence of the cancer were as low as if she'd never had cancer at all, which was a pretty spin on the truth: Her doctor had told her she could expect one good year, and after that—who knew? She made plans to attend the next Berkshire shareholder meeting, and to travel with Warren to New York City for their annual visit with old friends Sandy and Ruth Gottesman. The "geriatric gypsy" was back on the move.

No doubt everything Susie did, in those days, seemed like a minor miracle. Getting up, getting dressed, getting on an airplane. The trip to New York was especially remarkable, given that while she was

there, she sat for her first and only on-camera interview, a lengthy
conversation with Charlie Rose. She looked great, and apart from
a telltale lisp, spoke with ease, even when Rose pressed her on her
and Warren's unusual marriage, asking her why she'd moved to San
Francisco, and about her relationship with Astrid. "She took care of
your man for you?" queried Rose. "She's done me a great favor," Susie said, making her point of view on the matter perhaps a little *too*
clear.

Susie had a new love in her life. And, fortuitously, he was in town.
Bono hadn't met Susie, but he'd heard she was a fan, and he'd been
faxing her letters throughout her convalescence. "They were sort of
this giant thing to her," Susie Jr. later said. It was like Susie had a
schoolgirl crush. Was it mutual? Meeting Susie at the Plaza Hotel for
lunch, Bono brought along a portrait of her he'd painted from a pho-
tograph, overwritten with lyrics from the U2 song "One."

Not long after that, Susie and Susie Jr. were flying to Europe, having accepted Bono's invitation to join him at his mansion in the
south of France. "I've met my soul mate!" he cried, after a four-hour
heart-to-heart with Susie over dinner. Susie played U2 music on her
iPod the entire flight home.

As soon as she'd returned from Èze Bord-de-Mer, Susie was off
again, this time headed to Sun Valley for Herb Allen's honcho retreat. "I can't do it," Susie told her daughter when she came to pick
her up for a second day of hobnobbing. She ended up spending most
of her time in Sun Valley recuperating alone. She was spent.

Susie didn't want to be spent. She went to Omaha for the pre-
miere of *Spirit—The Seventh Fire*, a multimedia show staged by her
son Peter. (He'd worked on the film *Dances with Wolves*, which had
piqued his interest in Native American issues; the show featured
compositions inspired by Indigenous musical forms.) She escorted a
passel of grandchildren to her vacation home in Laguna Beach, and
then she prepared to head back to the cowboy state of Wyoming,
for Herb Allen's annual post–Sun Valley jamboree. The last week of

July 2004, Susie Buffett reunited with Warren in high-altitude Cody where the cream of the Sun Valley crowd was gathered. Not everyone in the Buffett clan was happy with Susie exerting herself so much, but she wanted to go, and Warren didn't want to put a damper on her newfound high spirits, so he took her along. She was in fabulous form, right up to the moment when, chatting with Herbert Allen, she blinked and said there was "something funny going on" inside her head. Her legs buckled.

She'd had a massive cerebral hemorrhage. The doctor at Cody's West Park Hospital informed a pacing Warren that Susie likely wouldn't make it through the night.

What did Warren's mind turn to, as he sat at the bedside of his wife, his watering can, his best friend, and waited for her to die? Did his mind turn to childhood, and memories of sitting in the family pew at church, calculating the life spans of hymn composers? He'd realized all the way back then that there was no correlation between goodness and a long life. Why had he supposed that Susie, who was so, so good, would outlast him?

Susie Jr. and Peter arrived at 4:30 a.m. and she took over the vigil. Soon after, she realized her mother was no longer breathing.

BACK TO SCHOOL

In 2005, Bill Gates turned fifty. And when a man reaches the half-century mark, he can sometimes get to thinking: What have I achieved with my life? Is it enough? Am I happy? How much more do I have to do? Some of these questions might have been easier for Bill to answer than your average quinquagenarian. But—*how much more is left to do?* Most people, looking back on similar achievements, would answer, "Not a lot." Not so Bill. As he celebrated his birthday, his foundation was gearing up for a major new project: transforming the way an entire continent grew its food. When your job is solving all the world's problems, your work never ends.

Bill's actual party was a small affair—Warren was there, of course, with Astrid. The guests wore matching red T-shirts printed with the words "Fabulous FIFTY." Warren—clearly grieving, in the eyes of his friends, but capable of high spirits—entertained them by performing a few push-ups on the deck. Wait—the deck? This small affair was held on the *Octopus*, Paul Allen's boat, one of the largest yachts in the world, replete with a movie theater, a recording studio, two helicopters, a sixty-three-foot tender, and a small submarine. While Warren showed off his push-ups, it was cruising off the coast of Tahiti. Astrid was delighted, but Warren was not quite so giddy; what he liked most about the *Octopus* was the chance to play a few good rounds of bridge. He summed up his experience in Tahiti with a shrug. "It beats home," he said.

Warren's seventy-sixth birthday rolled around the next year. On that day, he married Astrid Menks. Bill and Melinda weren't present—it was a civil ceremony, family-only, held in Little Sooz's Omaha backyard. Astrid wore white slacks and a turquoise blouse, and after exchanging vows, the couple went to dinner at Bonefish Grill, a chain seafood joint near Borsheims, where, using his discount, Warren had purchased Astrid's ring.

"Unconventional is not a bad thing," Susie Jr. told the *New York Times* apropos the nuptials. "More people should have unconventional marriages." Warren declined to comment.

WE CAN'T IMAGINE how Warren felt after Susie's death in July 2004. But we do know he didn't go to Susie's funeral. Much has been made of this; there's no use belaboring the point. He didn't go. He couldn't handle it. Everyone who did attend pretty much understood. Family and a few of Susie's most loyal pals were there to pay their respects, and to hear Bono serenade the dearly departed with a rendition of "Sometimes You Can't Make It on Your Own."

But Susan Buffett still had a surprise or two up her sleeve. At the reading of the will, some people expecting generous bequests from the deceased multibillionaire were unhappy to discover that the gifts were somewhat less generous than anticipated. Warren and the kids were taken aback to find out that, a year before her death, Susie had amended her will to leave her tennis coach John McCabe $8 million. Warren wasn't pleased, but in his grief, he took the revelation in stride; it wasn't like he hadn't known about Susie's relationship with McCabe. For Astrid, however, who'd been kept in the dark, the bequest might have seemed an affront. For years, she'd kept herself behind the scenes, quiet, patient, propping up the illusion that was Warren's marriage. For this?

Somehow, Warren had managed to share a home with Astrid for twenty-six years—about as long as he'd lived with Susie, in fact—without properly appreciating the degree to which she'd subjugated herself. Perhaps sorrow made him porous, for he understood now. In the months after Susie's death, he made an effort to give Astrid more of a public role in his life. He opened up to his children, too, checking in on Susie Jr. as she expanded—in compliance with her mother's last wishes—the Susan Thompson Buffett Foundation to reflect—after Susie's bequest injected $3 billion—its new size, then whooshed to Washington, D.C., for the launch of Peter's *Spirit* show when it played on the National Mall; bonding with Howie, who, in the end, had done his dad proud pursuing interests related to his love of nature and farming. He sent checks to most of his grandkids—"most" because he didn't consider Peter's adopted daughters, Nicole and Erica, his grandchildren. (Warren's financial generosity went as far as paying for Nicole and Erica's education; beyond that they were recipients only of his go-forth-and-fend-for-yourselves doctrine.) And in a supremely avuncular act, he invited Bill Gates to join the Berkshire Hathaway board, filling Susie's vacant seat.

Adding one of the most successful businessmen in the world to his company's board might not seem like an act of emotional outreach on Warren's part; given his tight bond with Bill, it almost seems like a no-brainer. But with the exception of Warren's short-term, covert purchase of Microsoft stock at the start of the antitrust contretemps, Warren and Bill's relationship had always been unfettered by business ties. Given Warren's consuming passion for Berkshire, you can interpret his addition of Bill to the board as anointing his brilliant friend, his bridge partner, as a kind of godfather to his beloved baby. More pragmatically, the move gave Warren the opportunity to observe Bill's business mind at close range, seeing how he handled knotty issues as and when they came up, rather than discussing them in the way of pals, after the fact. Why might Warren have wanted to gain this insight into his friend, and why now? Was

Berkshire in dire need of new guidance, or did he have something else in mind for Bill, down the road?

About a year and half later, on June 16, 2006, to be exact, Bill dropped a bombshell by quietly announcing his decision to step down, in two years' time (effective July 2008), from full-time executive duties at Microsoft, dedicating the bulk of his abundant energy to his foundation instead. This was big. Warren must have wondered: A man of Bill's talents and vitality and focus, redeploying all those mental gifts and mighty resources on . . . *charity work*? What was surely a great day for philanthropy must have forced a day or two of heavy reckoning for one Warren Buffett. What was *he* going to do next? Did he have a big play in response to his old bridge partner, the East to his West, going "dummy" and turning his cards faceup while his partner "led"? No spring chicken, Warren knew that holding good cards was only one small part of playing the perfect hand. When and how you laid 'em down, that was the trick, that was the magic. This would take some thinking about . . .

Warren's own approach to philanthropy had always been simple and unevolving. His personal fortune would compound, compound, compound, every day he drew breath. And then, once he died, Susie would give it away. All of it. "Susie would have enjoyed overseeing the process," he said later. "She was a little afraid of it, in terms of scaling up. But she would have liked doing it, and would have been very good at it. And she would really have stepped on the gas."

But with Susie gone, who was going to fill that role? Well, maybe the kids. When the younger Buffetts were in their early thirties, Warren began gifting them $100,000 a year to give away as they pleased. Circa the turn of the millennium, Susie and Warren had upped the ante, handing Susie Jr., Howie, and Peter $35 million each to donate as they saw fit. Susie Jr. donated to organizations such as Girls Inc., a 150-year-old nonprofit focused on mentoring young women. Peter was interested in supporting the arts. Howie, of gorilla costume fame, focused on conservation work, opening a cheetah reserve in the coming years. Among other activities.

Neither Warren nor Susie ever told their children how best to bequeath their millions. In a way, it was practice money: The Buffett kids' foundations were starter accounts that allowed them to learn the ins and outs of philanthropy before the real money came pouring in after Warren died.

But could they manage it? Did the younger Buffetts really have what it took to dispose of tens of billions of dollars? All the Buffett foundations were lightly staffed and tightly focused. Meanwhile, Warren's "third son" was already jetting around the world, shedding vast amounts of money wherever he went. He employed a small army of operatives—world-renowned experts in medicine and health policy, investment managers overseeing the endowment, publicists, administrative assistants, and on and on down the line.

So where should Warren place his fortune and his trust? How to fill the Susie-shaped hole in his once lead-lined legacy plan? Whom did he know who knew more than anyone else in this field? They'd need to possess enormous acumen in this area, for one thing, and boundless energy. They would, what's more, need to pass the rigorous Buffett test, the same test he'd imposed on all whom he'd ever allowed into his inner sanctum: They'd have to possess a peerless record of performance, a reliable track record of results year over year, decency, frugality, honesty, intelligence, transparency. Here, as well, he'd need someone who could adhere to the same rules that had made him a multibillionaire. Think loooooonnnng term. Look to the future, not the past. Innovate. Be patient. Learn from your mistakes. Soak up what others have to tell you. Be ready, because anything can happen . . .

In his home office sits a computer, the computer Bill persuaded him to buy, the computer on which Bill could be reached to play bridge online, the computer that runs on Bill's software system. Let us imagine Warren moving to this computer, awakening it, staring at the blank Explorer search window that greets him with its blinking cursor, representative of the questions pulsing gigantically inside the second richest man in the world, and also of the blank space in this man's life that needs filling and filling fast. With two tentative index fingers might he type Foundation, before pausing, then entering two names that logically loom in the forefront of his mind, at the top of his mental list: Bill and Melinda Gates.

Searching . . . He waits as the computer generates results.

AS BILL WAS learning, though, even an *Octopus*-size foundation could run into choppy waters.

For starters, the Gates Foundation was still actually *two* operations running under one roof. There was the international program, which scoured the globe for problems to fix: vaccinating kids, cleaning up dirty water, educating women, ending poverty, all the good stuff. And then there was the U.S. program—and that's where things start to get dicey.

The Gates Foundation's domestic program had just one major stated goal: fixing America's public school system. You can say this for Bill and Melinda: they don't go for easy challenges. About six months before his birthday shindig in Tahiti, Bill stepped to the podium at the National Education Summit on High Schools and proceeded to lob a hand grenade: America's high schools, he told the crowd, were "obsolete."

> *By obsolete, I don't just mean that our high schools are broken, flawed and under-funded—though a case could be made for every one of those points.*
>
> *By obsolete, I mean that our high schools—even when they're working exactly as designed—cannot teach our kids what they need to know today. . . .*
>
> *I'm not here to pose as an education expert. I head a corporation and a foundation. One I get paid for—the other one costs me.*

But both jobs give me a perspective on education in America,
and both perspectives leave me appalled. . . .

Our foundation has invested nearly one billion dollars so far to
help redesign the American high school. We are supporting more
than fifteen hundred high schools—about half are totally new,
and the other half are existing schools that have been redesigned.
Four hundred fifty of these schools, both new and redesigned, are
already open and operating. Chicago plans to open 100 new
schools. New York is opening 200. Exciting redesign work is un-
der way in Oakland, Milwaukee, Cleveland and Boston.

Bill went on to say that the fix for obsolete American high schools
boiled down to three things. One: States had to affirm that all students can and should graduate high school ready for "college, work,
and citizenship." Two: Metrics, the relentless pursuit of quality data
on school performance. Three: Make schools stop failing and open
new schools. "Every state needs a strong intervention strategy to improve struggling schools," Bill asserted. "This needs to include special teams of experts who are given the power and resources to turn
things around."

Well, he had the experts. They'd put their big brains to this admittedly mega-complex task, and—in classic Gates Foundation form—
they'd come up with a brilliant tech-industry-style hack that would
finally give every kid in America, especially Black and minority
kids, especially the disadvantaged and discounted, the education
they deserved.

"Disaster" isn't a particularly kind word for what followed. Neither is "catastrophe." Let's just call it a fuckup.

THE ARCHITECT OF the Gates Foundation's schools strategy was Tom
Vander Ark. Hired in 1999 to lead the foundation's educational ini-
tiatives, Vander Ark was something of an outlier in its brain trust:
Whereas the leaders of the teams working on global health issues

were world-renowned experts in their fields, Vander Ark's primary education credential was his five-year term as superintendent of the Washington State Federal Way school system, a tenure that began with a teacher walkout on his first day, and ended with a parent-teacher committee pledging to reverse one of his signature schemes, the replacement of letter grades with numerical evaluations. "I was clearly quite inept," said Vander Ark. So how in hell did he get his Gates Foundation job? Vander Ark seemed to have impressed Bill as a "smart guy," in Microsoft parlance—someone willing to work long hours and bore into details.

Vander Ark was also a big-idea guy, and in his case, the big idea was thinking small.

"A good size for high school is roughly four hundred students," he told an interviewer in 2003. "Recent studies have shown that, all else being equal, students in small high schools pass more courses, graduate, and go on to college more frequently than those in large ones."

Okay, then, let's run with that.

That summer, Melinda stepped out from the shadows to deliver a speech on education, giving much the same spiel. "In cities, suburbs, and rural areas, too often we see a tale of two high schools: One system for children whose parents live near good public schools or can afford to pay for private schools," she said. "And the other for the students stuck in large struggling high schools. Their classes aren't challenging or relevant. Their teachers are less qualified."

"So what should we do?" she continued. "We must reinvent our high schools so that they give all students a new version of the three R's: rigor, relationships, and relevance." The key, Melinda went on to say, was to rubbish the traditional large public high school, and replace those artifacts of the industrial age with boutique learning centers. "The fact is, we know what great schools look like," she asserted. "It should be a place where you walk in the door and you say, 'That's where I want to put my son or daughter.' Those are the kind of schools we need," said Melinda. "And usually they are small."

Melinda's speech set the stage for a rollout of grants to create small public high schools. Milwaukee, a hotbed of school reform, got $17 million. Chicago had received about $20 million, Boston $13.6 million. And in the splashiest outlay of all, New York City landed a $51 million grant to help it open sixty-seven new small schools, a gift that served as an endorsement of the disruptions to the nation's largest public school system spearheaded by Mayor Michael Bloomberg and his new schools chancellor, Joel Klein. Yes, *that* Joel Klein.

After stepping down from the Department of Justice following Judge Jackson's ruling to break up Microsoft, and a brief stint in publishing, Klein had gone on to seize the reins of New York City's public schools. He had no background in education—a fact Mayor Michael Bloomberg for some reason considered a plus—and his mandate was to impose fiscal discipline on the bloated school system, improve test scores and graduation rates, and, in aid of the first two goals, embark on an aggressive expansion of the city's charter school program. (For readers new to this topic, a charter school is one that receives government funding but operates independently of the established state school system in which it is located; the teachers who work there are not unionized.)

In September 2003, Klein was once again face-to-face with Bill Gates at the Bronx's Morris High School, as a grinning Mayor Bloomberg announced that "small high schools are a concept that has been proven to work." What on earth were those men thinking? Was Joel Klein wondering how he'd wound up begging for bucks from the formerly most-reviled tycoon in America, now a best pal of Bono and Nelson Mandela? Was Bill picturing the pinball machine Melinda had gotten for him during the Microsoft trial, with Joel Klein's face the target of the pinging balls? It was only a matter of months since the settlement in the case had been reached; there was no way Bill had cut a $51 million check to Klein without a second thought, was there?

Indeed, there wasn't. The path to the grant ran in part through the

nonprofit organization New Visions for Public Schools, which operated schools throughout New York City. The New Visions schools
weren't charters—they were public schools supervised by the city's
Department of Education staffed by unionized teachers. Largely
funded by donations from members of the financial community,
New Visions' schools landed right in the Gates Foundation sweet
spot: The organization took over large high schools and split them
up, and had been given broad authority to both institute new curricula and "excess" teachers they didn't like and replace them with
a younger staff committed to the mission. Once established, the city
paid New Visions to run the schools. The foundation had thrown
about $10 million at schools run by New Visions a year or so prior to
Joel Klein's taking the chancellor job; after his appointment, Klein
says, "I'm sure [Bill] thought long and hard about whether he'd give
any more."

"We were really impressed by what Joel was trying to do, and everyone on the staff wanted to do it," Melinda recalled to journalist
Steven Brill. "But on the afternoon we presented it to Bill, he hesi-
tated for a minute, which we completely understood." Bill said he
needed to sleep on the proposal. When he got up, he told Melinda,
"Klein is a smart, effective person, and now he's doing something
important that we should get behind."

When the press gaggle at Bronx's Morris High School wrapped
up, one of the principals of the five small schools it had been split
up into, came up to Klein and shook his hand. "Fifty-one million.
That was pretty impressive," the man said. Klein thanked him, and
the man added: "Imagine how much you would have gotten if you
hadn't sued the son of a bitch."

BY THIS POINT, the Gates Foundation had already done plenty of work
making its small schools dream a reality. By the end of 2003, the
foundation had committed nearly $600 million to help establish or
shore up 1,600 schools, most of them high schools, in impoverished

areas. Mountlake Terrace, a school right in the foundation's backyard, was one of its test cases. Nestled in the Seattle suburbs, the
1,800-student Mountlake was the first nonurban school to get the
Gates treatment, receiving a grant of $832,969 in 2001 to transform
itself from one large high school into several small ones, all housed
on the same campus.

"Students would be enrolled in one of five new Mountlake
schools," explained the *Seattle Weekly*. "Achievement, Opportunity
and Service (AOS), a 'traditional high school experience in a small
school setting'; Discovery, where students 'design [their] own projects instead of taking tests'; Innovation, 'aimed at creative thinkers:
writers, artists, inventors'; Renaissance, a bridge to four-year colleges
with the bulk of Mountlake's advanced placement classes; and Terrace Arts and Academic School (TAAS), a 2-D and 3-D arts–oriented
program." In September 2003, the converted Mountlake opened for
business.

At first, faculty and students were tentatively impressed with the
changeover. Smallness fostered greater intimacy among teachers,
administrators, and kids, just as Vander Ark had anticipated. But
there were unexpected wrinkles, too. "All the math teachers used to
share rooms, calculators, math tiles," said one faculty member. "Now
that we're broken up, we're spread throughout the building and we
have to buy five sets of things." The foundation had insisted that students not be allowed to switch from one mini-school to another, or
take electives at schools other than their own—a frustration for, say,
a "creative thinker" enrolled at Innovation who wished to sign up for
one of Renaissance's advanced placement courses. The five schools
found themselves competing for students, a situation Vander Ark
saw as a feature of the system, not a bug.

"We do think a system of managed choice is productive," he said.
"Will that create some competition? Yes, and generally we think
that's a good thing."

Another wrinkle? Kids being kids.

"There are so many different stereotypes," said one senior, referring to a kind of class stratification that emerged between the mini schools. "This has really divided us."

"Kids say AOS is the preppy, white school, Discovery is the Asian, gangsta, druggie school," echoed a freshman.

"A lot of students think that because the periods are longer in the Discovery School, the kids are stupid—they can't learn as fast," added a recent graduate.

As the first school year under the conversion scheme came to a close, almost one-quarter of the teaching staff quit. Mountlake Terrace principal Mark Baier and vice-principal Steven Gering left as well. Meanwhile, the all-important data was not yet painting a rosy picture.

"We can conclude," conceded Vander Ark, "that for large, struggling high schools, conversion is a very difficult entry point." Translation: Hang on, we need time.

But in school districts across the country, Gates-funded reform was storming ahead. Take another major beneficiary of the foundation's largesse: Manual High School in Denver, Colorado. Once, this had been the flagship institution for Denver's Black community—but by the time the foundation rolled into town, it had hit the skids. Denver abolished court-ordered busing in 1995; by 2000, Manual was the worst-performing high school in the entire state.

The Gates Foundation got to work. Manual was split into three schools: Leadership High School, Arts and Cultural Studies High School, and the intriguingly named Millennium Quest High School. Almost immediately, there were problems. For instance, what do you do when a crate of textbooks arrives, addressed not to Leadership, Arts and Cultural Studies, or Millennium Quest but to Manual High School? Suddenly, you have three principals bickering over who gets what. One principal, who'd waited two years for her micro-school to get its own science lab, gave up and started hanging the drywall herself over the summer. District officials ordered it knocked down.

Eventually, it was impossible to disguise how badly the experiment had failed. Manual High was closed down for a year in June 2006. But for hundreds of students, that wasn't the end. Three years later, University of Colorado researchers found that "only 52 per cent of students who were juniors when Manual was closed went on to graduate. The school previously had a 68 per cent graduation rate."

Oh, and by the way? That data Melinda and Tom Vander Ark had been so excited by, the figures showing that students do better at smaller schools? In 2006, the statisticians Howard Wainer and Harris Zwerling decided to re-crunch the numbers to interrogate such claims. Looking at schools in Pennsylvania, they found that smaller schools were indeed overrepresented among the top 3 percent in the state. They were also overrepresented among the *worst* 3 percent in the state. Turns out that when you have fewer students, a few exceptionally bright or extremely slow students will have an outsized impact on average test scores. The MO of the Gates Foundation had always been to follow the data and see what worked. Could they really have spent all that money, and possibly messed things up for thousands of kids, simply because they read the stats wrong?

THE FIRST BIG question here, one that even the harshest critics of Bill and Melinda must first address, is this: When the Gates Foundation screws up, could someone else have done a better job? Or are some of these problems they're running up against intrinsic to philanthropy itself? What are the dangers inherent in this type of gate-crashing philanthropy, when private persons step into the public sphere with an eye on (constructively) improving things?

Here's the crux of the matter: The Gateses, and the several other billionaire philanthropists who had taken an interest in education reform (among them Betsy DeVos, the Walton family of Walmart fame, and the late L.A.-based real estate titan Eli Broad), weren't starting new private schools and paying to send kids to them; what they were doing was chipping away at established schools, almost all of them terribly underfunded, by setting up privately run schools within the larger public system. Whether you were for or against this, there was no denying that one effect of that strategy was the diversion of resources away from the established schools, which had neither dollars nor talent to spare. Bill saw the foundation's investment in charter schools serving as "R & D" for the educational system as a whole: Taking the venture philanthropy approach, he reasoned that by funding a whole bunch of experiments, you'd find out what worked and what didn't, and then you could scale up the programs that posted positive results, all of which would be assiduously measured. Critics of this kind of reform complained it was tantamount to turning kids into lab rats. Charter schools would have great leeway in how they designed their curricula, how teachers taught, and how kids were disciplined, and it wasn't entirely clear who had the final say in determining what was kosher and what was not.

Was Bill Gates now *too much* in charge?

That idea rubbed a lot of people the wrong way. As David Callahan writes in *The Givers*, the Gates Foundation has come to be viewed as "a nine-hundred-pound gorilla on the K–12 scene, bulldozing forward with ideas that have sometimes turned out to be half-baked."

There's a philosophical question here, too: whether billionaires' tinkering with the American public school system is fundamentally *undemocratic*. What qualifies a bunch of tycoons to decide what's good for America's children? No one elected them. Are they even qualified?

And remember, what goes for schools also goes for everything else Bill was pouring his billions into. Back in 2001, he told an audience at Davos about one of his early projects. "We gave a grant for malaria," he said. "I think it was a fifty-million-dollar grant, and somebody said to me 'That's going to cause a fifty percent increase in the amount of research that goes on in malaria.'" In expressing his dismay at the countless unnecessary deaths in poor countries that are not even acknowledged by the denizens of rich countries, he was trying to inspire others to give more. But what his grant meant was that Bill Gates had more influence on global malaria research than everyone else on the planet combined. Is influence bad? Well, it is if you don't trust the influencer. And what if you don't like the impact this influence is having? To whom do you then appeal? The lack of regulation and oversight gives the influencer, in effect, carte blanche to experiment—to act, then evaluate. To some degree at least, the public is at the mercy of this fine altruistic impulse.

So, what was Bill and Melinda's view on their school's experiment? Was it a Eureka moment, one of reckoning, in which they learned valuable things about what *not* to do in future?

The foundation's report of 2008, subtitled *Reflections on the Foundation's Education Investments 2000–2008*, declared that their efforts provided hundreds of thousands of students new opportunities for learning, reshaped the debate on education in America, and improved data gathering so parents could go online and find out how their child's school was doing. It concluded: "As we learn from the past eight years of education investments, we recognize that we'll never reach our ambitious goal if we continue to focus primarily on the structure of public schools. To get transformational results requires us to expand our focus to the heart of the educational experience: the learning partnership between teacher and student."

Bill offered his own mea culpa in January 2009 in the first of the open annual letters he penned about his work and lessons learned at the foundation: "Many of the small schools that we invested in did not improve students' achievement in any significant way," he wrote. "Unlike scientists developing a vaccine, it is hard to test with scientific certainty what works in schools. . . . Based on what the foundation has learned so far, we have refined our strategy. We will continue to invest in replicating the school models that worked the best. Almost all of these schools are charter schools."

And in 2018, Melinda, looking back in the annual letter (titled that year *The 10 Tough Questions We Get Asked*) also allowed that mistakes had been made: "We recently announced some changes in our education work that take these lessons into account. Everything we do in education begins as an idea that educators bring to us. They're the ones who live and breathe this work, who have dedicated their careers to improving systems that are failing many students today, especially minority students." By 2018, the foundation was spending about $500 million a year in the United States, most of it on education. In 2022, the foundation donated $290 million to American schools, later announcing that it'd be devoting even more resources to programs that focus on improving math education. They were, and are, learning on the job.

IN THE DECEMBER 2005 issue of *Time* that named Bill and Melinda and Bono its "Persons of the Year," an accompanying article highlighted the Gates Foundation's global health initiatives, as had a lengthy feature published in October in *The New Yorker*. The latter piece paid particular attention to the foundation's efforts to eradicate malaria, but it also highlighted the transformations that came in the wake of Bill and Melinda's decision to focus on treating ills affecting the world's poorest. "It would be hard to overstate the impact that the Gates Foundation has had," wrote Michael Specter. "The research programs of entire countries have been restored, and fields that had languished for years, like tropical medicine, have once again burst to life."

Alongside noting, as profilers of Bill always do, his tendency to rock when agitated and his superhuman ability to vacuum up data, Specter captured Bill in a variety of moods: eyes glazing over as he politicked with health ministers at a WHO conclave; in high dudgeon, railing against the idea that suffering the world over should be met with a sense of futility; playing the happy warrior, preaching his update on Carnegie's *Gospel of Wealth*: "Capitalism is an unusual system, in that somebody can have so much wealth," he told Specter. "But then again, it's an unusual system because money can actually flow from the luckiest to the unluckiest and hopefully in clever ways so that it's not just writing checks."

"It's fun," he added, of his philanthropic endeavors. "And it is also an enormous responsibility."

The same month Bill, Melinda, and Bono's *Time* cover hit newsstands, Warren Buffett gave a talk at Harvard Business School. "What are your plans for the Buffett Foundation?" he was asked. By now he was used to answering questions about his future philanthropy, and people were waiting for some version of his stock reply, namely that all that could wait till after he was dead. But this time, he paused, then replied that he didn't see much value-add in letting his money continue to compound. He was thinking of giving it away.

Not at some point in the future.

Not when he died.

Like, *tomorrow.*

10

THE GIFT

The scene is set. A kitchen in Omaha. It's Wednesday at Warren's. There's Cherry Coke on the table, and McDonald's hamburgers on china plates. Warren, Astrid, Bill, and Melinda are playing bridge. It's the sixth or seventh hand of the night, and the ladies have just about had it, but they keep playing because Bill and Warren could play and play until sunrise—and would, if Bill and Melinda didn't have to jump back aboard their private jet to make it to New York City for a morning meeting at the UN. Astrid is scowling at her cards, half contemplating her bid and half making the next day's grocery list, when Warren drops the news. Drops it like it's nothing—a bit of dander floating through the conversation—that he intends to give the Gates Foundation the bulk of his fortune, the single biggest act of monetary generosity in the history of the world. While the others stare at him, open-mouthed, incredulous, he sips his Cherry Coke and says: "Astrid, your turn." Then Melinda asks him to repeat what he just said; not the bit about whose turn it is, but the thing before that. And so, Warren, with a straight face repeats it, and, with Astrid nodding her confirmation, Melinda and Bill finally understand, breathlessly, that Warren means it, that it's for real. Melinda clasps a hand to her mouth in shock, her eyes—in close-up—widening as she processes, at lightning speed, its significance to her, to the founda-tion, to the global poor. And that's when Melinda and also Bill set down their cards, and begin to cry.

This is, at least, as I would like to have imagined the scene. Call it the Norman Rockwell version of how this monumental moment might have gone down. It's not entirely clear, you see, how it *did* go down, because the central characters in the drama have stayed largely schtum on the specifics. But what we do know is this . . .

We know that in the spring of 2006, Warren informed Bill of his intentions—Bill alone, so it's reasonable to suppose the conversation occurred to one side of a Berkshire board meeting. Or maybe it did happen over a hand of bridge. Maybe it was a follow-up to many pre-vious conversations—Warren brainstorming, testing the idea. If so, then maybe Bill asked Warren if he *was* serious this time, and maybe Warren said something to the effect of, "If your goal is to return the money to society by attacking truly major problems . . . what could you find that's better than turning to a couple of people who are young, who are ungodly bright, whose ideas have been proven, who have already shown an ability to scale it up and do it right?" Which is what he'd say a short while later to Carol Loomis when she inter-viewed him for *Fortune*.

Or maybe Warren and Bill just batted around ideas about how the gift should be structured—two rationalists ducking meaning in favor of logistics. Either way, Bill went home and reported back to Melinda, after which they went for a long walk. And they both cried.

Melinda later recalled: "We said to each other, 'Oh my gosh, do you know how responsible we're going to feel giving someone else's money away?'"

A short time later, Bill and Warren phoned Bono, who later told CNN that Bill was still reeling from the news, still trying to find the right words to fit his emotions, but that when he passed the phone to Warren, the Oracle would calmly say, "The money has no utility for me," adding that Bill and Melinda were the right people to do the right thing with the biggest individual gift in history.

The public announcement came on June 26, 2006, when Warren told the world that he would give away 85 percent of his Berkshire Hathaway stock—a portion then worth $37 billion—to an assortment of foundations. Five out of six shares would go to the Gates Foundation. He'd give out the stock in installments, with the requirement that his money be spent as it was given; he didn't want to create a charitable institution like the Ford or Rockefeller Foundations that lived on for generations after his death. Each of his children's foundations would get a total of $1 billion—more than Peter, Howie, or Susie Jr. had ever anticipated receiving—and $3 billion would go into the coffers of the Susan Thompson Buffett Foundation. "The man who was, at the time, the second richest person on earth was giving away his money without leaving a trace of himself behind," Alice Schroeder writes. There would be "no Buffett hospital wing, no college or university endowment or building with his name on it."

That said, Warren's gift wouldn't go unnoticed: He, Bill, and Melinda staged a press conference in New York City, and, later the same day, sat for a joint interview with Charlie Rose that had been plugged with a full-page ad in the *New York Times*. A *Fortune* magazine cover story was already in the works.

"I looked at a lot of foundations, Charlie," Warren explained. "And there are a number that I admire, but there's none that are in the same class, in my view, as the Bill and Melinda Gates Foundation. And not just because of size."

They really have looked at the world without regard to gender, color, religion, geography, and they said, how can we do the most good for the most people, and particularly for the people that have gotten the short straws in life?

Warren's gift to the Gates Foundation was unprecedented: No person as rich as Warren had ever eschewed the opportunity to hang out his own shingle, and instead, after studying his options, decided to give his fortune to a philanthropic organization he considered better able to dispose of his money. Yet in another sense, the gift is unsurprising. Warren had built his fortune running Berkshire Hathaway, a business that invested in other businesses. And though it's certainly true that Warren had a hand in managing those companies, either because he wholly owned them or because he was a major shareholder who sat on their boards, his preference was to delegate to people he considered masters of their particular realms.

Take, for instance, Rose Blumkin.

One of eight children born to a rabbi in a village near Minsk, Rose Gorelick Blumkin conceived her American dream in 1899, when she was six. She'd just found out about the pogroms. She began her journey to the land where streets are paved with gold at age thirteen, walking barefoot for eighteen miles to catch a train to the nearest town, where she talked her way into a job at a dry goods store. Three years later, petite Rose was bossing around six male employees, and six years after that, she fled the chaos of the Russian Revolution to join her husband, Isadore Blumkin, in Fort Dodge, Iowa, getting there via China, then Japan, then a boat across the Pacific, then a brief sojourn with the Hebrew Immigrant Aid Society in Seattle. She spoke no English.

The Blumkins resettled in Omaha. Rose gave birth to four children, and then the Depression struck. Isadore's secondhand clothing shop was about to go under—until Rose stepped in, slashing prices and launching a promotion to outfit a man from head to toe for five bucks. Her marketing scheme worked: The store took in $800 in a single day, more money than it had made the entire previous year.

In 1937, Rose borrowed $500 from one of the brothers who'd arrived in America before her, and opened Blumkin's, predecessor to the soon-to-be-legendary Nebraska Furniture Mart. Her philosophy was "Sell cheap, tell the truth, don't cheat nobody." Other local furniture sellers tried to muscle her out of the business, leaning on wholesalers not to work with her, because she priced her goods so low; Rose responded by "bootlegging," traveling all around the Midwest to locate overstock merchandise that she'd buy for 5 percent over wholesale and sell for just a bit more. Pioneering a business model that would later be adopted by retailers such as IKEA and Inditex, owner of Zara, she made up for her ultrafine margins by trading in high volume, at one point renting out the Omaha Civic Auditorium and stuffing it like a Thanksgiving turkey with sofas and tables and appliances. "This is it! The Sale of Sales!" proclaimed the ad for the event. "We can't eat 'em! We must sell 'em!" A quarter of a million dollars' worth of merch went out the door in three days.

By the early '80s, Rose and her war hero son, Louie, had built Nebraska Furniture Mart into the largest furniture store in North America. Customers from all over the Midwest made pilgrimages to its three-acre showroom in downtown Omaha, buying $100 million worth of furniture each year. Naturally, local boy Warren had taken note, observing with admiration the pint-sized, elderly widow with the bouffant black bun who whizzed around her empire in a golf cart, yelling at her employees, many of whom were immigrants and refugees she'd hired on the principle that "you don't need English to count." The first time Warren tried to buy the store, she waved him off, saying: "You'll try to steal it."

Warren had dealt with tough cookies like Rose Blumkin before, however. She was of the same ilk as National Indemnity's Jack Ringwalt and Associated Cotton Shops' Ben Rosner, entrepreneurs whose identities were inseparable from the companies they'd built, and who, quite simply, loved to work. Rose—or Mrs. B, as everyone called her—spent six and a half days at it each week, and on Sunday afternoons, her time "off," she'd drive around town with Louie, staking out the competition. "I plan an attack on the shopkeepers, thinking, 'How much hell can I give them?'" If Warren could be a dolt about things like, say, his wife's feelings, one yearning of the human heart he understood was the ache to work. And so, in 1983, when he got wind that the Blumkins might be ready to sell to another buyer, he went straight at Rose's soft spot, writing to Louie: "Such a buyer—no matter what promises are made—usually will have managers who feel they know how to run your business operations." Whereas Warren figured that no one could possibly manage the Furniture Mart better than Mrs. B and her son, and should they sell to Berkshire Hathaway, he'd insist they continue doing so.

Warren and Rose shook hands on a $55 million all-cash deal on his fifty-third birthday. He didn't take inventory, and he didn't ask for an audit. Congratulations, Rose told him. "You bought an oil well on your birthday."

Of all the folks Warren Buffett got into business with in the course of his long career, Rose Blumkin may have been the person he admired most. "Put her up against the top graduates of the top business schools or chief executives of the Fortune 500," he said, shortly after Berkshire assumed majority control of the Furniture Mart, "and, assuming an even start with the same resources, she'd run rings around them."

Rose had brains, and she had grit. And she was thrifty as hell. Mrs. B was a woman after Warren's heart when it came to making money. She died in 1998, at the age of 104, involved in day-to-day operations of her business nearly to the end.

As for choosing Bill and Melinda, as Warren told Charlie Rose:

> *If you've got something important in life to do—let's say I was going to play the golf match of my life, you know—and I could get somebody to substitute for me like Tiger Woods, I would do it any time. And if I had to sing on television, you know, and I could just mouth the words and get Sinatra in the back room doing it for me, I'd do it. So, the idea that you have to—you have various responsibilities in this world, and this money*

is a responsibility, but if you can get somebody better at doing something that needs to be done in your place, you know, I'm used to that.

Within days of the announcement of Warren's gift, other rich people began lining up behind him. Jackie Chan announced he would part with half his wealth. (He later said he would give all of it away to his foundation.) Li Ka-shing, then the richest man in Asia, said he would give a third of his $19 billion fortune to his own foundation. As it would turn out, that was just the start.

BUT EVEN WARREN'S largesse had its limits. Around the same time that he was dotting the i's and crossing the t's on the gift to his third, nonbiological son, other distant extremities of the Buffett clan were causing him grief.

April 2006 saw the release of a documentary titled *The One Percent*, courtesy of Jamie Johnson, filmmaker scion to the Johnson & Johnson fortune. A follow-up to Johnson's 2003 exposé *Born Rich*, which featured Ivanka Trump, Georgina Bloomberg, and the perfectly named Josiah Cheston Hornblower, heir to the Vanderbilt and Whitney fortunes, *The One Percent* tackled wealth inequality, a hot topic in 2006. Some of the luminaries on-screen this time included economist Milton Friedman (who walked out of his interview in a huff, accusing Johnson of promoting socialism), Steve Forbes of *Forbes* magazine fame, Bill Gates Sr. (on-hand to advocate higher taxation of the wealthy)—and one Nicole Buffett, who spoke up for the relatively unspoiled "Buffett" way of life.

Nicole was Peter's daughter. Well, not biologically. She was the daughter of Peter's ex-wife, Mary, from a previous relationship. Peter and Mary divorced in 1993, and though he'd adopt her daughters and give them the Buffett name, were the girls still part of the family? Clearly, Warren didn't think so. (He had paid for the education and related expenses of all his grandchildren, including Nicole and

Erica's.) The documentary gave Nicole a platform to express her sentiments. Soon after its release, Oprah invited Nicole onto her show to elaborate. Referring obliquely to the fact that Susie had remembered her in her will but that Warren had warned her she'd be forgotten in his, Nicole told Oprah she was "at peace" with not having inherited wealth, but also complained about her exclusion from the family's charitable endeavors. "It would be nice to be involved with creating things for others with that money," she said. Nicole also sent Warren a letter asking why he'd disavowed her.

"I have not legally or emotionally adopted you as a grandchild," he replied, "nor have the rest of the family adopted you as a niece or cousin. . . . It is simply a fact that just as [your mother] is in no respect my daughter-in-law, her children are not my grandchildren."

"Buffett to kin: You're Fired!" had bleated the *New York Post*, after getting hold of Warren's letter. The phrase had been meme-ified by Donald Trump, who'd recently taken up residence on the reality show *The Apprentice*, a fake billionaire playing a fake business whiz. To Warren, a real billionaire and real business whiz, it must have seemed like Nicole was making him into some kind of reality TV spectacle, too. Who was she to offer tutorials on the inconsistencies underlying Buffett-style humility and thrift? If you wanted to see how *that* worked, Astrid Menks Buffett was the woman to observe: She kept her head down, and was mostly known in Omaha for treasure-hunting in the city's secondhand shops. "People see her around town," Buffett biographer Andy Kilpatrick told the *Guardian*. "She'll be out looking for bargains for the house, shovelling snow or doing errands for him."

Nicole Buffett would instead be sitting for an interview with *Marie Claire*, supplying its editors with a card from Warren signed "Grandpa."

WHEN WARREN SIGNED over his gift to Bill and Melinda and his children, he probably didn't expect that one upshot of his generosity would be Nicole upbraiding him on *Oprah*. But that's the trouble with philanthropy—even when you're trying to do good, there are always unintended consequences.

Jean Strouse has a good anecdote in her *New York Times Magazine* article about the World Health Organization's efforts to control the spread of malaria back in the 1960s. The story—worthy of Hans Christian Andersen—begins with WHO fieldworkers in Borneo spraying houses with the pesticide DDT. Mosquito genocide ensued. Success! Except that, as Strouse notes, the campaign had "side effects."

"House lizards ate the dead bugs, then cats ate the lizards and died from the accumulated insecticide," Strouse writes. "Without cats, the local rat population exploded—rats that could carry plague and typhus. Neighboring states donated cats to [Borneo's] affected upland regions. For the remote interior, the W.H.O. and Singapore's Royal Air Force devised a maneuver worthy of Disney called Operation Cat Drop: They packed cats into perforated containers and sent them plummeting into upland villages by parachute."

The road to hell is paved with et cetera et cetera.

Setting aside the obvious question—*What happened to those cats?!*—what is the moral of this story? It's not that attempts to do good are always futile, or that would-be do-gooders should be paralyzed by fear of failure. The point is that not all consequences of aid can be foreseen, and thus do-gooders must proceed with caution when they meddle with the status quo. Unintended consequences come in a variety of forms—as in the anecdote above, they can arrive in a cascade of knock-on effects, or, equally likely, are wired into a campaign's faulty design, because, blinders-on, the designers didn't get answers to questions they hadn't thought to ask. The infamous Khanna study funded by the Rockefeller Foundation is an example of the latter.

Between 1953 and 1960, a team of Harvard researchers conducted a study of the effectiveness of oral contraceptives in limiting fertility in the Punjab region of India. Eight thousand people in seven villages were surveyed, with the women being given birth control tablets and asked monthly about highly personal matters such as their menstrual cycles and frequency of sex with their husbands. At the end of the study, the researchers were surprised—and embarrassed—to find that the birth rate among women who had received the pills was *higher* than that of women in the control group. It turned out that many of the subjects didn't understand what the pills did, or what the study was about—some of them believed it had to do with building roads—and they were accepting the pills out of politeness, but not taking them.

Unintended consequences. But the Khanna study also illustrates the problem of *intended* consequences: When the Punjabi women discovered that the aim of the study was to get them to have fewer babies, they were horrified. And furious. For these desperately poor families, children were viewed as necessary to economic survival—an idea your average wealthy Westerner may have trouble comprehending, but that's the point. The Rockefeller Foundation had one notion of what constituted "the good"—a reduction in fertility—and the people the foundation believed it was helping thought otherwise. Who gets to decide?

And it's not just philanthropic aims at issue here. It's philanthropic process, too.

The Green Revolution of the 1960s and '70s—another campaign spearheaded by the Rockefeller Foundation—has been widely lauded as a miraculous success, credited with saving over a billion people from starvation thanks to the transformation of farming across the developing world. And it's true that many, many people lived who might have starved, and that farming *was* transformed. The way it was transformed is a story of intended consequences: Agronomist Norman Borlaug, considered the "father of the Green Revolution," advocated for the cultivation of high-yield grains such as dwarf wheat, the shipping of seeds, and the promotion of industrial agricultural practices in countries in Latin America, Asia, and

Africa; small farms were to be replaced by large ones that utilized tractors, modern irrigation, chemical pesticides, and nitrogen-based fertilizers. "The good," for the Green Revolutionaries, wasn't just a reduction in food scarcity; it was also the advancement of Western ideas about the primacy of efficiency in the growing of food, and the weaving of developing nations into the global commodity network. Is that a good? The answer depends on how you view a lot of things: globalization, GMOs, sustainability, and more. Unintended consequence: Neither Borlaug, who won the Nobel Peace Prize in 1970, nor his foundation funders anticipated that former subsistence farmers consolidated off their land and fieldworkers displaced by mechanization would stream into cities and take up residence in slums.

"What at the time appears to be astonishing progress, over the longer term is often revealed to be a poisoned chalice," writes David Rieff in the *New Republic*, noting that fifty years after the introduction of Green Revolution–style farming in Punjab, an area once seen as a lodestar of the program's success, farmers are dealing with aquifers tainted by runoff from chemical and petroleum-based fertilizers they depend on, but cannot afford except by trapping themselves in endless cycles of debt. "The Green Revolution in Punjab did indeed fuel India's economic development," Rieff adds, "but if anything further impoverished India's rural poor."

Rieff is an outspoken critic of philanthrocapitalist fixes, so his view on the Green Revolution needn't be taken as definitive. There are those who would argue that aiding India's economic development is a major accomplishment, and not something to be written off in a quick aside—a point Rieff himself concedes, going on to describe the Green Revolution in South Asia as "both a triumph and a tragedy." Again, the matter turns on how one chooses to define "*the good*." You arrive at the same conundrum reading John Perkins's massive study *Geopolitics and the Green Revolution*: Perkins makes the case that the U.S. government got behind global agriculture reform not out of concern for the world's poor so much as a desire to keep them from taking to the streets to demand left-wing regime change. A less cynical take would be that Cold War–era American officials saw helping the poor and staving off socialism as two sides of the same pretty coin.

One person who perhaps understands all this complexity better than many is Howie Buffett. His interest in sub-Saharan Africa only sharpened in the years after Susie's death, and now, with the coffers of his own foundation full, he was trying to figure out why food insecurity remained so stubbornly prevalent throughout the region. The Green Revolution never took there—indeed, African farmers suffered as a result of it, investing in worthlessly expensive fertilizer and seeds and then competing for local market share against newly cheap grain imported from Asia. As a farmer and a onetime board member of Big Ag conglomerate ADM, Howie viewed the failure of the Green Revolution in sub-Saharan Africa as a puzzle; as a man, he was moved by the plight of famine victims, like the ones in Malawi he saw eating termites on CNN. Shocked by the images, he booked a trip to the country, and met up with a representative of the United Nations' World Food Programme (WFP) in the capital, Lilongwe.

When Howie recounted his aghast response to the termite-eaters, the WFP rep laughed. Then he pointed out the window of their car at the stalls where roadside vendors were grilling something that looked like shish kebab. It turned out, termites were a delicacy in Malawi—and people who couldn't afford to buy grilled termites were delighted to eat fresh bugs plucked out of the ground. Mice, boiled whole and gobbled fur-on, were another treat favored by locals in southern and central Malawi.

Malawians' taste for mice wasn't just an interesting bit of trivia. Digging deeper, Howie found that mouse hunters played an important role in the rural ecosystem. Mice would burrow holes beneath crop residue from cornfields owned by local tribes; the hunters flushed the rodents out by clearing the residue and setting a small fire. "As you travel the countryside, you will see puffs of smoke rising from the savanna," Howie noted. Tribes permitted the hunters on their land because they considered them a boon: Not only were they controlling a mouse population that constantly threatened to overrun their villages, but they also did the work of clearing the crop residue, which farmers thought of as trash. This created a conundrum for aid workers trying to promote soil improvement practices, one component of which is "leaving crop residues on the ground after harvest to improve the soil's organic matter and retain moisture," as Howie explains. Thus, he goes on to point out, there is a certain diplomacy involved in negotiating an accommodation among villagers, farmers, and mouse hunters—such as suggesting to tribal chiefs that hunters be asked to replace crop residue they'd burned.

"You may give clear information to farmers about the importance of leaving crop residues, and you may have a stack of papers and material to back it up," wrote Howie, "but if you are in southern or central Malawi and don't factor in the mouse hunters, you're going to have trouble."

Local knowledge is key, in other words. Superlocal knowledge. When Howie mentioned the eating of mice to an NGO worker from the northern part of Malawi, he was informed: "If you tried to give a boiled mouse to a member of my tribe to eat, we would vomit."

As Howie notes, "You have to be on the ground to understand the fundamental dynamics of agriculture and food."

But Howie wasn't the only beneficiary of his father's billions to start developing a serious interest in this stuff. And while Bill was racing around the world, juggling vaccines and U.S. education and everything else, Africa would end up being where his plans and Howie's started to collide.

BACK IN 2004, UN Secretary General Kofi Annan had issued a call for African farmers to wage their own Green Revolution. "A revolution that is long overdue," he said in a rousing speech in Addis Ababa, "a revolution that will help the continent in its quest for dignity and peace." And soon after, the Gates Foundation began brainstorming ways to support the effort—inspired, no doubt, both by Annan and by Bill and Melinda's own dawning understanding of the degree to which food, poverty, and the diseases they were attempting to treat were all inextricably interlinked.

Their first port of call was, of course, the Rockefeller Foundation, still the leader in philanthropy-spurred agricultural development. In 2005, the presidents and vice presidents of the Gates and Rockefeller Foundations sat down together to begin hammering out a plan. What emerged was the Alliance for a Green Revolution in Africa, or AGRA, founded in 2006, headquartered in Nairobi, with a $100 million donation from the Gates Foundation and $50 million from the Rockefeller Foundation. Kofi Annan was named chair, and heavyweights from all over Africa were recruited to the AGRA board.

So why did the first Green Revolution never quite take hold or, as critics say, fail in Africa? For lots of reasons—the landscape of Africa is incredibly heterogeneous, and sociocultural conditions as well as the politics and related governance issues across the continent are just as diverse. There was simply no way to apply a one-size-fits-all philosophy. Some soil in Africa is beset by drought, other soil by inundating rains. Some soil sees a bit of both, erratically. Different types of pests bedevil farmers operating in different microclimates. The same difficulties the Gates Foundation encountered in delivering medicine and vaccines to remote villages applied in reverse for farmers trying to get their goods to market, and/or obtain seeds, tools, fertilizer, and pesticides. The folks at and behind AGRA took stock of all this, and promised they had no intention of trying once again to graft a one-size-fits-all solution onto Africa's complex, varied terrain. Noted Joseph DeVries, who led AGRA's seed research program, to David Rieff, "I don't need our critics to tell me what was wrong with the first green revolution. We're not talking about repeating that experience uncritically, whatever they think." (In 2022, AGRA rebranded, dropping "Green Revolution" from its name.)

The critics were on the case early. AGRA Watch, a project of the Seattle-based Community Alliance for Global Justice, was launched virtually in tandem with AGRA itself. Food First, a research and advocacy organization based in Oakland, sprinted to counter the claims and promises in AGRA's first mission statement, issuing a policy brief in October 2006 that listed ten reasons why AGRA "will not solve the problems of poverty and hunger in sub-Saharan Africa." Along with the usual warnings about loss of biodiversity and the probability that reliance on genetically engineered seeds and chemical fertilizers and pesticides would ensnare poor farmers in debt traps, the three PhDs who authored the Food First report made one particularly striking claim: "Hunger is not primarily due to a lack of food," wrote Eric Holt-Giménez, Miguel Altieri, and Peter Rosset, "but rather because the hungry are too poor to buy the food that is available."

"AGRA claims that by raising yields, they will help the region's 180 million smallholders feed themselves and the rest of the Sub-Saharan poor.... But a good food production-population ratio does not necessarily indicate that famine will not occur," the trio wrote, echoing the work of Nobel Prize–winning economist Amartya Sen. "Famines have occurred in Asia during periods of high agricultural output and were due to speculative stockpiling, unemployment, and low purchasing power—not food shortages."

The folks at AGRA saw the situation in very different terms. In their view, the key problem was absolutely one of yield: The population of sub-Saharan Africa was exploding; communities were trying to keep up with demand by razing forests to create new farmland, and in the meantime, farmers eked out more production not by improving the efficiency of their fields but by further cutting down on crop rotation, a maximizing effort due to pay sharply diminishing returns as soil was depleted of basic plant nutrients. An environmental catastrophe was in the offing, in short.

"The choices that confront African farmers and the world at large," noted Joseph DeVries, are simple and stark. "Either we will increase agricultural yields on the lands now under cultivation, or the combination of low yields and population increase will force smallholders to cut down virgin forest lands and cultivate them. There are no other realistic possibilities."

Rajiv Shah, then-Gates Foundation's agriculture honcho, appeared to believe that both AGRA and its critics had a point. The population/yield calculus was frightening, exacerbated by climate change, and exacerbating it in turn. On the other hand, as Shah admitted to persistent skeptic David Rieff, global institutions had played a major part in fomenting Africa's present troubles. Philanthropist organizations had done wrong in asking poor farmers to adopt cultivation practices that relied on fertilizers and pesticides they couldn't afford. The insistence of loan agencies, such as the World Bank, that African governments adhere to strict fiscal discipline had led those governments to neglect agricultural development and orient food production toward export, which had the effect of "further marginalizing the small-holding farmers who are in the majority in Africa," Shah told Rieff. Treading gingerly, he seemed to be expressing the opinion that change on the continent demanded paradigm shifts not just at the bottom but at the top—the folks who convene at Davos were going to have to adjust some of their assumptions about how the global economy ought to work.

Was this perspective endorsed by Bill and Melinda Gates?

At any rate, Shah wanted to colloquy with his critics. He met with the Food First people, and with Raj Patel, a disillusioned former World Bank staffer, author of *Stuffed and Starved: The Hidden Battle for the World Food System*, and an ardent disbeliever in Gates-style "creative capitalism" that relies on market-based solutions. Shah heard them out, but did he listen? "It seemed so up in the air," said Patel of the conversation. "I'm happy to impute the best possible motives to them. But Gates' success in imposing his [philanthrocapitalist] terms on the debate strengthens the status quo rather than doing what needs to be done—which is to transform it."

In 2007, Howie visited Ghana. There, he found a cheap, locally developed, ecologically sound farming practice. *Proka* was a traditional technique that had fallen into disuse; the gist of it, Howie says, is "mulch: plant residues and other organic matter left on or even carried to the rows in between the planted crops."

"The mulch helps the soil retain moisture," he notes, and as it decomposes it also raises the biomass and organic matter in the soil. Farmers tend to be an ingenious lot: Systems similar to *proka* can be found all over the African continent, and include traditional systems of pest control.

From Howie's perspective, Bill and Melinda looked ready to bulldoze all these important local systems with their big continent-wide Green Revolution. By itself, that would be bad enough. But to do it with his own father's money?

FOR WARREN HIMSELF, though, things were looking up. For one, Berkshire Hathaway was having a banner year. On October 23, 2006, BRK became the first American stock to trade over $100,000 per share. On December 10, 2007, a single share of Berkshire would be selling for $149,200.

But then, some people just don't care about good news. Like the activists tut-tutting at Warren for Berkshire's investment in PetroChina, whose parent company was implicated in China's sidelong complicity in the genocide in Darfur. Warren's position was that inasmuch as PetroChina was owned by the Chinese government, the company didn't have any say in how its profits were used. A billboard overlooking a major freeway in Omaha appeared, posing the question: "Will your conscience let you off on a technicality?"

Some months later, Warren unloaded his PetroChina shares, showing—finally, perhaps, just perhaps—the same receptivity to criticism and a willingness to learn and to change course that he demands from those in whom he invests. Warren had always been famed as an oracle, but maybe now he was really learning to be *wise*.

One Halloween over the coming years, Melinda held a Camelot-themed costume party in Seattle. Bill was Arthur, of course, in a fake ermine stole and a plastic crown. (You have to wonder why he didn't just buy a real one, possibly from some decaying European monarch.) Warren came as Merlin, in golden robes with a long, lustrous fake beard. Maybe we shouldn't read into these things, but the symbolism is almost too rich. Bill had the power: the wealthiest philanthropic foundation in human history, an operation spending billions in every corner of the globe. He was the king of his particular realm. And Warren, his Merlin, was the man who'd helped put him on his throne. His methods would be subtler. A seat on the Gates Foundation board. A word in an ear. A swish of a magic cape.

Well, if you have your Arthur and your Merlin, what's next? A Round Table, maybe, and a few knights to populate it. Which was, in fact, exactly what Bill and Warren had in mind.

11

OUT OF THE SKY

In a secret location somewhere in New York City, some of the richest people on the planet had sat down for a dinner to talk philanthropy. This is how Warren's old friend Carol Loomis describes the furor that arose:

> The Chronicle of Philanthropy *called it "unprecedented"; both* ABC News *and the* Houston Chronicle *went for "clandestine"; a* New York *magazine parody gleefully imagined George Soros to have been starstruck in the presence of Oprah. One radio broadcaster painted a dark picture: "Ladies and gentlemen, there's mischief afoot and it does not bode well for the rest of us."*

Loomis has a pretty good idea of who might have let slip to the press what was taking place here: Chuck Feeney.

In a room full of interesting people, including Warren and Bill, David Rockefeller Sr. and David Rockefeller Jr., George Soros, Mayor Michael Bloomberg, CNN founder Ted Turner, and Oprah Winfrey, duty-free magnate Chuck Feeney might have been the most unusual. He is, as things stand, the only example of a billionaire giving away all his money during his own lifetime, and possibly the only person to have *deliberately* left the Forbes 400 list. Today, having donated virtually all $8 billion of his wealth—the last of it in a $1.5 billion sprint—Feeney, who co-founded Duty Free Shoppers, lives in a modest rental apartment in San Francisco. It took him thirty-eight years to dole out most of his dough, both because he targeted his giving in highly personal ways—for instance, by choosing to fund schools and universities in Ireland—and because his fortune grew as he went along, for a while faster than he could give it away. (Feeney was an early investor in Facebook, not the ideal investment for a guy avid to un-rich himself.) But he was highly motivated to die poor, and so he kept at his wealth-ridding mission.

The news about this secret meeting didn't break in the *New York Times* or the *New York Post*, or even any of the punchier little outlets that spend their time following people like Oprah around. Instead, one of the bigger stories of the year broke on a website called Irish-Central.com. And what, pray tell, is IrishCentral.com? According to the publishers, it's a site whose "focus is on connecting the Irish and friends of the Irish across the globe and working to keep them informed and inspired." But the site's founder, Niall O'Dowd, happens to be a longtime friend of one Chuck Feeney. So, one mystery potentially solved.

Thanks to a later article in *Forbes*, we actually know a good deal about this clandestine gathering. It was held at the President's House at Rockefeller University—a swish midcentury manse that serves as an official residence for the university's head, and an events space whenever the Rockefellers wanted it. The whole thing had been Warren's idea. Turns out, his big gift to Bill and Melinda didn't mark the end of his philanthropic journey—if anything, it left him with the determination to do even more. But, ever the delegator, he decided he needed help. So, how about a kind of Avengers ensemble of charitable giving, an alliance of the world's most superpowered philanthropists? He even came up with a name for the team he wanted to build: "The Great Givers."

It sucked and didn't stick.

"If you had to depend on Warren to organize this dinner," Bill later recalled, "it might never have happened." Luckily, Warren had some very capable people around him—people like Bill and David Rockefeller Jr.—to handle the tricky work of choosing a venue and printing out some nice invitations. (And when you get an invitation signed by Warren Buffett, Bill Gates, and a Rockefeller, how do you say no?) When the dinner itself rolled around on May 5, Warren played the MC, or, in David Rockefeller Jr.'s words, "the enlivener." Warren, in his usual unfussy style, spoke for around fifteen minutes about his adventures in philanthropy, and then invited his guests to do the same. Quick back-of-the-napkin calculation: twelve of the fourteen total attendees, each speaking for fifteen minutes—that's a *three-hour* colloquium on giving your money to charity. But Warren set the tone well. He didn't spend his quarter hour gloomily sizing up the vastness of the problems in the world, and he didn't spend too much time on self-congratulation either. Warren kept it light, and the guests were rapt.

Dinner was served, and the guests started brainstorming ways to get more of their fellow billionaires to give away more of their fortunes. They didn't come to any firm conclusions and some of the ideas (such as a nice shiny presidential medal for great philanthropists) were a little shakier than others. But on that night, a snowball started rolling.

Of course, some aspects of the dinner remain shrouded in mystery. For instance, what was on the menu? Steak and snails? Something from Dairy Queen? On that front, you'll have to use your imagination.

BUT WHILE NEW York society was gripped by talk of secret billionaire dinners, another of Warren's personal crusades was hitting the news in a pretty major way.

In his 2003 letter to shareholders, Warren penned one of the more famous lines ever written about investing, calling derivatives "financial weapons of mass destruction." Back then, this might have been big news for the kind of people who know what a derivative is. For most of us, though, it was just more inscrutable finance-babble. For those that slept through the lesson that came about five years later, a derivative is any financial product spun out of an asset.

The Big Short is a good movie that aims to explain the causes of the 2008 crash. If you want a crash course in the big-bank-built WMDs that blew up the economy—such as derivatives and CDOs (collateralized debt obligations) as well as gouts of good old greed, including a passing reference to Warren—go there. Why was Warren mentioned? Because Warren Buffett is the guy who tried to warn everyone about the coming meltdown. In the same 2003 letter to the shareholders, he'd also described derivatives—a stake in a package of thousands of mortgages, some good, mostly bad—as "time bombs." And just as no one paid him any heed during the dot-com bubble, no one listened to Warren and Charlie Munger when they warned that the explosion in derivatives was likely to lead to a global run on the banks. But it did. In an apocalyptic way.

In the summer of 2006, the housing bubble silently burst. By early the following year, everyone was being hurt, but especially poor and minority homeowners. On October 19, 2007, the Dow went into free fall. Central banks frantically cut interest rates. The CEOs of Citigroup and Merrill Lynch got booted. Countrywide, the United States' largest mortgage underwriter, went up for sale at a clearance price. The trouble seemed to culminate on March 13, 2008, as a bank run began on Bear Stearns: In a near-perfect echo of the Salomon Brothers crisis years earlier, lenders were refusing to roll over Bear's short-term loans, and the bank was on the brink of collapse.

"What happened at Bear Stearns was the first true demonstration of what the crisis looked like, because it was a crisis of confidence," explains *Too Big to Fail* author Andrew Ross Sorkin. "Bear Stearns owned a huge piece of the housing business, and they had taken on some of the worst risk. All of a sudden, all sorts of investors on Wall Street said, I don't think that Bear Stearns is good for the money. And not only do I not think they're good for the money, but I've got to get my money out of there *immediately*."

Bear Stearns honcho Ace Greenberg dialed up his old pal Warren Buffett. Might he be interested in a Salomon-like salvage operation? Warren said, no thanks. So, the Federal Reserve stepped in, guaranteeing $30 billion worth of Bear Stearns's debt—that is, digesting a bunch of its garbage—and orchestrating JPMorgan Chase's acquisition of the bank. The markets breathed a sigh of relief. It would be their last for a while.

"The economy is definitely tanking," Warren told his biographer Alice Schroeder at the time. "It's not my game, but if I had to bet one way or another—everybody else says a recession will be short and shallow, but I would say long and deep."

And long and deep it was.

BILL GATES STEPPED down from Microsoft on June 27, 2008.

In a teary farewell speech delivered to Microsoft employees at its headquarters in Redmond, Bill took leave of his full-time executive role at the company. This exit, which would enable him to focus squarely on the Gates Foundation, had been in the offing for two years—his departure had been announced, with little fanfare, in 2006, just before the flamboyant reveal of Warren's gift. This day, Bill poked fun at his unfamiliarity with the concept of "downtime" as he delivered his final address as company chairman. Assuming his new, avuncular persona, and clad in a suave combo of pale-lavender button-down and dark-lavender pullover, Bill introduced a video spoof of The Office showing him working out with his personal trainer, played by Matthew McConaughey, auditioning for Steven Spielberg, and cutting a rap track with Jay-Z. "Killed it, Billy G," Jay-Z says, before adding, to the camera, "Somebody got to tell him: It's horrible." That's the main joke of the short, which also features Barack Obama, Hillary Clinton, *Daily Show* anchor Jon Stewart, George Clooney, and, of course, Bono: Bill poking his nose into everybody's business, and getting treated with kid gloves. It's funny.

Bill was leaving the company at a perilous time. The good news: Video game console Xbox was a roaring success, bringing Microsoft hardware into millions of homes. Windows, the operating system the company had made into the default computer interface, and which had been the crux of the Justice Department's antitrust case, continued to dominate, even as Apple rose from the dead and coaxed clone users to switch to iMacs and MacBooks. Microsoft was still the go-to for business-related software, especially its flagship Office package. The Redmond coffers were still flush with cash.

But in the years between the onset of the antitrust case and Bill's exit, Microsoft had witnessed a string of setbacks. Playing catch-up with Apple's iPod, it launched the dismal Zune—seven months prior to Apple's release of the first iPhone. "There's no chance that the iPhone is going to get any significant market share," said Steve Ballmer. Google had gone public in August 2004 and was swallowing the search market whole—not to mention stealing away Microsoft talent. Nothing to see here, said Ballmer. "Google's not a real company," he fulminated as Microsoft engineers set to work on the ill-fated search engine MSN Search, one of the several precursors to Bing. "It's a house of cards." Despite the fact that Microsoft had a ten-year head start on development of an e-reader, it ceded the market to Amazon, which launched the first Kindle in August 2007. Bill Gates, not Steve Ballmer, may be to blame for that one: Shown a prototype Microsoft e-reader in 1998, Bill gave it a thumbs-down, declaring it off-brand because it didn't feature a Windows-style interface; unmoved by arguments that people wouldn't want to look at Windows gewgaws while they were paging through books and articles, he folded the e-reader initiative into the group creating software for Office, where it got chewed up by pressures on the division to report profits straightaway. Social networking was another missed boat. And Windows Vista, the much-ballyhooed update meant to compete with Apple's sleek OS, launched after several delays in 2007, and was promptly declared the "biggest disappointment" of the year by *PC World* magazine.

Whence the rot? When journalist Kurt Eichenwald interviewed current and former Microsoft employees, everyone—every single person—brought up Microsoft's employee review system, known as "stack ranking." Following bell curve logic, every unit within the firm "was forced to declare a certain percentage of employees as top performers, then good performers, then average, then below average, then poor."

"If you were on a team of 10 people, you walked in the first day knowing that no matter how good everyone was, two people were going to get a great review, seven were going to get mediocre reviews, and one was going to get a terrible review," one former software developer told Eichenwald. "People planned their days and their years around the review, rather than around products. You really had to focus on the six-month performance, rather than on doing what was right for the company."

Stack ranking created an atmosphere of internecine warfare among staffers: People working in the same unit competed against one another, unit managers competed against other unit managers rather than collaborating across projects, and everyone jockeyed for the attention and affection of top execs, so a company once famed for its argumentativeness became a hotbed of brown-nosers and yespeople. Can you blame Bill for wanting to hightail it out of there and concentrate on eradicating polio?

But Bill couldn't escape Microsoft entirely. It was where he'd cut his teeth, and where he'd sourced some of the initial staff for his foundation. Some of the problems bedeviling Microsoft were already creeping into the foundation's work. And once again, the arena would be America's public schools.

SEPTEMBER 2008 WAS a doozy. Fannie Mae and Freddie Mac crashed. Lehman Brothers collapsed. That month, ordinary people who usually flipped the channel when the business news comes on had to start paying attention, because the housing crisis had metastasized into a full-blown financial panic, and the global economy was on the brink of collapse. Markets all over the world were going berserk. Wall Street was in a meltdown—even gold-plated Goldman Sachs seemed wobbly. "We were a few days away from the ATMs not working," then-president of the New York Fed Timothy Geithner recalls. Treasury Secretary Hank Paulson and Federal Reserve Chairman Ben Bernanke started throwing cash at companies like they were at a Tampa nudie bar throwing it at dancers, and returned to Washington to try and ram a $700 billion bank bailout package down Congress's throat.

Reenter Warren Buffett. On September 23, Warren jogged in from the sidelines to play his accustomed savior role, announcing that Berkshire would invest $5 billion in Goldman Sachs, but his terms were steep and self-serving. Warren freely admitted that his decision to plunk a fifth of $25.2 billion of Berkshire's cash reserves into Goldman was based on his intuition that the government was not going to let the bank fail—and then he got out on the hustings to call on Congress to protect his investment. Failure to bail out the big banks would result in an "economic Pearl Harbor," he said.

Congress responded by voting down a bailout. The Dow responded by plummeting 777 points, then its steepest-ever one-day fall. Warren responded by snapping up $3 billion worth of General Electric, one in a series of sizable prop-up investments he'd make in the coming months. Soon, Congress reversed course and passed the $700 billion Emergency Economic Stabilization Act. Both presidential candidates John McCain and Barack Obama said they'd consider naming Warren Buffett Treasury secretary if they were elected.

So, politics worked, everything was fine, and we all lived happily ever after.

We kid! Nothing was fine. The savings and loan bank Washington Mutual had collapsed—the biggest bank failure in American history. The FTSE in London continued to tumble, as did Japan's Nikkei index; virtually every business in Iceland went bankrupt. In the United States, consumer credit had dried up, and volatility continued to plague the markets. Hank Paulson was wracking his brain trying to figure out a way to dump additional cash directly into bank coffers, to stoke lending.

One night, as Paulson was sleeping, his phone rang. Drowsily, he picked up. "Hank, this is Warren," said the voice on the line.

"And my mind—I'm thinking, my mom has a handyman named Warren, why is he calling me?" remembers Paulson. Warren pitched Paulson on forcing the big banks to sell billions of dollars of preferred shares of their stock to the U.S. government—basically, to get the taxpayer to play the same role Warren had in buying a piece of Goldman, acting as lender-of-last-resort, and stipulating onerous repayment terms. As Paulson and Ben Bernanke love to point out, taxpayers wound up turning a healthy profit on the deal. It also might have kept the United States from sliding into a years-long depression.

But America, and Warren, were far from being out of the woods.

Berkshire was having its worst year ever. Moody's, the rating agency that Warren had long cherished, and that Berkshire now owned 20 percent of, was implicated in the crash. And more broadly, Warren bemoaned the giddy stupidity that had propelled the housing bubble: Though it was perfectly reasonable to assume that, over time, thanks to inflation, a home a person lived in would rise in price, that didn't mean home prices could *never* fall, or that naïve Americans ought to be lured into taking out "liar loans" or signing up for mortgages with too-good-to-last "teaser rates."

Clayton Homes, Berkshire's mobile home subsidiary, was the instructive counterexample for Warren: "Why are our borrowers—characteristically people with modest incomes and far-from-great credit scores—performing so well?" he asked rhetorically.

The answer is elementary, going right back to Lending 101. Our borrowers simply looked at how full-bore mortgage payments would compare with their actual—not hoped-for—income and then decided whether or not they could live with that commitment. Simply put, they took out a mortgage with the intention of paying it off, whatever the course of home prices. . . .

Jimmy Stewart would have loved these folks.

Warren wasn't letting irresponsible borrowers off the hook. But his criticism of Wall Street wizards who believed housing was a no-lose bet was far sharper. "The stupefying losses in mortgage-related securities came in large part because of flawed, history-based models used by salesmen, rating agencies and investors," he explained.

These parties looked at loss experience over periods when home prices rose only moderately and speculation in houses was negligible. They then made this experience a yardstick for evaluating future losses. They blissfully ignored the fact that house prices had recently skyrocketed, loan practices had deteriorated and many buyers had opted for houses they couldn't afford. In short, universe "past" and universe "current" had very different characteristics. . . .

Investors should be skeptical of history-based models. Constructed by a nerdy-sounding priesthood using esoteric terms such as beta, gamma, sigma and the like, these models tend to look impressive. Too often, though, investors forget to examine the assumptions behind the symbols.

"Our advice?" added Warren. "Beware of geeks bearing formulas." Despite his chagrin, Warren shifted into his Atlas mode, hoisting America onto his back. He penned a widely shared op-ed for the *New York Times* announcing that his personal investments—as opposed to the ones he made on Berkshire Hathaway's behalf—were all in American equities, and he was feeling bullish. "Bad news is an investor's best friend," he wrote. "It lets you buy a slice of America's future at a marked-down price."

Voters seized on their own version of President-elect Barack Obama's campaign catchphrase "Hope." In his slender form, Obama—a man completely unknown a decade earlier—embodied America's dreams about itself. That a person could emerge from the masses and rise to the highest office in the land. That racial reconciliation was possible, and maybe even inevitable. That a hero, measured and eloquent and fair, could ride to the rescue and, armed with a bunch of wonky proposals, fix everything that had gone sour over years of misrule. This time everything was fine, and we all lived happily after.

Right?

WARREN'S MERLIN ACT with Bill was starting to bear fruit. Well, some fruit. Bill was still less cautious than he should have been about nerds with formulas—but he did take a page from his mentor's book when it came to getting the message out. In early 2009, Bill penned his first annual letter as the head of the Gates Foundation. Warren had encouraged him to duplicate the format of his communications to shareholders—point-by-point rundowns of each division of the business, plus commentary. "In this letter I want to share in a frank way what our goals are and where progress is being made and where it is not," Bill began. "I won't be quoting Mae West or trying to match [Warren's] humor, but I will try to be equally candid."

Bill's letter isn't nearly as granular as any of Warren's annual missives to Berkshire Hathaway shareholders, but it does paint a picture of his top-line thinking about each of the Gates Foundation's areas of focus: global health, agricultural development, and education in the United States.

Fifty percent of Gates Foundation giving was directed at global health, Bill said, and the primary aim within this category was to reduce deaths of children under age five. That number stood at 10 million a year as of 2005, with a few diseases, including diarrhea, malaria, and pneumonia, accounting for more than half of the deaths. "The key to eliminating these conditions is the invention of a handful of new vaccines and getting them into widespread usage," Bill stated. He'd elaborated on this philosophy in a speech in 2008 at the World Economic Forum in Davos, saying "There are two great forces of human nature: self-interest, and caring for others" and explaining that the Gates Foundation reconciled them by offering pharmaceutical companies financial incentives to enter markets in the developing world and conduct research they wouldn't otherwise pursue.

In his letter, Bill goes on to note that improving child mortality rates sets in motion a virtuous cycle: When families can trust that their kids will survive and thrive, they have fewer of them, and when families and governments can dedicate more resources to every child, nutrition and education improve, and eventually, whole communities see a steady rise in living standards, thanks to succeeding generations of young people yet more ready, willing, and able to take on the world.

It's an appealing pitch. It may even be true.

While making no reference to it here, Bill has acknowledged elsewhere another major factor in global poverty, war. In *40 Chances*, Howie Buffett recounts a trip he and his son took to Sierra Leone in 2008, where they met with former child soldiers and toured the countryside. "By the time we visited Sierra Leone, there had been a stable peace for a half dozen years," he writes. "But the consequences of the conflict would forever haunt the people who had lived through it. We learned that many had been forced off their land so that the government could sell diamond mining rights to foreign corporations . . . Huge numbers of former combatants with no skills and no other way to support themselves . . . now worked in diamond mines for pennies a day."

War is a factor in endemic poverty, as Howie's anecdote makes clear; so, too, is exploitation, as when foreign corporations muscle their way into countries in order to extract resources, a sorry story that began under colonialism and hasn't yet ended. To cite but one example, in the 1990s, the Ogoni people of the Niger Delta rose up against the oil company Royal Dutch Shell, whose hundred or so wells they blamed for poisoning their fertile land, polluting their water supply, and, thanks to twenty-four-hour gas flares, making the air periodically unbreathable and creating intolerable constant noise. The number of jobs Shell and other oil companies provided to Ogoni tribespeople didn't make up for the ones lost to environmental devastation and the breakup of farms by pipelines; nor did these companies offer anything in the way of local infrastructure, other than what was required to maintain its workforce. Presumably, the heads of these firms believed it was the Nigerian government's job to take care of governance, which it was; however, the fact that oil accounted for 80 percent of Nigeria's export revenue—and that the country's military rulers and their cronies were creaming riches off the business—made the government turn a blind eye to Ogoni concerns. And when the tribespeople rose up, the regime responded by executing the protest leaders, playwright and activist Ken Saro-Wiwa among them.

What, you may be wondering, does any of this have to do with the Gates Foundation?

"Justice Eta, 14 months old, held out his tiny thumb," begins a story published in the *Los Angeles Times* on January 7, 2007, and datelined from the town of Ebocha in Nigeria. "An ink spot certified that he had been immunized against polio and measles, thanks to a vaccination drive sponsored by the Bill & Melinda Gates Foundation.

"But polio is not the only threat that Justice faces. Almost since birth, he has had respiratory trouble. His neighbors call it 'the cough.' People blame fumes and soot spewing from flames that tower 300 feet into the air over a nearby oil plant. It is owned by the Italian petroleum giant Eni, whose investors include the Bill & Melinda Gates Foundation."

The article goes on to note that the foundation had also invested hundreds of millions of dollars in Exxon Mobil, Chevron, Total of France, and Royal Dutch Shell, "the companies responsible for most of the flares blanketing the delta with pollution beyond anything permitted in the United States or Europe." Drilling and refining in the region weren't just causing problems adjacent to the Gates Foundation's health mission; it was also causing the spread of illnesses the foundation had explicitly committed to fight: Oil bore holes filled with stagnant water became breeding grounds for malaria-carrying mosquitos; rivers clogged with leaked oil incubated cholera and other waterborne diseases. In response to the *Los Angeles Times* investigation, which found that the Gates Foundation had about $8.7 billion invested in companies that seemed to "contravene" its mission and good works, then-CEO of the foundation Patty Stonesifer penned a letter to the editor accusing the reporters of naïveté and stating that changes in the foundation's investment practices "would have little or no impact on these issues."

Note that at time of this writing, and in another example of learning as you go, the Gates Foundation has recently divested itself of direct holdings in all oil and gas companies, something that cannot yet be said of Berkshire Hathaway, which continues to invest.

And what of the foundation's record with Big Pharma corporations such as GlaxoSmithKline and Merck? "It's more like [the Gates Foundation] are selling technology than solving problems," one health researcher based in Ghana told *No Such Thing as a Free Gift* author Linsey McGoey. That this researcher declined to be named tallies with a 2008 piece in the *Seattle Times* noting that the foundation's position as both thought leader and money pump made on-the-ground critics wary of piping up: "Particularly in the field of global health, where funding for diseases in the developing world was anemic before Gates' $9.5 billion infusion, few are willing to risk wrath by pointing out flaws in the foundation's approach."

"It would be suicidal for someone who wants a grant to come out and publicly criticize the foundation," said Mark Kane, a former leader of a Gates-funded immunization program who spoke to the *Seattle Times*. "The Gates Foundation is very sensitive to PR."

Speaking to a reporter from the *New Internationalist* magazine, Dr. David McCoy, then a researcher at University College London, said he believed the relative lack of criticism was simply the result of the foundation's influence—it had the power to enforce consensus. "The Foundation is more than a collection of grants and projects," McCoy pointed out. "Through its funding it also operates through an interconnected network of organizations and individuals across academia and the NGO and business sectors. This allows it to leverage influence through a kind of 'group-think' in international health." McCoy's analysis was echoed in a leaked memo by Arata Kochi, then head of the World Health Organization's malaria program, who voiced fears that the foundation was elevating the findings of research it had funded and shutting out dissenting views.

The foundation, for its part, was alert to the echo chamber problem. "The danger isn't in what people do tell you—it's in what they don't," noted Patty Stonesifer in 2007 in her final annual report as Gates Foundation CEO. "It's amazing what people won't tell you when you have billions of dollars to give away."

Criticisms that *did* emerge sometimes verged on the conspiratorial. To wit, accusations that the foundation was merely a stalking horse for Western pharmaceutical companies who wanted to test their medicines quickly and cheaply on people in the developing world. But, as the saying goes, just because you're paranoid, it doesn't mean they're not after you: The cost of conducting lengthy clinical trials in the United States and E.U. had exploded, and companies were having trouble recruiting test subjects, so, "since the late 1990s, drug companies have routed this dilemma by exporting their clinical trials for new drugs to developing countries, where the sick and desperate abound," noted investigative journalist Sonia Shah in 2007.

There are plenty of cranks out there with strange beliefs about vaccines. It's easy to dismiss those worries when they spiral into tinfoil-hat fantasies about power-mad lizard people bent on euthanizing the world's poor. When they're in the form of a structural analysis proffered by one of the Gates Foundation's putative allies, it's . . . less easy.

In his first annual letter, Bill writes presciently at some length of the difficulty of refrigerating vaccines, an issue that would later come to occupy the entire planet during the Covid crisis. "Adding a new vaccine," he explains, "like one for rotavirus, that needs a lot of refrigerator space, requires increasing the refrigeration capacity at every stage of the entire delivery chain, including very remote areas that don't have electricity." Back then, in 2010, the newsletter failed to mention the difficulty of vaccinating people who suspect they are being used as guinea pigs, or that one of the reasons electrification was spotty in swathes of the developing world is because of an even greater issue: sovereign debt.

"When resentment builds because of . . . the burden of unfair debt, that are debts, by the way, that keep Africans poor? That's not a cause, that's an emergency." So sayeth Bono, in his May 17, 2004, commencement address at the University of Pennsylvania. As he stated, debt is perhaps the most decisive factor in third-world poverty, and by extension, the persistence of easily treatable disease. In Africa, the IMF and World Bank strictures forced governments to cut back on spending on infrastructure and healthcare. In Ghana, for instance, where universal healthcare had been guaranteed since the country gained independence in the 1950s, Linsey McGoey writes, "jobs at publicly funded hospitals were slashed" through the '80s and '90s "to appease IMF development experts."

The point of raising these issues isn't to blame the Gates Foundation for the world's problems, or to suggest that it isn't being effective or making massively beneficial contributions, because it inarguably is. (In 2002, it gave seed money to fund Bono's DATA—which stands for Debt, Aids, Trade, Africa—in order to continue the work of Jubilee 2000's campaign to cancel debts owed by the poorest countries.) Even its toughest critics affirm that the foundation has done much good in the realm of global health. And its cheerleaders—Bono among them—believe the foundation is doing God's work. How could you not be moved by the story of Saru, a woman in western Nepal, whose service as a Female Community Health Volunteer (FCHV) is recounted in the 2009 Gates Foundation Annual Report? After losing her son to diarrhea, Saru joined the Gates-backed FCHV program, through which volunteers "distribute vitamin A and deworming tablets to young children, offer family planning counseling . . . manage cases of pneumonia with first-line antibiotics [and] treat diarrhea with zinc and oral rehydration salts (ORS)," the report explains. "By latest counts, in a single year, FCHVs had treated 236,000 children with pneumonia and distributed 854,000 packets of ORS and 1.8 million zinc tablets. All told, these efforts save an estimated 12,000 lives each year."

It's perfectly proper for Bill to tout this type of progress when evidence of progress helps draw others to the cause. And there are other healthy signs that the foundation continues to learn from its activities as it evolves. Take, for instance, Bill's approach to climate change. In 2019, Bill angered some activists when he argued that the movement to divest investment funds from fossil fuels stocks—a movement that even counts the Rockefellers among its members—was not particularly effective. "Divestment, to date, probably has reduced about zero tonnes of emissions," he told the *Financial Times*. In his 2020 annual letter, he spent some time with the subject—although again, his approach focuses more on adaptation: ways to help people survive in a warming world; for instance, by supplying farmers with drought and flood-resistant crop strains. But that doesn't mean he's all effects and no causes. In fact, the following year, he published a book called *How to Avoid a Climate Disaster*, in which he outlines his vision for the technologies that can save our planet, both the "solutions we need to deploy in a big way now and where we should pursue breakthroughs because the clean alternatives aren't cheap enough"—and as always with Bill, this isn't just idle speculation.

Since 2016, Bill has raised more than $2 billion for Breakthrough Energy Ventures, an investment group dedicated to funding projects for zero-carbon energy. Tricky engineering problems, you might recall, are sort of his thing. TerraPower, a company he founded in 2008, has some pretty audacious designs. It is working on a project to generate electricity from spent nuclear waste, providing safe nuclear energy while also finding a new use for the estimated 90,000 metric tons of nuclear waste in the United States. (For scale, TerraPower said, consider that 8 tons could power 2.5 million homes for a year.) And it's not just domestic energy; the company is also exploring ways to power oceangoing ships with small zero-carbon atomic batteries. And then there's his abiding interest in clean water, and sanitation, working with designers to revolutionize the humble toilet in the developing world, a huge issue given that half a million children under five die each year from drinking water contaminated by human waste. So, it's true that you won't find Bill Gates protesting outside an oil company's headquarters. But he might put them all out of business yet.

AS 2009 WORE on, Bill and Warren were holding ever more dinners with ever more billionaires, with a view to convincing them to start giving their money away to good causes. There was a second event in Manhattan, held at the New York Public Library, and another in Menlo Park, California, birthplace of both Apple and Google. But while the world of billionaires is small, it also tends to sprawl over national borders. Before long, Bill and Melinda had taken the Great

Givers international. Dinners in London. Dinners in India. Dinners in China. Wherever people had amassed enormous fortunes, Bill and Warren were there, trying to think of ways to separate those people from their money. But now they had a new idea.

And, maybe just as importantly, they had a name. for it: the *Giving Pledge*. They wanted the super-rich, starting with the Forbes 400 list of the Americans with highest net worth, to pledge at least 50 percent of their net worth to charity during their lifetimes or at death. "The idea of aiming for a 50% slice of net worth was pragmatically pulled from the sky," Carol Loomis explains, "being less than the principals would have liked to ask for but perhaps as much, at least initially, as they [could] get."

Forbes estimated the total net worth of its American 400 to be $1.2 trillion in 2009. Loomis dug into the available numbers on billionaire giving, and calculated that they gave about $15 billion in total each year; if you assume that out of half of $1.2 trillion, or $600 billion, 5 percent (the minimum required by the pledge campaign) would actually be donated each year, the pledge would double the amount of 400-listers' charitable contributions. "A ten percent increase in charitable giving would elevate the resources of the non-profit world to a level we'd normally not see for several years to come," noted a columnist for the *Chronicle of Philanthropy*. "But a one hundred percent increase would mean access to resources today that otherwise would not appear for a generation."

Though it may have been "pulled from the sky," that 50 percent figure was still an interesting one to have alighted on. When the affluent are asked how much money they'd need to truly feel wealthy, they double their current net worth. If they've got $10 million in the bank, they say they'd need $20 million. For these people, $10 million is considered "entry-level rich," as former *Wall Street Journal* Wealth Report columnist Robert Frank writes in his book *Richistan*, a study of America's contemporary upper class. "Yet even billionaires are starting to feel common," Frank adds.

The Giving Pledge offered a different measure of wealth: Are you rich enough to give away half of what you have?

This is a massively audacious recalibration of what it means to be wealthy, and perfectly plays to the psyches of alpha types, turning into an exciting challenge something that might otherwise feel onerous and deflating.

"It costs me nothing," Warren has said of his Gates Foundation gift. "I've had everything in life—*everything* in life—I've ever wanted." This is a stunning bit of psychological jiujitsu, a jibe at wealth hoarders too insecure to part with their money.

The pitch worked. Better than either of the two men could have hoped.

In June 2010, the Giving Pledge was formally announced. By August, forty billionaires had signed their names to it. Seventeen more joined the club before the end of the year.

The work of socialists, cried letter-writers to conservative magazine *The Weekly Standard*. Clearly, they were confused. And enraged. And they weren't the only ones: Outside, far away from Warren and Bill's secret dinners, with their earnest talk, something strange was happening on America's streets.

There was a lot of anger in the years after the 2008 crash. Hundreds of thousands had lost their jobs, their businesses, and/or their homes. And as the Tea Partiers saw it, Obama's federal bailout was a giant subsidy for the billionaire classes and also, as the galvanizing rant from CNBC's Rick Santelli put it, for the various "losers" who couldn't pay their mortgages. Strange, then, that so much of the financial muscle behind the Tea Party's electoral triumph came from a pair of billionaires, the Koch brothers, and their super PAC Americans for Prosperity Action.

The Koch brothers unsurprisingly never signed the Giving Pledge. But they, like many of those who did sign, have given upward of $1 billion to various charities. They're most famous for their political activism, but it hardly ends there. MIT's cancer research institute is named after David Koch, and he also helped set up research and treatment centers from Mount Sinai to Johns Hopkins to Stanford. And that's not to mention their other interests, which range from addiction recovery to poverty reduction to culture. It's likely New York City wouldn't have remained the ballet destination it has without the largesse of David Koch. In 2014, five years before his death, Koch was asked what he wanted his epitaph to read. His response could have come from Warren or Bill. "I'd like it to say that David Koch did his best to make the world a better place," he said, "and that he hopes his wealth will help people long after he has passed away."

Laudable indeed. But how are we to measure the Koch brothers' commitment to curing cancer against their documented role in giving it to people? In the 1990s, OSHA-mandated tests started finding that workers at Koch Industries oil refineries had abnormal levels of benzene, a known carcinogen, in their blood. To make matters worse, the workers often weren't informed in time. Refineries were also emitting illegal quantities of benzene into the air, and Koch Industries was concealing it in its reports to the environmental authorities. Koch Industries ended up paying out tens of millions in fines and settlements. So, when the Kochs start funneling money into cancer treatment, is this making the world a better place—or damage control?

It's all very well asking billionaires to give away more of their money. But give it to whom? And see *what* done with it? Oh dear—we might cynically think—the slings and arrows of gifting an outrageous fortune . . . and yet, step into their shoes for a moment and realize that these deeds are not easily done.

12

BROTHERS AT WAR

For the son of a billionaire, Howie Buffett hasn't had an easy ride—but then, not every billionaire is like Warren. When Howie started working in the family firm, it wasn't with a seat on the Berkshire Hathaway board but with a mop and bucket, cleaning the floors at a See's Candies store in Los Angeles. When he got remarried, his dad bought the new family a farm out in Nebraska—only to charge them rent, fluctuating according to Howie's girth. If Howie weighed more than 182.5 pounds, he owed his father 26 percent of the farm's gross receipts; if less, it was 22 percent. "He's showing he's concerned about my health," said Howie. Warren's interest in the farm was purely financial: Howie loved plowing his rows of soybean and corn, and begged his father to visit and take the John Deere tractor for a spin. "I can't get him to come out and see how the crops are going," he was complaining around the time Warren met Bill, who must have seemed to Howie like the son his dad had always wanted.

It had to be a relief when, in late 2011, Warren announced that he would like Howie to succeed him as chairman of Berkshire Hathaway. A paternal decision, maybe, but also a pragmatic one: Howie, the Nebraska, and now Illinois, farmer with a lot of muck under his fingernails and no college degree, would be a guardian of the Buffett family values. Simplicity. Unfussiness. Thrift. That sort of thing. He accepted the role with a classic Buffettism. "As long as I can keep farming," he said, "I'm okay."

The announcement was publicized in an episode of CBS's *60 Minutes*. Here's Howie on his farm, looking delighted as he charges around in a big tractor. Here's Warren, full of praise for his son. Journalist Lesley Stahl prods Warren into admitting that his elder son isn't exactly a chip off the old block. "He likes doing big things," says Warren. "You know, moving dirt."

And then, Stahl goes for the jugular. And Howie does, too.

"Here's the irony," says Stahl. "Bill Gates is spending a huge chunk of Warren Buffett's money on poor farmers in Africa, giving them hybrid seeds and synthetic fertilizers. It's exactly the kind of high-tech approach Howard tried and now feels is doomed to fail with farmers who make barely a dollar a day."

> HOWIE BUFFETT: *They're pushing a system that really is similar to what we have outside this door.*
> LESLEY STAHL: *But doesn't—isn't that wonderful?*
> HB: *No. What I would argue is that at some point those guys are going to go home and the money's gonna not be there. It's exactly the same thing we did, and I don't feel it worked.*
> LS: *Well, you know Bill Gates. Have you said to him, "Eighty percent of what you're throwing down there in Africa is not going to work?"*
> HB: *Well, I've said it a little differently, I think. And that is that we need to quit thinking about tryin' to do it like we do it in America.*

At this point, the segment cuts to an interview with Bill. "Howie's the farmer here," he chimes in. "I'm the city boy on the panel."

> LS: *So, your father gives all this money to Gates. You come out and tell us what he's doing is all wrong.*

HB: *I'm not saying it's all wrong.*

LS: *Well, a lot of it's wrong. Little bit of sibling rivalry there?*

HB: *No.*

LS: *Maybe.*

HB: *No—you know, once in a while we call him Brother Bill. But—*
But—[chuckle] But—

LS: *Exactly.*

HB: *No, I—you know what? Bill Gates is the smartest guy in the*
world next to my dad maybe. I better say that if I'm on tape.

You can tell that Howie's choosing his words very carefully. Bill is
doing the same. But just like Howie, he knows that country boys and
city boys don't always get along.

AROUND THE SAME time that Warren's predictions about financial
derivatives were all coming horribly true, another financial crisis
was also engulfing the world. Between 2006 and 2008, the prices of
staple food commodities soared. The price of rice rose by 217 percent. Wheat went up 136 percent, corn 125 percent, soybeans 107
percent. Food riots broke out in dozens of countries: Bangladesh,
Burkina Faso, Egypt, Haiti, Indonesia, Mexico, Nepal, Peru, Uzbeki-
stan, Yemen—the list goes on. *The Economist* calculated that the "real
price" of food was higher than it had been at any point since 1845,
when it began measuring it. So, what happened? The Gates Foundation had thrown its efforts into improving yields, but the problem
wasn't that we were simply running out of food. Instead, it had all
the signs of a speculative bubble. According to a report from the
UN's Special Rapporteur on Food, Olivier De Schutter, the years
before the crisis saw a whole host of new investors, such as pension
funds, hedge funds, and banks, betting on food commodities. "This
was simply because other markets dried up one by one: The dotcoms
vanished at the end of 2001, the stock market soon after, and the
U.S. housing market in August 2007." It must have seemed like a safe

bet—people will always need wheat, right? But the more investors got involved, the higher the prices soared, in a sort of tulipomania that left millions around the world hungry, even while more and more food was being produced.

And what was the Gates Foundation doing in the middle of all this? Well, they were helping set up complex financial markets for African agricultural products, and creating a brand-new class of commodity traders. But here, Bill and Melinda were posting a success story about one of the programs they'd funded.

The program in question was called Purchase for Progress, or P4P. The idea is simple, at least on its face: The World Food Programme, a major buyer of food crops—$1.1 billion in seventy-three developing countries in 2008, when the five-year pilot program was launched—committed to procuring 10 percent of its supply from smallholder farmers. It'd buy these crops at a guaranteed price in advance of the harvest, helping to insulate farmers against market forces and providing security against which they could take out loans. One beneficiary of the program, singled out in Gates Foundation promotional materials released in 2012, is Odetta Mukanyiko, a smallholder in Rwanda who is part of a farmers' cooperative participating in P4P. "Thanks to WFP training, [members of the cooperative] were able to sell their surplus maize and beans to the WFP and other buyers. For the first time in anyone's memory, these farmers earned a handsome profit for their harvests. Odetta's income more than quadrupled, earning her enough money to replace her two-room thatch roof hut with a four-room, metal-roofed home."

The good news goes on. "With the help of a loan she was able to buy a larger piece of land allowing her to grow more maize and beans. She has adopted the two children of a desperately poor relative, so now she's supporting four children and paying for their school fees and medical insurance. What's more, she's provided part-time employment to eight of her neighbors who help with planting and harvesting."

"People here used to grow maize in despair," says Christent Bi-
ziyaremyi, president of Odetta's co-op. "Now we see the value in
what we're doing."

Even hardened Gates Foundation critic Linsey McGoey has written approvingly of P4P, which operated in Central America as well
as in Africa. The program "helps to foster sufficiency among local
smallholders," she notes, "ensuring a stable market regardless of
whether yields flounder or flourish in a given year." And though P4P
hasn't yet replaced imported food aid, McGoey points out that it is
helping "to dislodge large US and European multinationals from
their dominant position in global food chains."

Another Gates–Green Revolution skeptic who has spoken approvingly about the program? Howie Buffett. In fact, he's been part
of it from the very beginning in 2008: Howie's foundation sank
$13 million into the program, and doesn't seem to have any regrets.
"P4P is one of the most important projects we have ever invested in,"
he announced in 2011 as he handed over another $2.4 million. "It
truly has the potential to be a game changer."

But as the indefatigable Frederick Kaufman points out, writing
in *Harper's*, P4P's guaranteed price system looks quite a bit like the
practice of buying commodity futures. "P4P was designed to mimic
sophisticated global markets," Kaufman writes. "In some cases, P4P
would not purchase a farmer's grain immediately but would instead
encourage him to warehouse his product and receive a receipt. . . .
The receipt allowed the farmer to register with his countrywide exchange, a place in the capital city where all the grain from all the
country's farmers could be bought and sold. Henceforth," Kaufman
adds, "the rural farmer could follow fluctuating prices with the
technology of his mobile phone. The once indigent peasant could
become a commodity trader and peg his sale to any time of the year."

Kaufman doesn't waste any time wondering whether "once indigent peasants" might *want* to be commodity traders, if that earns
them better prices for their crops, but then, his concern is with food

security, and the probability that bets on staple commodities will lead to hoarding and price shocks. This is a valid concern. But, as yet, a speculative one.

But it's the Gates Foundation's ties to agribusiness giants such as Cargill and Monsanto (acquired by Bayer in 2018) that have raised the most alarm. It was revealed in 2010 that the Gates Foundation had purchased 500,000 Monsanto shares, worth around $23 million, and also that the foundation was teaming up with Cargill on a $10 million project to "develop the soya value chain" in Mozambique—news heralding "the big time introduction of GM soya in southern Africa," as the *Guardian* pointed out at the time. Opinions of genetically modified crops differ, but setting that debate aside, the Cargill deal and others like it indisputably serve as market-making for foreign corporations seeking a foothold in Africa. Bill and Melinda would no doubt insist that's a side effect of their belief in biotechnology, but looked at from another angle, market-making can seem the main point. To wit, not long after the Cargill deal and Monsanto investment came to light, the Gates Foundation was knee-deep in negotiations for the New Alliance for Food and Nutrition Security, a cooperation framework agreed to in 2012 by the G8 nations, African countries, donors, and private sector firms. Intended to "lift 50 million people out of poverty over the next ten years through inclusive and sustained agricultural growth," the framework was denounced by many as a corporate land grab, with USAID, the World Bank, and like-minded entities cornering African governments into setting aside huge parcels of land for foreign investment, reforming their laws to promote commodity exports, and carving out generous tax incentives for foreign corporations operating inside their borders.

Tanzanian MP Zitto Kabwe was one of several observers who decried the New Alliance's emphasis on industrial agriculture, noting that smallholders had not participated in an agreement that augured a wholesale shift in their social, economic, and political arrangements. "With large-scale farming, you are turning small farmers into mere labourers," he told the *Guardian*. "There may be improvements in rural infrastructure. But this will not liberate people from poverty." Kabwe also feared that small farmers would have no negotiating leverage against large corporations drawing them into their supply chain. "Who determines the contracts?" he asked. "The fear is that at the end of the day you have small-scale farmers being exploited."

Although improving nutrition and food security was a stated goal of the New Alliance framework, there were no targets set and no process put in place for gauging whether and how investment was translating into attainment of these goals—a sharp contrast to the Gates Foundation's emphasis on performance metrics. "Without a clear theory of change indicating how increased investment in large-scale agriculture will lead to poverty reduction [and] improved food security or nutrition," noted Colin Poulton, a research fellow at the School of Oriental and African Studies in London, "the New Alliance is so far primarily an initiative to commercialise agriculture in Africa."

A land grab, in other words. Olivier De Schutter summed up the situation thusly: "There's a struggle for land, for investment, for seed systems, and first and foremost there's a struggle for political influence."

Let's give Bill Gates the benefit of the doubt and assume that the part he played in New Alliance negotiations was to advocate for the primacy of poverty reduction and food security and nutrition in the framework's design. And that he got outvoted. Bill wasn't the only power player in the room, after all—and the G8 summit that gave rise to the New Alliance coincided with a State Department campaign to boost exports of GM crops and GM seed technology, two areas of global trade wherein the United States generated a trade surplus. And the said State Department campaign coincided with a contemporaneous report written by a Chicago-based think tank and funded by the Gates Foundation: Titled "Renewing American Leadership in the Fight Against Global Hunger and Poverty," it called for the United States to run point on "spreading new technologies"– not only because it would boost trade, but also because it would "strengthen American institutions."

You don't have to be a tinfoil-hat conspiracy theorist–or even a Marxist–to see something amiss in all this. Neither of those types tend to publish many op-eds in the *New York Times*, but eighteen months after Howie critiqued the Gates Foundation on CBS, the paper put out an impassioned screed against "philanthropic colonialism." Oh, and the author of this particular jeremiad? One Peter Buffett. Yep. *That* Peter Buffett.

Peter's work on the *Dances with Wolves* soundtrack had led to a long-standing engagement with Native American traditions and activism. More recently, he–like his brother–had started getting seriously into Africa. For instance, in 2009, he released the charity single "Blood into Gold" featuring the Senegalese-American R & B artist Akon. The song begins: "When I go to sleep at night / I wonder why I don't feel the pain / From where the sun is shining bright / But empty shells of lives remain."

Okay, Bob Dylan it ain't. But Peter was dedicated to his cause. The song's debut wasn't at a stadium, and it wasn't on radio or a streaming service; it was in a live performance at the UN General Assembly concert hall.

Peter doesn't name any names in his op-ed, but he does warn that he might "upset people who are wonderful folks and a few dear friends." He writes that much of the do-gooding he's observed does little more than reinforce an unjust status quo, and that philanthropists parachuting into far-flung countries touting blanket agrofixes, for instance, are engaged in a form of "conscience laundering." "But this just keeps the existing structure of inequality in place," he writes. "The rich sleep better at night, while others get just enough to keep the pot from boiling over,"

"It's time for a new operating system. Not a 2.0 or a 3.0, but something built from the ground up. New code," continues Peter. "Albert Einstein said that you cannot solve a problem with the same mindset that created it."

Make no mistake: It might have looked less like a brawl and more like a quiet game of bridge, but Bill and the Buffett sons appeared to no longer be playing on the same team.

MAYBE IT WAS in the hope of tamping down this little spat that Warren had decided to double his contribution to his children's foundations, sending his children a letter announcing the extra billions. "I knew you would apply your considerable brains and energies in order to make the most of the funds," he wrote. "However, you have exceeded my high expectations. Your mother would be as proud of you as I am. I see her influence in what you are accomplishing."

A clever play. But while his coffers were swelling, Howie was getting a taste for conflict.

In probably his most daring exploit, Howie flew into a war zone to aid one of his fellow philanthropists. In 2011, Shannon Sedgwick Davis of the Bridgeway Foundation was deeply involved in the hunt for the Ugandan warlord Joseph Kony, to the extent that she'd recruited Eeben Barlow—the go-to guy if you were in the market for a crack team of commandos—to train a squad of Ugandan soldiers to scour the jungle for Kony and his Lord's Resistance Army, which had spent a quarter century sowing death and despair in the Great Lakes region of Africa. "By December 2011, three hundred Ugandans had passed through Barlow's intensive three-month course at an Army base in Arua, near the border with Congo," as Elizabeth Rubin later reported on newyorker.com. The newly minted special-op guys once got tantalizingly close to Kony, but he remained on the loose, and money was drying up fast.

Enter Howie. "It was May 2012, and the temperature was over one hundred degrees. I had flown into this remote camp in a Cessna Caravan turboprop just minutes before, and the sweat was pouring out of me," he writes of his visit to a forward operating base. "There were tents and Mi-8 transport helicopters and Mi-24 attack helicopters parked under camouflage tarps." The Bridgeway Foundation couldn't cover all the expenses on its own, so Howie—whom Warren nicknamed "the Indiana Jones of philanthropy"—stepped in to help foot the operating bills for a helicopter and a Cessna, and a canine unit to sniff out some of the thousands of children Kony had brainwashed into serving as soldiers and/or turned into sex slaves. As of this writing, Kony remains on the run, his army, forced into hiding, is said to number no more than a hundred men and to no longer pose a serious threat to the region.

This wasn't Howie's only trip to a combat zone: He and his son, Howard Jr., had also visited Afghanistan; he returned with his father, taking a Black Hawk helicopter to meet with farmers in Jalalabad. His foundation ended up funding an agricultural institute at the local university. The following year, he spearheaded a program to jump-start farming in the newly created country of South Sudan, staying the course as fighting broke out again in the region. "You can't start a $10 million program in South Sudan and then pull out when the bullets start flying," he would explain.

And if real tensions had lingered between Howie and Bill, it appears these had dissipated, at least by October 2011, when the World Food Program USA, a nonprofit that supports the UN's WFP, chose to give out its McGovern Leadership Award in honor of the Purchase for Progress program. This meant that then-Secretary of State Hillary Clinton—who was presenting the award—gave out two identical trophies to the two men who'd done the most to spearhead the initiative: Bill Gates and . . . Howie Buffett. Howie was his usual gregarious self at the ceremony, while Bill, receiving the award, looked more than a little sheepish, but since then the two foundations have continued collaborating on multiple projects, including something close to Howie's heart: soil quality. To date, Bill has poured millions into Howie's project to improve African soils with crop rotation and nonchemical fertilizers. Howie has a name for this. He calls it the "Brown Revolution."

Of course, there are *three* Buffett children (not counting Brother Bill). What's Little Sooz been up to, while the menfolk were rattling their sabers?

Well, quite a lot, it turns out. But you won't find Little Sooz choppering into war zones. She's very much her mother's daughter: She works as quietly as possible, and tries to do the most good she can. After all, Susie is the one running her mother's own foundation, along with the Buffett Early Childhood Fund and the Sherwood Foundation, which mainly focuses on issues local to Omaha and Nebraska. One beneficiary of Sherwood largesse, for instance, was Project Everlast, a grassroots group helping current and former Omaha-area foster kids transition out of state supervision, assisting them with housing, transportation, health care, education, and employment. Sherwood has also long funded a range of organizations advocating—*ahem*—against charter schools, and its education-related donations have more recently extended into projects such as Seventy Five North Revitalization Corp., a nonprofit working to revitalize an abandoned Omaha neighborhood by building affordable housing, and partnering with a local school, transforming its campus into one that also houses job training and a medical center. Big Susie, champion of desegregation, is no doubt smiling down from heaven on that initiative. The Buffett Early Childhood Fund also emphasizes education for at-risk children: Its most prominent effort is Educare, a national network of twenty-five pre-schools that offer low-cost enrollment. Susie Jr.'s foundation first invested in Educare in 2003, and it was something of an accident—initially, with her dad's money burning a hole in her pocket, Susie Jr., proud graduate of Omaha Public Schools, had wanted to give back to the system she'd come out of. "I went to see our school superintendent," she recalls. "He basically said to me, 'Don't give me the money. See who's doing the best work in early-childhood education and spend it there.'"

A 2014 study by the University of Pennsylvania's Center for High Impact Philanthropy found that, in Omaha, children in grades three through seven who had attended Educare for at least two years performed 29 percent better on standardized reading tests than a control group of low-income students in the same district.

The Susan Thompson Buffett Foundation is where things get hairy, at least given the current political climate in America. Under Little Sooz's leadership—indeed, at her discretion, as the organization is lightly staffed, and she calls all the shots—the foundation has upped its giving to Big Susie's pet cause of reproductive rights. It is a top supporter of Planned Parenthood; the largest donor, by far, to the National Abortion Federation (NAF), the professional association of abortion providers; and one of the most generous private funders of international family planning services. For example, Ipas, which trains abortion providers around the globe, received nearly $150 million in grants from the Buffett Foundation between 2006 and 2016. Buffett has also provided grants to make IUDs more commonplace, with investments in both research toward better versions of the long-acting contraceptive, and programs to promote its use. "One foundation-backed effort to provide long-acting birth control to teenagers in Colorado helped lower the birthrate among teenagers across the state by a stunning forty percent from 2009 to 2013, and sharply cut the number of abortions, too," notes *The Givers* author David Callahan approvingly. What Callahan points out, though, is the Susan Thompson Buffett Foundation's utter opacity even as it cut bigger and bigger checks. As *Bloomberg Businessweek* put it, the foundation, which gave away almost half a billion dollars in 2013, most of it to organizations dedicated to reproductive health, "barely maintains a website [and] studiously avoids press," and almost all of its grants are credited to "an anonymous donor."

"The place is a case study in non-transparency," Callahan complained on Inside Philanthropy, the news site he founded to track foundations and wealthy donors. "While you can understand why a foundation that is deeply enmeshed in protecting abortion rights might want to keep a low profile, this seems excessive."

Is it? Abortion and birth control foes seem to have had little trouble ferreting out who's bankrolling groups such as the NAF: Susie and Warren have been named and shamed on innumerable right-to-life blogs (not to mention Fox News), and for anti-choice partisans, it no doubt causes no end of chagrin to discover what the profits from their GEICO premiums and Dairy Queen sundaes are going to. (Just as, for liberals, it's infuriating to think that their purchase of Brawny paper towels benefits the Koch brothers, and advocates of agriculture reform in Africa gnash their teeth as they type out policy papers in Microsoft Word.) Warren, for his part, may not be stepping forward to defend the Buffett Foundation's work, but he's not backing down either: Of all the charitable causes his Berkshire stock funds, reproductive rights seem the one most directly linked to his own strong convictions.

"For Warren, it's economic," explained Judith DeSarno, the Susan Thompson Buffett Foundation's former director for domestic programs, in a 2008 interview. "He thinks that unless women can control their fertility . . . you are sort of wasting more than half of the brainpower in the United States."

"Well, not just the United States," DeSarno added. "Worldwide."

THE BUFFETT BOYS might have been at loggerheads with their adoptive brother, Bill, but on this issue of reproductive rights, at least, the Buffett Foundation and the Gates Foundation were on the same page. Or, to put it more accurately, Sooz had a key ally in Melinda.

There's an anecdote Melinda's friend Charlotte Guyman shares in her 2008 *Fortune* profile—the first solo profile of Melinda, part of a PR push as she emerged from Bill's shadow, that she'd agreed to do—about a trip she and Melinda took to Calcutta in 2004, where they visited Mother Teresa's Home for the Dying. One woman at the home was suffering from AIDS and tuberculosis, and she'd been reduced to bones and an impenetrable zombie-like stare. "Melinda walks in, pauses, and goes right over to this young woman," Guyman recalled. "She pulls up a chair, puts the woman's hand in her hands. The woman won't look at her. Then Melinda says, 'You have AIDS. It's not your fault.' She says it again. 'It's not your fault.'" As Guyman remembers it, the woman turned her face to look directly at Melinda, and tears began rolling down her gaunt cheeks. Melinda continued sitting with the dying woman, hand in hand. "It seemed like forever," Guyman said.

The Moment of Lift is a collection of stories like this: stories about Melinda turning a soft gaze onto victims of disease and injustice, taking them in, and marching away from the encounter in equal parts unsettled by the tenuousness of her grasp on the harsh realities of the world and determined to help people, and help them *right now*. With Bill it's all charts and graphs and homilies, like how it ought to cost well under $100 to save "a year of a person's life," and if the foundation wastes $500,000, they are "wasting 5,000 years of life." From Melinda, you get the story in full about visiting Malawi and being moved to see mothers, who had walked great distances, queued up with their children, waiting for shots, and then she's brought up short by a question posed to her in retort, one mother asking her, *Where's my shot?* "She was talking about Depo-Provera, a long-acting birth control injection," Melinda explains. "She already had more children than she could feed. She was afraid of having even more. . . . [And] she was just one of the many mothers I met during my early trips who switched the topic of our conversation from children's vaccines to family planning."

"Increasingly on my trips, no matter what their purpose, I began to see and hear the need for contraceptives," Melinda goes on. "I visited communities where every mother had lost a child and everyone knew a mother who had died in childbirth. I met more mothers who were desperate not to get pregnant because they couldn't take care of the kids they already had. I began to understand why, even though I wasn't there to talk about contraceptives, women kept bringing them up anyway."

Contraception was, at the time, a tricky question for Melinda. She was, after all, raised in a staunchly Catholic family, and she's still steadfast in her Catholic identity. The position of the Vatican on this stuff is . . . let's just say it's well known, and leave it at that. On the other hand, Melinda had used contraceptives herself to make the best of her own life. And by *not* talking about contraceptives when she went to Africa or India, she was denying, by inaction, millions of women the chance to do the same thing.

Was it Little Sooz's influence that finally encouraged her to take a stand? Was it Warren? Or did Melinda balance one principle against another, long into the night, night after night, until she decided what was right?

In July 2012, Melinda spoke out on reproductive rights for the first time at a major public forum, appearing at the London Summit on Family Planning. Her speech was brave. Susie Buffett lets her money do the talking, but Melinda Gates, practicing Catholic, stood at a podium and asked the world to see birth control through the eyes of marginalized women who desperately wanted to take control of their reproductive destiny. "When you think about family planning from the perspective of the women who want to use it," she said, "everything changes. Your basic assumptions and long-standing policies begin to shift."

> *For example, many family planning programs consider a health clinic that has any form of contraceptive "stocked." They may only have condoms available and consider that success. That may make sense if you're thinking only about the supply side. But many women I talk to tell me they simply can't negotiate condom use with their partners.*
>
> *One woman said she couldn't ask her husband to use a condom. I asked why, and she said that asking would make him*

think she had HIV, or was worried he did. Now countries are changing their policies so that clinics offer women many options—including injectables and implants and IUDs—so they can use contraceptives the way they want, when they want.

Melinda's fight on behalf of family planning is a sterling example of Gates Foundation beliefs and methodologies translating on the ground. In her London speech, Melinda showed the crowd a photo of a piece of new technology—a Uniject device that Pfizer was testing for at-home administration of a new version of Depo-Provera, an injectable birth control popular in Africa. Given that women in rural sub-Saharan Africa may need to travel many miles to a clinic for their quarterly Depo injections, and that not all of them can make the trip consistently, at-home administration would be a game-changer. Private sector innovation, spurred by the foundation, could help, as Melinda put it, "clear away the obstacles that prevent women from having access to contraceptives."

Would the Gates Foundation be market-making for Pfizer? Yes. Would it be filling an urgent need? Also yes.

Melinda didn't just speak at the London summit; she also helped organize it. By the end of the conference, she'd gotten commitments from the United Kingdom to double its international family planning budget, just as the Gates Foundation was doing, and developing countries had pledged an additional $2 billion to the cause of making contraceptives available to 120 million additional women by 2020, the benchmark set at the summit's end.

The response was swift. Usually, when a devout Catholic decides they have to part ways with the Church on a matter of conscience, the turmoil is private. Not so with Melinda. The front page of *L'Osservatore Romano*, the Vatican's newspaper, blared forth disapproval, the columnist lamenting that Melinda had "gone astray." But Melinda held firm. "As a Catholic," she had told the *Guardian*, "I believe in this religion, there are amazing things about this religion, amazing

moral teachings that I do believe in, but I also have to think about
how we keep women alive." After all, as she pointed out, "a church is
made up of its members."

Melinda's newfound role as a feminist warrior queen didn't stop
there. And in this fight, she couldn't always count on her old allies.
As she confessed to the *Chronicle of Philanthropy*, circa the release
of her book, Bill fiercely resisted Melinda's request that she co-write
the foundation's 2013 letter. "I felt a keen sense of ownership over
our family planning work, and I wanted to write about it," she told
Chronicle editor Stacy Palmer. "He said he didn't see why things
should change."

"It got hot," she admitted. "We both got angry. It was a big test for
us. In the end, we survived, and though the letter went out under his
name, it included a family planning essay under mine."

By 2015, Melinda was co-writing the letter with Bill. Behind the
scenes, however, she might have continued to feel less-than-equal—
and to suspect that her strong convictions regarding female empowerment weren't *entirely* shared by her husband.

I am afraid we must pause our story once again, this time to discuss Jeffrey Epstein. It's a dismal task. For those who wish to look
further into the man himself—his mysterious rise to the upper rungs
of American finance; his spiderweb of shady connections; the well-
documented charges of abuse and exploitation of young women—
there's plenty of content out there; the book *Perversions of Justice*, by
Julie K. Brown, the *Miami Herald* reporter who originally unearthed
much of this sordid tale, is a good place to start. But for our purposes,
let's just say that by January 2011, when Bill first made Epstein's acquaintance, the financier had already been convicted in Florida for
solicitation of prostitution involving a minor, and he trailed various ugly rumors in his wake. But that didn't keep Bill from joining
grandees such as Prince Andrew, Harvard professor Steven Pinker,
famed attorney Alan Dershowitz, and—perhaps most famously—Bill
Clinton from enjoying Epstein's hospitality. Naturally, Bill's inter-

est in Epstein was philanthropical; I think we can take his word on this, that the initial handshake was made on the basis that Epstein was known to have a Rolodex stuffed with the names of rich men he cajoled into donating to causes dear to Bill's heart. Maybe that's all there was to it, a few face-to-face meetings, plus an abortive effort on Epstein's part to get a cut of Gates Foundation action by inserting himself into its for-profit investments in businesses related to global health. Nothing to see here. Or, a little something to see here, as Bill himself admitted after visiting Epstein's now-notorious Upper East Side townhouse for the first time, writing in an email that "his life-style is very different and kind of intriguing although it would not work for me," an aw-shucks disclaimer that has a whiff of Bill's "I'm just here for the pizza and people-watching" assertions regarding his visits to Boston's Combat Zone while he was in college.

But then again . . .

Maybe Bill *did* meet up with Epstein "dozens of times," as reported by the Daily Beast—and irately denied by Bill—and maybe he *did* use "the gatherings at Epstein's $77 million New York townhouse as an escape from what he told Epstein was a 'toxic' marriage, a topic both men found humorous," according to a person who attended the meetings. This too Bill has classified as "false," as he has denied ever receiving or soliciting personal advice of any kind from Epstein. So who can say what Bill really thought of Epstein and his entourage? Bill's not talking beyond expressing regret, and Epstein, as pretty much anyone with an internet hookup knows, died in jail in 2019 while awaiting trial on sex trafficking charges (under circumstances hard-nosed reporter Brown deems suspicious). What we can say with 100 percent certainty is that Melinda found Epstein noxious—and demanded Bill cut off the relationship. "I did not like that he'd had meetings with Jeffrey Epstein, no," Melinda told CBS's Gayle King in a March 2022 interview, and yes, she'd made that clear to him, in terms no less plain than she used to describe her instant aversion to Epstein after meeting him about a decade prior.

I also met Jeffrey Epstein, exactly one time. I wanted to see who this man was. And I regretted it from the second I stepped in the door. He was abhorrent. He was evil personified. I had nightmares about it afterwards. My heart breaks for these young women, because that's how I felt, and here I'm an older woman—my God, I feel terrible for those young women. It was awful.

In October 2014, Bill donated $2 million to the MIT Media Lab at Epstein's behest—a personal gift from Bill to one of Epstein's pet projects, not a grant dispersed by the foundation. After that, he cut off contact, either at Melinda's insistence or for reasons of his own. But Bill's willingness to hang chez Epstein—and his initial blithe take on Epstein's "lifestyle"—seems to have stuck in Melinda's craw. Nestled there beside, perhaps, rumors of Bill's predilection for hitting on underlings, one instance of which had by 2008 come to the attention of top Microsoft executives, and earned Bill a dressing down; separately, a prior sexual relationship with a Microsoft engineer was revealed to the board shortly before his (previously announced) departure from the company in 2020.

Anyway, it's safe to assume that Melinda had reasons to feel that her then-husband wasn't as wholeheartedly on board with the goal of women's empowerment as she had become, both in the lead-up to her 2012 speech in London, and then, ever more so, in its aftermath. Melinda's convictions on this point had been sharpened by one conversation in particular, over dinner with several high-powered women who had attended the London summit. The event had just wrapped, and Melinda was basking in the glow of a job well done; she was also totally exhausted, and unprepared for the coming reckoning. "That's when these women all said to me, 'Melinda, don't you see? Family planning is *just the first step* for women! We have to move on to a much bigger agenda!'"

According to Melinda, this exchange opened her mind to the idea that family planning was merely a weapon in a larger battle: The battle for gender equity. It was a fight that had to be waged on many fronts at once, and for it to be won, you couldn't work inside the structures that had produced the inequality. You had to dismantle the scaffolding of patriarchy and erect something else, something better in its place. A new operating system. Not 2.0 or 3.0. New code entirely.

Melinda decided she was done taking a back seat to Bill, and done with women taking a back seat to men in general. Her own moment of level-setting regarding the global female condition came in a chat with a group of women in Senegal raised in communities where female genital cutting was the norm; all of them had been cut, and some had held their daughters down to be cut, as well. But they'd turned against the practice. The translator refused to translate the most gruesome parts of their stories, for fear Melinda couldn't handle it. "[The women] believed they were telling me a story of progress, and they were," Melinda writes in *The Moment of Lift*. "But to understand in what sense it was progress required an understanding of how cruel and widespread this practice still was. They were telling me how far they had come, and were also revealing to me how awful things still were for girls in their country. The story was horrifying to me," she continues. "I just shut down. I saw the effort as hopeless and endless, beyond my stamina and my resources, and I said to myself, 'I *quit*.'"

Then she un-quit. "I had to accept that my job is to do my part, let my heart break for all the women we can't help, and stay optimistic."

The battle was joined.

13

ZERO

In 2015, Warren Buffett celebrated fifty years of owning Berkshire. In 2016, ten years after having made his pledge to the Gates Foundation, Warren turned eighty-six. And he bought himself an extravagant present: Precision Castparts, an Oregon-based aerospace parts manufacturer. At $32.3 billion, it was the largest single purchase he'd ever made. Warren might have been getting older, but he wasn't slowing down.

To mark all these propitious alignments, he also wrote two letters. In 2015, he wrote one to his Berkshire Hathaway shareholders. The other, the following year, was to Bill and Melinda.

Warren's first letter is classically sunny and frank, published under the unassuming headline "Berkshire—Past, Present and Future." Looking back on his history with the company that made him famous, he charts its evolution from a New England textile manufacturer whose industry was "heading south, both metaphorically and figuratively" to its present state, "a sprawling conglomerate, constantly trying to sprawl further." Whatever nightmares this image might conjure for a generation raised on *RoboCop*, Warren sees it as an unmitigated good. Because Berkshire does a bit of *everything*—when he was writing, it owned consumer brands like See's Candies and Coca-Cola, insurance firms, industrial manufacturers, a car dealership, and a railroad; it was the entire U.S. economy in microcosm—he is "perfectly positioned to allocate capital rationally and at minimal cost." If life insurance is making a steady return but more investment is needed in machine parts, he needs only to snap his fingers, and it's done.

Warren writes frankly about his mistakes, and the people (most of all, Charlie Munger) who helped him change his investment approach for the better. Ever the delegator, he's happy to admit that the process is still ongoing. The picture he paints of Berkshire is of a big joint adventure, a partnership, in which Warren makes some of the decisions (for good or ill) but is never too proud to listen to good advice. He concludes the letter by talking about a recent shareholder vote on a resolution, the text of which read:

> RESOLVED: *Whereas the corporation has more money than it needs and since the owners unlike Warren are not multi billionaires, the board shall consider paying a meaningful annual dividend on the shares.*

By an overwhelming margin, the Berkshire shareholders—maybe up to a million people, when they're all totted up—rejected the motion. They didn't want a payday; they wanted Berkshire to keep doing what it was doing: letting their money compound.

"I am a lucky fellow," Warren concludes, addressing all one million of them, "to have you as partners."

The letter was warmly received—not least by Bill Gates, who called it "the most important one [Warren] has ever written." So, in his second letter to Bill and Melinda, Warren suggested that they might like to do the same thing. Of hitting fifty years at the helm of Berkshire, he wrote, in part:

> *[I] used the occasion to write a special report to the company's owners. I reflected on what had gone particularly well or*

poorly, what I'd learned, and what I hoped would get done in the future.

As you might guess, I ended up being the prime beneficiary of this effort. There's nothing like actually writing something out to clarify thinking....

I thought you might enjoy writing a look backward and forward similar to what I did.

I'm not the only one who'd like to read it. There are many who want to know where you've come from, where you're heading and why. I also believe it's important that people better understand why success in philanthropy is measured differently from success in business or government. Your letter might explain how the two of you measure yourselves and how you would like the final scorecard to read.

Bill and Melinda did exactly that. Their letter is a bit slicker than Warren's, full of flashy infographics. The tragic subjects they address do not allow them Warren's folksy tone, but they do share plenty of his optimism. They point out that in the previous year, 1 million infants died on the day they were born. They note that 45 percent of childhood deaths are linked in part to the thorny problem of malnutrition—of children who aren't starving but aren't getting the right balance of nutrients they need to fend off diseases. They cite the 225 million women in the developing world who want to avoid pregnancy but don't have access to contraceptives. But in every case they argue that all these things are getting *better.*

This being a Gates presentation, they have the numbers to back it up: 122 million children's lives saved since 1990, in part because, as they write, "coverage for the basic package of childhood vaccines is now the highest it's ever been, at 86 percent. And the gap between the richest and the poorest countries is the *lowest* it's ever been." But some of the solutions they tout are astoundingly low-tech: Rwanda, for instance, managed to cut newborn mortality by 30 percent just by encouraging breastfeeding and skin-to-skin contact between mothers and their newborns.

For Bill and Melinda, one of the biggest problems doesn't even seem to be the actual heath issues themselves—it's the atmosphere of pessimism; the idea that things simply can't be improved:

> *Bill: Extreme poverty has been cut in half over the last 25 years. That's a big accomplishment that ought to make everyone more optimistic. But almost no one knows about it. In a recent survey, just 1 percent knew we had cut extreme poverty in half, and 99 percent underestimated the progress. That survey wasn't just testing knowledge; it was testing optimism—and the world didn't score so well.*
>
> *Melinda: Optimism is a huge asset. We can always use more of it. But optimism isn't a belief that things will automatically get better; it's a conviction that we can* make *things better. We see this in you, Warren. Your success didn't create your optimism; your optimism led to your success.*

What Bill and Melinda *don't* do in their letter, strangely enough, is take direct credit for the progress that's been made. They might have a quantitative approach to philanthropy, but the direct impact of these interventions is notoriously hard to quantify. If extreme poverty is falling, can Bill and Melinda look out into an improving world and see their accomplishments reflected in it? Or might they be greeted by the stern face of the Chinese Communist Party? (According to the World Bank, three-quarters of people who have escaped poverty since 1980 have been in China.) Which is not to say that these difficulties have stopped the Gateses' claiming any credit at all. For instance, Melinda took a bow when she appeared on an episode of David Letterman's Netflix series in 2019. Early in the chat, Letterman asked her, "The absence of polio from the planet, that's you, right?"

"That's Bill and me," she replied, with a satisfied nod, clarifying that they're "on the verge" of getting there. The audience erupted into applause.

The fight to eradicate polio began in 1988, but victory came into view only in 2000, when the Gates Foundation got on board. What the foundation did was tackle the hard cases—the countries where medical services were spotty at best, the regions that were racked by poverty and strife, the villages that were nearly impossible to reach. The Gates Foundation didn't do all of that on its own, but its money and its muscle had a galvanizing effect on governments, donors, volunteers, and NGOs. Despite poliovirus being detected in recent years in wastewater in London, New York City, and elsewhere, and its stubborn persistence in some parts of Pakistan and Afghanistan, it's quite likely that, in the next few years, polio will become the first disease since smallpox to be wiped off the face of the earth.

If—fingers crossed—polio disappears in the near future, it will have taken twenty years of Gates involvement to show an incontrovertible *result*. Who knows what future decades will bring?

Bill and Melinda save their most important number for the end of their letter: zero. "This," Bill writes, "is the number we're striving toward every day at the foundation. Zero malaria. Zero TB. Zero HIV. Zero malnutrition. Zero preventable deaths. Zero difference between the health of a poor kid and every other kid." It's an admirable goal, but one thing is certain: Getting there will involve more failure than triumph. There's no way around that. As charity evaluator GiveWell notes, many of the problems that philanthropy aims to address "are extremely difficult problems that foundations, governments and experts have struggled with for decades," and in consequence, "many well-funded, well-executed, logical programs haven't had the desired results." And so, as Bill and Melinda continue to spend their money, and Warren's, they'll be parrying shots from critics—who are just doing their jobs—with data points illustrating that they're on the road to progress, but it's a long road.

But there's one big difference between Warren's letter and Bill and Melinda's. Warren's letter was directed to the Berkshire Hathaway shareholders: hundreds of thousands of people who'd given him their money to invest, who were active stakeholders in everything he did. *This*, Warren could say, *is what we're doing.* Inclusive "we." Everyone's invited on this ride. Everyone who invests gets a vote. But Bill and Melinda's letter was directed *to Warren*. Whom else could they write to? The Bill and Melinda Gates Foundation doesn't have hundreds of thousands of shareholders. It's not accountable to anyone except the people it's named for. When Bill and Melinda say *This is what we're doing*, "we" means Melinda and Bill with Warren's money.

There's a danger here. Another piece of billionaire-related news you might remember from 2016 was the election of Donald Trump as the forty-fifth president of the United States. It would take a whole book to explain exactly how that happened, and plenty of people have taken a stab at writing precisely that book. But *one* of the reasons was that millions of ordinary Americans felt like they weren't being invited on the ride: Powerful people were changing the world without their consent, and nobody seemed to be listening to their story.

Warren had spent a long time teaching Bill how to communicate better. It was his idea for Bill to start writing annual letters explaining the foundation's work; he helped turn the Microsoft tech tyrant into one of the most admired philanthropists in the world. But now he might have to help teach Bill how to *listen*.

WHEN THE WRITER of Melinda's 2008 *Fortune* profile asked Warren if he'd have given his billions to the foundation if Melinda weren't involved, he admitted he was "not sure." Bill is "smart as hell, obviously" Warren said, "but in terms of seeing the whole picture, she's smarter." He likens Melinda's effect on Bill to Susie's on him. "Bill is an awkward guy," Warren pointed out. "He's lopsided, but less lopsided since he's with Melinda. Susie made me less lopsided, too."

It's tempting to see Bill and Melinda's partnership as a yin-yang split: He's the ledger thinker, running the numbers, and she's the person worried about the human beings the numbers on the ledger represent.

"You can't save kids just with vaccines," Melinda told *Fortune*. "I'd go into rural villages in India and think, 'Okay, we saved this child. But the cows are defecating in the stream coming into the village. There are other things we need to be doing."

If Bill is Warren's third son, Melinda might be his second daughter. She's certainly much more in line with the philanthropic traditions established by Howie, Peter, and Little Susie. Whether spreading the gospel of traditional farming practices or filling the coffers of grassroots groups in Omaha, the Buffett children tend to adhere to the approach Peter describes in his book *Life Is What You Make It*, which is "to provide support for people who identified *their own* needs and evolved *their own* solutions."

Listening is Melinda's preferred method of unpacking the problems-inside-problems matryoshka doll, and if she weren't engaged in constant listening, the Gates Foundation would be deprived a key agent of self-correction. In its direction of some of its health money to low-tech interventions such as insecticides-sprayed bed nets and condoms rather than staying laser-focused on the hunt for vaccines; and in the climb-down on small schools, one can infer Melinda's influence—recall how long and how doggedly Bill fought the government's monopoly case, because the only way he could interpret the data before him was to read it as affirming his view that he was *right*.

And remember, it was by *listening* to all those women she met in her travels abroad that Melinda finally ended up emerging as one of the planet's most forceful advocates for reproductive rights and gender equity.

After all, what improved access to contraception means is that millions more people suddenly have a *choice* over what goes on in their own lives, especially in Africa, where—due to the threats posed there by huge population growth estimates—her work may wind up doing more to ameliorate their troubles than all the GM seeds Monsanto can provide.

It's a rerigging of the rules that govern the ovarian lottery, and so it's unsurprising that this is the part of the foundation's work that's dearest to Warren's heart. "This is the No. 1 thing that Warren and I talk about," Melinda told the *New York Times* in 2016. "I can't come off of an event with him, whether it's the foundation's annual meeting, whether it's an event he and I go to with the other billionaires who are part of our Giving Pledge, that Warren doesn't catch me backstage and say, 'Melinda, I think this is the most important thing you are doing at the foundation, the most.'"

Melinda is at her detailed best in the section of *The Moment of Lift* where she discusses the relationship between gender and agricultural development. She provides a revealing blow-by-blow of debates inside the foundation about whether and how to add gender equity for women and girls to its mix of activist concerns—one "highly placed person" fought back by saying, "We don't do 'gender'" and another said, "We are *not* becoming a social justice organization."

So, the Gates Foundation is *not* a social justice organization? Really? Are we *sure*?

IN MAY 2021, news broke that Bill and Melinda Gates were getting a divorce. The statement they supplied to the public was opaque and to-the-point: "After a great deal of thought and a lot of work on our relationship, we have made the decision to end our marriage," they tweeted, separately, from their individual accounts. "We no longer believe we can grow together as a couple." For most observers, the fracture came out of nowhere; Bill and Melinda had always presented a united front. Naturally, there was a great deal of speculation about the cause of the rift, some of it salacious. Much was read into the revelation of Bill's affair in 2000 with a Microsoft employee and his habit of making "clumsy approaches to women in and out of the office," as the *New York Times* put it in one article after the news of the split. And there was chewier grist for the mill—namely, Bill's ill-considered entanglement with Jeffrey Epstein. According to several reports, Melinda was so incensed by revelations in a 2019 *Times* investigation into Bill's ties to Epstein, she was moved to engage a team of divorce lawyers. Later reporting by the *Wall Street Journal*, in 2023, revealed that Bill may have had an affair circa 2010 with much-younger professional bridge player Mila Antonova; Epstein learned about the relationship, and seems to have been trying to blackmail Bill over it. A tangled web, indeed.

Following the announcement of Bill and Melinda's separation, more details emerged, including gossip among Gates Foundation staffers that Melinda saw *l'affaire Epstein* as yet another instance of Bill revealing a lack of regard for her crusade for female empowerment. She might have had similar frustrations with Bill's handling of workplace misconduct complaints against Michael Larson, the man who managed most of the couple's money, as well as the Gates Foundation Trust. Further reporting, by *Vanity Fair*, furnished additional rumors of marital discord—such as that "someone in Melinda's circle" had hired a private investigator in the time leading up to the divorce filing, a claim Melinda's spokespeople *have* emphatically denied. It's not clear if the PI was tasked with finding out if and when Bill was cheating on her, the underlying implication being that she suspected him of having had affairs.

Given all this, it's worth revisiting that argument recounted in *The Moment of Lift*, about whether the Gates Foundation was or should be "a social justice organization." Squinting between the lines, it seems apparent that this was a Bill and Melinda fault line—he framed the foundation's mission in strictly technocratic, problem-solving terms, while she had come to see it as a vehicle for advancing larger aims, particularly with respect to women's equality. In that light, you can see why the Epstein thing may have been Melinda's line in the sand: "Problem-solving" often entails doing business with shady characters; "crusading" allows less quarter.

We'll likely never know the whole story. But the news of marital strife did manage to crack open the black box of the Gates Foundation as reporters began examining its internal operations and atmospherics, its global influence, and, perhaps most intriguingly, its finances; one report from March 2020, in *The Nation*, uncovered more than $2 billion in tax-deductible donations from the Gates Foundation to for-profit businesses, including $250 million in grants to companies such as Merck and Unilever in which it is simultaneously invested. Grants to companies *it holds a stake in*? Is that kosher? When, then, is a grant not a grant? In some cases the overlap was accidental—a matter of the foundation's grant-makers not knowing what its investment managers were up to, and vice versa—and in other cases it was strategic, as with its $7 million equity stake in the start-up AgBiome, which received a $20 million donation to develop pesticides for African farmers. (What does Howie Buffett make of *that*?) The scrutiny extended to Bill and Melinda's financial interests outside the foundation, exposing the holdings of a fortune that exceeds Morocco's annual GDP, as the *Times* estimated, and charting the sharply different courses they each took in investing some of that money: Melinda, via her female-empowerment-focused vehicle Pivotal Ventures, and Bill with his stakes in various businesses focused on ameliorating climate change. Following the money revealed Bill and Melinda's individual priorities—not chalk and cheese, exactly, but distinct enough to raise questions about how the divorcés could possibly continue sharing the reins of the Gates Foundation, as they assured the public they would.

Divorce is a private matter. But the future of the Gates Foundation is of public concern—as Bill and Melinda obliquely acknowledged in issuing a statement designed to allay worries that the foundation might splinter or be recast in a new form. Or completely implode. *Steady on*, was the message—a bit like Susie Buffett telling Warren,

We already lead separate lives, so nothing of consequence would change if she moved to San Francisco. One wonders if Warren took the Gateses' split especially hard—if it opened old fears of his, that Bill was too "lopsided" to be trusted with Warren's money alone, and that having Melinda on team Gates was a condition of Warren's beneficence. Presumably, the Gateses duly reported their plans to divorce to Warren well before the public found out about the split, and one can only wonder about the private conversations and ruminations about the future of the foundation that the dissolution of the Gates marriage galvanized—but one shock was soon followed by another, as, in June 2021, Warren announced that he was resigning as a Gates Foundation trustee. "For years, I have been a trustee—an inactive trustee at that—of only one recipient of my funds, the Bill and Melinda Gates Foundation," Warren said in a statement. "I am now resigning from that post, just as I have done at all corporate boards other than Berkshire's." Later that summer, Warren would turn ninety-one, and it's not unreasonable to assume that the desire to reduce his workload played some part in this decision.

Warren's departure raised concerns inside and outside the foundation. Mark Suzman, the foundation's CEO since 2020, assured staff, in an email, that he had been "actively discussing with [Warren], Bill, and Melinda approaches to strengthen our governance to provide long-term stability and sustainability . . . in light of the recent announcement of Bill and Melinda's divorce." But on July 7, 2021, just two weeks later, Suzman, announced that actually, Bill and Melinda were embarking on a kind of trial, during which they'd see if they were able to co-run the foundation as exes. "They have agreed that if after two years either one of them decides that they cannot continue to work together, Melinda will resign as co-chair and trustee," Suzman informed foundation staff. And if Melinda were to resign, she "would receive personal resources from Bill for her philanthropic work." Later in the year, Melinda published a Giving Pledge letter under her own name that also mentioned her investment vehicle, Pivotal Ventures—which is *not* a charity, it must be noted, but through which Gates is supporting gender-parity related causes in America and that, at time of writing, has a staff of 90 and has made more than 150 philanthropic investments. By February 2022, by which time the *Wall Street Journal* was reporting that Melinda did not plan to give the majority of her post-divorce wealth to the Gates Foundation, it seemed clear which way the wind was blowing. Two years post-divorce, however, Melinda French Gates remains on the foundation board—alongside six recently appointed additional trustees, Suzman among them.

As for Warren, he hasn't given up on the foundation either. One might have assumed the $3.2 billion donation of Berkshire Hathaway shares he made to the foundation on announcing his resignation was a parting gift, but in fact, it's been followed by more largesse. In June 2023, he donated another 10.45 million shares; the transfer brings his total giving to the Gates Foundation to date to more than $39 billion. Other gifts were announced at the same time—2.2 million shares split evenly between charities led by Warren's children, and another 1.05 million shares to the Susan Thompson Buffett Foundation, which has been growing in recent years. In 2022, just a couple of days before the Supreme Court's overturning of *Roe v. Wade*, the *Wall Street Journal* reported that the Susan Thompson Buffett Foundation had been hiring additional staff, and gearing up for a large influx of cash. Large, like, in the range of $70 to $100 billion, according to the *Journal*, following up on rumors that this philanthropy championing reproductive rights will reap the bulk of Warren's (still-compounding) wealth when he passes away. Should the report be largely correct, it would be a homecoming of sorts—Susie and Warren reunited in the afterlife, fighting for a cause so dear to both their hearts.

Not that the Gates Foundation will ever find itself short on cash—even as its original protagonists divert more of their attention, and funds, to other pursuits. Bill himself is increasingly preoccupied by activities outside the foundation; most of his climate-change-related interests in innovation and low-carbon technologies, for instance, are outside its fold, and he's handed over much of the responsibility for shaping and communicating the foundation's priorities to Suzman, who since 2022 has penned its annual letters. The Gates Foundation seems to be evolving, then, into a sturdy institution not so different from the Ford or Rockefeller Foundations. With that has come a change in tone: In his January 2023 letter, Suzman took on criticisms of the foundation's deficit of transparency and accountability head-on, saying, "We have an obligation to be clear about how we try to use our influence and why." No longer a monologue, but a dialogue. It's a start.

WHEN YOU BOIL it down, the chief frustration people have had with the Bill and Melinda Gates Foundation is that its founders won't get into arguments. At least not publicly. They long ago set a course of action and plowed forward, brushing off critics' doubts and fears as so much "pessimism," until some data point came along that caused them to adjust their thinking. Good faith critics all presume that Bill and Melinda sincerely want to alleviate as much suffering as they can, and they acknowledge that the pair could easily be spending their days sunning themselves on a superyacht rather than marching off to urban slums and remote rural villages to see what their dollars can do for the desperate.

But they also wonder why Bill and Melinda were so allergic for so long to engage in, say, a frank dialogue about the pros and cons of a technocratic approach to treating hunger that relies on GM seeds and chemical fertilizers and liberal trade policies and corporate partnerships, as opposed to, say, the "right to food" movement in India. By contrast, the Zero Hunger program enacted in Brazil in 2003 did receive research funding from the foundation, so there were exceptions, indicating that there is no particular opposition to working with governments who will fulfill their obligations to their citizens. Still, for Bill (the foundation's dominant personality), "politics" for a long time was anathema, a dirty word—fine for social justice warriors, if that's what they're into, but sidelong to the task he's set himself as a philanthropist, which is to be a problem-solver, trusting in innovation and efficiency fixes to address our biggest problems. The irony remains, however, at least for this author, that solving the problems in an extant system *is* perforce a form of politics, an undeniable vote in favor of the political status quo.

In a lengthy interview Bill once conducted in March 2014 with *Rolling Stone*, Bill made a clear distinction between innovation and politics:

> *Before 1700, everybody was poor as hell. Life was short and brutish. It wasn't because we didn't have good politicians; we had some really good politicians. But then we started inventing—electricity, steam engines, microprocessors, understanding genetics and medicine and things like that. Yes, stability and education are important—I'm not taking anything away from that—but innovation is the real driver of progress.*

This may be the most Bill Gates-y thing Bill Gates has ever said. He's not merely ignoring the fact that innovation drives not just "progress" but also political change—case in point, the breakdown of the landed aristocracy in Europe in the wake of the Industrial Revolution—he's saying that innovation and politics are entirely distinct from one another. They are quite separately at work on the same problem: the alleviation of suffering. It's just that technology is way better than politics at getting results.

The problem with this viewpoint is that any change has built-in political consequences, with huge social consequences as well, so that it is superdangerous to ignore this relationship, as nice as it might be to think that innovation can purely speed on its own tracks, without looking to the left and right, leaving only gifts to humanity in its wake. Innovating home-administered contraceptive shots *is* political. Innovating charter schools and Common Core standards *is* political. Just as innovating a new way to view the racial divide in America—as Martin Luther King Jr. did—is also political. And "progress" itself is political; what looks like improvement to some seems a setback to others, and more often than not, the terms are set by those wielding power.

Citizens of the United States, the United Kingdom, and the European Union are mired in the consequences of this mindset *right now*. When innovation is treated as inexorable and value-neutral, you wind up with large populations furious that their jobs have been outsourced or automated or turned into temp labor assigned by an algorithm greasing the gears of the global supply chain. You get people ardently convinced that the "elites" who benefit from this innovation don't give a shit about them or their kids or their communities, and who resent those same elites for assigning themselves the authority to fix what's broken in the system by implementing a patch here and a patch there and then shrugging and saying, "Oh well" when the patches need patching. You get anti-vaxxers skeptical of science and Fox News viewers skeptical of "facts," because the elites keep running their mouths about data and meanwhile *you've* still got problems, so what do they know? You get hysteria about immigration. You get Brexit. You get Donald Trump.

Anyway, it's not like Bill doesn't understand politics. In 2018, he delivered a speech in Abuja, Nigeria, to an audience that included Nigerian president Muhammadu Buhari. The speech's theme was "human capital," and without mincing words, Bill told the crowd that Nigeria, with its "unmatched economic potential" would be wading into perilous waters if it didn't start investing in its people.

"What do I mean by investing in your people? I mean prioritizing health and education," Bill said. "The World Bank World Development report that just came out makes it clear that education leads to improvements in employment, productivity, and wages. Today, though," Bill added, "more than half of rural Nigerian children can't read and write."

"The conclusion is inescapable," he continued. "Nigeria's economy tomorrow depends on improving its schools today."

Bill went on to point out that for Nigeria to invest in its schools, and by extension, its people, the country's government needed to improve its collection of taxes. And doing that, he noted, was going to require *political will*. You'd have to take on entrenched interests, and convince the powerful—by some combination of carrots and sticks—to adjust their expectations about how "the system" is supposed to work. And because that task would be difficult, you'd have to get numbers on your side, engaging the broad populace by making it clear—through action—that their voices were being heard.

Given the power the Gates Foundation now wields, isn't it appropriate to ask them to do better themselves, where summoning political will is concerned?

THE COVID-19 PANDEMIC laid bare the importance of that question. It laid bare a lot of other things, too. Monopoly is a hot topic again, as companies like Amazon consolidated market share while small businesses went under. The crisis exposed global supply chain frailty and shone a spotlight on the vulnerability of the poor and working class in an age of extreme inequality: "Essential" workers got sick on the job and returned to crowded homes to infect their families and neighbors, many of whom fear eviction now that government-mandated moratoriums have "sunsetted." Watching as the American education system unraveled, inventing distance learning techniques on the fly and leaving technologically disadvantaged kids far behind, you may have wondered what all the billionaires so preoccupied with education reform were doing to help matters. (Or *are* doing: These problems are ongoing.) They, the billionaires, are of course just fine—returning to the jet set after sheltering in place at their vacation homes, and keeping a beady eye on moody

Mr. Market, whose current ill humor poses no real threat to their households' bottom lines.

And of course, the issue most front and center in all of this is that Gates Foundation specialty: vaccines. This has emerged as a tale of two Bill Gateses.

We'll tell the accurate story first.

On April 3, 2015, Bill issued a now prophetic warning, telling a TED conference crowd in Vancouver that "if anything kills over 10 million people in the next few decades, it's most likely to be a highly infectious virus rather than a war." No one paid much attention at the time. Which is fine, in a way—as Stanford's Rob Reich argues in *Just Giving*, the form of philanthropy most complementary to democracy is the use of the wealthy's spare billions as society's "risk capital," with investments best directed into potential fixes for *low-probability catastrophes* such as, say, a major global pandemic.

Of course, the point Bill was making in his talk was that a pandemic wasn't so low-probability—it was simply that we'd been lucky thus far. But few gamblers leave a hot table, so the world kept spinning and Bill, Cassandra-like, kept pressing his case. In 2016, he raised the issue with then-president-elect Trump. At the 2017 Munich Security Conference, he urged world leaders to approach the threat of a pandemic with the same hypervigilance they would in stopping a terrorist from developing a new weapon that could efficiently kill millions. A year later, he was at it again, giving yet another speech suggesting—nay, begging—that governments and NGOs team up to stage outbreak simulations and training exercises, "so that we can better understand how diseases will spread and how to deal with responses such as quarantine." Finally, in October 2019, the Gates Foundation partnered with the World Economic Forum and the Johns Hopkins Center for Health Security to run something called Event 201. This was a "3.5-hour pandemic tabletop exercise that simulated a series of dramatic, scenario-based facilitated discussions, confronting difficult, true-to-life dilemmas associated with response to a hypothetical, but scientifically plausible, pandemic." In practical terms, what this means is that fifteen people—one was the director general of the Chinese Center for Disease Control and Prevention—sat around for an afternoon and imagined what they'd do in the event of a global pandemic. They watched a few dramatized news broadcasts, more for atmosphere than anything else. In the scenario, a new disease emerges in pig farms in Brazil and spreads around the world, killing 65 million people in eighteen months.

Searching for a plausible vector, the organizers decided that this terrifying new disease should come from a *novel coronavirus*.

Yeah, right.

Cut to January 17, 2020. Just as COVID-19 was sweeping through Wuhan Province in China, the Gates Foundation, the World Economic Forum, and Johns Hopkins released a joint statement on Event 201, offering seven proposals to governments worldwide to enhance their pandemic preparedness. The last item on the list addressed the need for quick action to "combat mis- and disinformation."

Anyway, we all know what happened next. And here we encounter the *other* Bill Gates, the creation of conspiracy theorists who need a famous figure to latch on to if their theories are to gain any purchase in the public mind. Pandemic? Bill Gates must be behind it. Suddenly, outrageously, Bill was the bogeyman of those peddling an alternate version of the above history. A sample claim: "In this whole saga the ever-present Gates Foundation, has just announced another funding venture for worldwide control of every person, with a new project called Trust Stamp," naturopath Ross Walter posted on Facebook. "This is a vaccination-based digital identity program . . . Trust Stamp will link your biometric digital identity to your vaccination records and your financial and banking access." Walter goes on to suggest that this is part of a "war on cash," as well as an aid to development of *Minority Report*-style predictive policing. Elsewhere in the fever swamps, tweets with the hashtag #exposebillgates assert, among other things, that Bill Gates himself developed COVID-19 in a lab, that he's patented it, that he intends to use a COVID vaccine to microchip everyone on earth—a cousin to Walter's claims about Trust Stamp—and that, uh, this is all somehow related to 5G wireless and Bill Gates is in on it. *Sigh.*

I've aired a lot of critiques of the Gates Foundation in this book. I've done so because I believe that legitimate critique is important, but there's another reason for giving space to thoughtful naysayers: In a vacuum of serious public debate, conspiracies rush in to fill the void. When the mainstream media props up an image of Bill and Melinda as genius do-gooders at large, without diving into the details of their work—where the efforts are always well-intentioned, if the outcomes are unavoidably imperfect—it invites random naturopaths posting on Facebook to assume the role of critical authority. "The posts on social media about you and coronavirus are considered the most widespread coronavirus falsehoods that exist," *CBS Evening News* anchor Norah O'Donnell pointed out to Bill in a July 2020 interview. "So . . . to be clear: Do you want a vaccine so that you can implant microchips into people?" Bill kept his cool. Just shook his head. "No," he said. "There's no connection between any of these vaccines and any tracking-type . . . thing . . . at all."

The fact that Bill had to shift attention away from his vital work fighting COVID to counter crazy claims that he was using the coronavirus as an excuse to brand innocent people with the Mark of the Beast suggests that both the world and the Gates Foundation could benefit from a more sober and thorough debate about the role we want big money to play in our lives. More transparency—and more democracy—in the years to come can only help.

In a more perfect world, the news that should have been flooding Facebook was that in this crisis, the Gates Foundation's work was proving vital. To start with, its long experience with issues of immunology bolstered the research of scientists and epidemiologists throwing body and soul into defeating COVID. Beyond that, Gates

Foundation efforts as of the long, hot summer of 2020 included committing $350 million to improve detection, isolation, and treatment of the virus and accelerate the development of vaccines; and working to protect at-risk populations in Africa and South Asia. Bill also took a page from the Warren Buffett playbook, jawboning in private and in public: Behind the scenes, he was on the phone with power players like US chief medical adviser Dr. Anthony Fauci, and the rest of the time, it seemed, he was offering science-backed guidance to nervous citizens, tweeting furiously, writing op-eds, and showing up via Zoom on TV. "He is in his element right now," former Gates Foundation CEO Jeff Raikes told the *Washington Post*.

One striking aspect of Bill's jawboning was his insistence that any vaccine that was created be treated as a "global public good." Speaking to a remote conference hosted by the International AIDS Society in July 2020, he declared, "If we just let drugs and vaccines go to the highest bidder, instead of to the people and places where they are most needed, we'll have a longer, more unjust, deadlier pandemic." Instead of "market-driven factors," he suggested, the distribution should be based on a notion of "equity."

Or, maybe, in other words—justice?

Bill is still a big fan of private-sector innovation. One decidedly non-tinfoil-hat critique of him that emerged in the midst of the pandemic addressed his lobbying efforts to retain patent protections on COVID vaccines, even as organizations such as Doctors Without Borders and, er, the Biden White House argued that putting the technology in the public domain would speed vaccinations in poor countries. Here we saw Bill's concern for "the common good" running straight into his bedrock belief in the inviolability of intellectual property rights—a flag he's been waving since his early skirmishes with the Homebrew bootleggers when they were ripping off Microsoft code.

But then again, time has a way of transforming people. The speed-racing wunderkind counting *cars* in the Microsoft parking lot becomes a statesman-like do-gooder counting *lives saved*, thanks to efficient dispensation of oral rehydration salts. The press-shy Catholic mom turns into one of the world's most forceful spokespeople for reproductive rights. People do change. Sometimes. And in sometimes unexpected ways. Jonas Salk refused to patent his polio vaccine; so perhaps the day will come when Bill, receiving the welcome report that polio has been eradicated, thanks in large part to his efforts, will take up the full measure of Salk's legacy and decide to soften his stance on intellectual property rights and market mechanisms.

This fantasy is less far-fetched than it may seem. Over the past twenty years, the Gates Foundation has evolved—sometimes more slowly than critics might hope, but the arc is clear. In 2018, for instance, Bill and Melinda made a big announcement: They were once again expanding the Gates Foundation remit, and this time the focus would be on domestic poverty. The first big grant in this program area was $158 million to study the causes and consequences of poverty in the United States, as well as the barriers to economic mobility. As remarks by then-foundation CEO Sue Desmond-Hellmann made clear, Bill and Melinda intended to approach this problem in the Gates way, investing in data because "you can't measure outcomes and be nimble and adjust if you don't have good data on what others are doing, and how you can generate results." So, some things *don't* change—but the anti-poverty campaign, and the international education grants the foundation rolled out at the same time, speak to the evolution of the foundation's thinking about its philanthropy. Addressing poverty in America and education abroad augurs a more holistic approach to the problems Bill and Melinda previously sought to solve with silver bullets.

Another new endeavor was the Bill & Melinda Gates Medical Research Institute in Cambridge, Massachusetts. A nonprofit world-class biotech research facility, capable of running its own clinical trials, this institution shows that Bill is putting his money where his mouth is, where declarations of (limited) independence from drug companies is concerned. It's not crazy to suppose that the Gates Foundation of the future will introduce other changes that make it look very different from the Gates Foundation of the past—less an exercise in private billionaire philanthropy, and more an expression of our common efforts to make this world a better place.

WAY BACK IN 2000, Melinda gave her first big philanthropic speech at the Washington Women's Foundation Convention. It's a strange document to read now—there's so much less of the bravado and self-assurance you associate with a Gates Foundation oration. Instead of starting the speech by making big global-scale statements about poverty and disease, she talks about the long walks she and Bill like to take around their neighborhood. "My husband and I," she said, "are really just beginning our journey in philanthropy. And I can't think of any better way to describe it than to say that it is a long walk we hope is in the right direction."

Well, there have been some twists and turns on that path, and you never really know if it was the right direction until you get there. It'll be up to the future to decide; this story certainly isn't over yet. But if there's one thing the Gates Foundation has been getting better at, it's *getting better*. That future, when it comes, might be a better place than it would have been if it weren't for Bill and Melinda Gates.

OH, AND WARREN? He's still Warren. Still living in the same house, wearing the same rumpled suits, drinking the same Cherry Coke. Still rich. Of course. How rich? Despite all that giving, very rich. The *Forbes* 400 list has been a little volatile of late, with Elon Musk and Jeff Bezos constantly overtaking each other for the top post, but Warren's never been too far behind. (Sidenote on Mr. Bezos: He is the only member of the top five as of 2020 to not have signed the Giving Pledge—giving away half of your worth in your own lifetime—though his ex-wife, MacKenzie Scott, did, in 2019. He had, however, given $2 billion to fund organizations serving the homeless and create preschools for children from low-income families, among other grants, and during an interview with CNN in 2022 surprised everyone by saying he now plans to give away "most" of his then $124 billion fortune in his lifetime.)

Charlie Munger, a man with whom Warren said he'd never had one argument, died in December 2023, one month shy of his one hundredth birthday. Warren's eulogy was simple: "Charlie has given me the ultimate gift a person can give to somebody else. I've lived a better life because of Charlie."

Warren remains, at ninety-three as of this writing, a loyal friend to Bill and Melinda, still offering and receiving advice. Who could have known how significant, for himself, and now also for so many in dire need around the globe, his first meeting with Bill, way back in 1991, would become? He surely could never have imagined it.

His philanthropic response to COVID-19? Bill and Melinda are of course now spending his money whenever the Gates Foundation doles out cash for such emergencies. But we have no precise figures. We do know he dumped all his airline stocks and lent his company's private jets to fly N95 masks from China to Mount Sinai Hospital in New York. Also, he appeared in an animated public service announcement for children on how to properly wash their hands. And, for the first time, he had to deliver his 2020 Berkshire sermon to his faithful *online*!

He's into technology now—back in 2016, he became a big investor in Apple. And the guy who read *Moody's Manuals* on his honeymoon now makes time to hang out with his grandkids and great-grandkids. He also plays bridge online with Bill and others several times a week on the platform Bridge Base. On the bridge circuit, the word is that his game is still in top shape. There are monthly outings to—where else?—Dairy Queen, where the clan pigs out on Dilly Bars and Blizzards. Grandpa Warren goes for a plain old sundae. Because of course he does. Because he's the world's most regular guy: a formerly quasipolyamorous multibillionaire who rescued two Wall Street banks from collapse, propped up the U.S. economy, raised a daughter who's just about single-handedly preserving the right to abortion in America, a son who composed an award-winning multimedia song cycle on the plight of Native Americans, and another son who, last we checked, had withdrawn from the race to be a sheriff in Illinois. Just a regular guy who decided to give away more money than anyone else ever has, because his sleep was troubled by the idea that he was *lucky*. Whose modesty extends to the fact that he's declined to put his name on anything, not even the company he built from scratch and that made him, for a time, the richest man in the world. Every working day, $100 million rolls into Berkshire Hathaway—cash from subsidiaries, stock dividends, interest—and Warren, eyeballing one hundred, is there, sitting at his desk in Kiewit Plaza, trying to figure out what do with it. The fuckups are part of the fun.

As Warren has often said: "If you played golf and you hit a hole in one on every hole, nobody would play golf. You've got to hit a few in the rough and then get out of the rough."

"That," he adds, "makes it interesting."

JUST A GAME

Warren Buffett and Bill Gates are very different people. Their friendship probably wouldn't have ever been as significant if they weren't both avid bridge players.

The rules of bridge—or, as players call them, the "laws"—are famously complex, but here's how a game starts. You begin with four players, two teams—with the team mates sitting opposite each other—and a deck of cards. The cards are dealt and privately viewed by each player, and then the "auction" begins. Here, all the players compete to declare how well they think their team will do with the cards they've been dealt, and whoever makes the most extravagant promises gets to make the contract.

Businessmen tend to like bridge: It's a game that rewards focus and strategy, where you need an eye for the long game and a killer instinct, patience and decisiveness both. You need to know how to absorb your losses, because—just like in business, or philanthropy, for that matter—you can't win every time. But you can see why a game like this would appeal to someone like Warren in particular: It's his "ovarian lottery" in a nutshell. Just like with every other card game, you don't ever get to choose the cards you've been dealt, and every so often, every player gets a terrible hand. The difference is that in bridge, nobody goes out into the world alone. Your partner is just across the table from you, and it's their job to help turn your bad hand into a winning play.

Throughout his life, Warren has sought out worthy partners, people like Rose Blumkin and Charlie Munger and, well, Bill Gates. Just like with Warren's businesses, a good partnership in bridge requires a common goal and good communication. Partners aren't allowed to openly tell each other which cards they're holding, but they can send "signals" to each other in prearranged code—for instance, you could respond to a high card with a very low card to indicate that your hand is weak, or conversely play a much higher card than necessary to hint at your strength. Warren Buffett, need we mention, is probably the greatest business communicator of our age. There's a reason his annual letters are devoured by thousands of people who've never spent a dime on Berkshire Hathaway stock. This stuff is in his blood.

Bill, too, might have found something in bridge to fit his temperament. After all, this is a game about making promises and then *backing them up*. It's all very well taking the contract by promising you'll win every trick—if you can't deliver, you lose the game. And Bill is a man who built his career on making extraordinary promises and then delivering the goods. Back in 1975, he promised that he could write a version of BASIC that would work on the 8080 chip, and won himself a contract. He delivered. Fast-forward almost fifty years, and Bill is promising to end all preventable deaths from AIDS and polio and so many of the other terrible products of poverty. It's a powerful bid. And everywhere across the globe, the Gates Foundation is working to make good on it.

Of course, a cynic could point to some other features of the game of bridge that cast a gloomier light on Bill and Warren's philanthropy. After the auction, the winner is known, for the rest of the hand, as the "declarer," for this person has decided what suit is trumps. Their partner is thereafter known as the "dummy," and must play no further part in the game, turning their cards faceup for all to see. All the dummy's moves are then made by the declarer. Which is to say: These partnerships are never quite equal. As we've documented, there are plenty of people in India and Africa and elsewhere across the world who might be feeling a little like the dummy in this game Bill and Warren are playing. While the billionaires plot and strategize, their cards are laid open—and even if they end up winning the hand, there are many who feel they haven't gotten to play much of a role. Perhaps, in philanthropy, this is just one of the rules of the game.

Over the course of a game of bridge, the score is kept on a piece of paper divided into two columns, headed "We" and "They," for the two teams, with a horizontal line partway down. When a side has scored 100 or more points below the line, it has won a "game." To show this, the scorekeeper draws a horizontal line across the score sheet, below the score that ended the game. This signifies that the next game will begin.

Sharon Osberg, whom you might remember as Warren's bridge coach, describes the difference between Bill's and Warren's playing styles in words that could equally well describe the two men in general. "Bill is very scientific," she told the *Washington Post*. "He reads and studies on his own. Warren enjoys playing. Warren has good instincts." Warren really does enjoy playing. As he once said, he wouldn't mind going to jail if his three cellmates played bridge. According to Warren, at least, providing he's not playing Sharon Osberg, he usually comes out on top. "I probably play 100 times as often as Bill, so that probably is the only game in the world where I would have a slight edge with him," he told CNBC in 2019. "Very slight edge," he admitted.

As for the ever-competitive Bill—here, at least, he doesn't seem to mind losing occasionally. As he's spent the last decade telling his fellow billionaires, the feeling that winning delivers lasts but a moment, precious though it is, and you must never forget that you can't take it with you, so why not make your preparations for the final defeat now, that eternal unwinnable rubber against a relentless foe; oh, and while you're at it, why not settle your score card to ensure that, before you fold 'em for eternity, the last check you ever write bounces.

ACKNOWLEDGMENTS

Several people have assisted me greatly in the preparation of this book. Principal in this are my researchers, Maya Singer and Sam Kriss, who lent great aid and support and forensic nouse in helping to penetrate the often opaque world of billionaire philanthropy. I also wish to thank the steadfast support and editorial input of Noah Eaker at HarperCollins, and that of my agent and, better yet, friend, Jennifer Joel at ICM/CAA. Lastly, my thanks to my publishers in Germany, Diogenes Verlag, for their support over more than two decades.

BIBLIOGRAPHY

Bibliographic Note

This book began its life in 2017 as a stage play: *Wednesday at War-ren's, Friday at Bill's*, the third part of what would become the Worship Trilogy, three plays that explore disputed arguments in the worshipped worlds of Religion, Art, and, finally, Money. In this third case, I was drawn without fixed opinion to the question of whether superphilanthropy was, on balance, a good or a bad thing for society, and I was especially intrigued by not only the domestic aspects of the friendship between Warren Buffett and Bill Gates but also the influential roles played by Melinda Gates, Susie Thompson Buffett, and Astrid Menks Buffett in a four- and five-way friendship that would develop, seemingly casually and over a series of innocent bridge game evenings and other encounters, into what remains as the biggest single philanthropic commitment in history.

As I have twice before found to be the case—this book marks the third instance—an impulse to create a work of speculative fiction for the stage or screen, perforce obliged an enormous amount of prepa-ratory research so that no gross injury was done to history. This took the form, finally, of another work of nonfiction, with all its stringent demands for unbending accuracy.

The preparation of this particular book, then, relied upon a great number of sources, but I wish to single out for special mention the following titles.

Paul Allen's *Idea Man* granted a unique perspective on Bill, as did Stephen Manes and Paul Andrews, while Howard Buffett and Carol Loomis and notably Alice Schroeder did the same for Warren. Melinda's *The Moment of Lift* was full of bracing candor. Walter Isaacson gave a fine overview of the digital upheaval we have, in our lifetimes, all experienced. More penetrating analyses of the costs and benefits of superphilanthropy were provided by, among others, Linsey McGoey, in her *No Such Thing as a Free Gift: The Gates Foundation and the Price of Philanthropy*, David Rieff in his *The Reproach of Hunger: Food, Justice, and Money in the Twenty-First Century*, and David Callahan in his *The Givers: Wealth, Power, and Philanthropy in a New Gilded Age*. A final mention for Robert Cringely if, for nothing else, the title of his book: *Accidental Empires: How the Boys of Silicon Valley Make Their Millions, Battle Foreign Competition, and Still Can't Get a Date.*

Books

Allen, Paul. *Idea Man: A Memoir by the Cofounder of Microsoft*. New York: Portfolio/Penguin, 2011.

Brill, Steven. *Class Warfare: Inside the Fight to Fix America's Schools*. New York: Simon & Schuster, 2011.

Buffett, Howard G. *40 Chances: Finding Hope in a Hungry World*. New York: Simon & Schuster, 2013.

Callahan, David. *The Givers: Wealth, Power, and Philanthropy in a New Gilded Age*. New York: Alfred A. Knopf, 2017.

Cringely, Robert X. *Accidental Empires: How the Boys of Silicon Valley Make Their Millions, Battle Foreign Competition, and Still Can't Get a Date*. Boston: Addison-Wesley, 1992.

Doerr, John. *Measure What Matters: OKRs—The Simple Idea That Drives 10x Growth*. New York: Portfolio/Penguin, 2018.

Doogan, Kevin. *New Capitalism?: The Transformation of Work*. Cambridge, UK: Polity Books, 2009.

Federici, Silvia. *Wages Against Housework*. London: Falling Wall Press, 1975.

Fleishman, Joel L., J. Scott Kohler, and Steven Schindler. *Casebook for the Foundation: A Great American Secret*. New York: PublicAffairs, 2007.

Frank, Robert. *Richistan: A Journey Through the 21st Century Wealth Boom and the Lives of the New Rich*. London: Piatkus Books, 2008.

Gates, Bill. *How to Avoid a Climate Disaster: The Solutions We Have and the Breakthroughs We Need*. New York: Alfred A. Knopf, 2021.

Gates, Melinda. *The Moment of Lift: How Empowering Women Changes the World*. New York: Flatiron Books, 2019.

Giridharadas, Anand. *Winners Take All: The Elite Charade of Changing the World.* New York: Alfred A. Knopf, 2018.

Graubard, Margaret E. M. *In the Best Society.* Bloomington, IN: iUniverse, 2008.

Hays, Charlotte. *The Fortune Hunters: Dazzling Women and the Men They Married.* New York: St. Martin's Press, 2007.

Isaacson, Walter. *Steve Jobs: A Biography.* New York: Simon & Schuster, 2011.

———. *The Innovators: How a Group of Hackers, Geniuses, and Geeks Created the Digital Revolution.* New York: Simon & Schuster, 2014.

Kovacs, Philip E., ed. *The Gates Foundation and the Future of US Public Schools.* New York: Routledge, 2011.

Lesinski, Jeanne M. *Bill Gates: Entrepreneur and Philanthropist.* Minneapolis, MN: Twenty-First Century Books, 2009.

Loomis, Carol. *Tap Dancing to Work: Warren Buffett on Practically Everything.* New York: Portfolio/Penguin, 2012.

Lowe, Janet. *Bill Gates Speaks: Insight from the World's Greatest Entrepreneur.* Hoboken, NJ: John Wiley & Sons, 2001.

Lowenstein, Roger. *Buffett: The Making of an American Capitalist.* New York: Random House, 1995.

MacFarquhar, Larissa. *Strangers Drowning: Voyages to the Brink of Moral Extremity.* London: Allen Lane, 2015.

Manes, Stephen, and Paul Andrews. *Gates: How Microsoft's Mogul Reinvented an Industry—and Made Himself the Richest Man in America.* New York: Doubleday, 1993.

Mayer, Jane. *Dark Money: The Hidden History of the Billionaires Behind the Rise of the Radical Right.* New York: Doubleday, 2016.

McGoey, Linsey. *No Such Thing as a Free Gift: The Gates Foundation and the Price of Philanthropy.* London: Verso, 2015.

Muraskin, William. *Crusade to Immunize the World's Children.* Morrisville, NC: Lulu Press, 2005.

Plath, James, ed. *John Updike's Pennsylvania Interviews.* Bethlehem, PA: Lehigh University Press, 2016.

Reich, Rob. *Just Giving: Why Philanthropy Is Failing Democracy and How It Can Do Better.* Princeton, NJ: Princeton University Press, 2018.

Rieff, David. *The Reproach of Hunger: Food, Justice, and Money in the Twenty-First Century.* New York: Simon & Schuster, 2015.

Schroeder, Alice. *The Snowball: Warren Buffett and the Business of Life.* New York: Bantam Books, 2008.

Wainer, Howard. *Picturing the Uncertain World: How to Understand, Communicate, and Control Uncertainty Through Graphical Display.* Princeton, NJ: Princeton University Press, 2009.

Articles

Ackman, Dan. "Bill Gates Is a Genius and You're Not." *Forbes,* July 21, 2004.

Alberts, Hana R. "Legal Adversary Turned Ally." *Forbes,* June 25, 2008.

Alpert, Gabe. "If You Had Invested in Berkshire Hathaway When Buffett Took Over." *Investopedia,* May 21, 2020.

Andrews, Paul. "Bill Gates, Version 38.0." *Seattle Times,* October 28, 1993.

Andrews, Paul, and Stephen Manes. "Power User—He Saw the Future and It Was Him." *Seattle Times,* January 10, 1993.

Armstrong, Robert, Eric Platt, and Oliver Ralph. "Warren Buffett: I'm Having More Fun Than Any 88-Year-Old in the World." *Financial Times*, April 24, 2019.

Bailey, Jeff, and Eric Dash. "How Does Warren Buffett Get Married? Frugally, It Turns Out." *New York Times*, September 1, 2006.

Bajaj, Vikas. "Freddie Mac Tightens Standards." *New York Times*, February 28, 2007.

Beam, Alex. "Lifestyles of the Rich." *New York Times*, June 10, 2007.

Bishop, Todd. "Bill Gates Patched Things Up with Paul Allen, Hoped to Travel the World with Microsoft Co-founder." *GeekWire*, February 12, 2019.

Bloomberg News. "Buffett Reluctantly Discloses Berkshire Stake in Microsoft." *New York Times*, February 23, 2000.

Bowman, Andrew. "The Flip Side to Bill Gates' Charity Billions." *New Internationalist*, April 1, 2012.

Buffett, Peter. "The Charitable-Industrial Complex." *New York Times*, July 26, 2013.

Buffett, Warren E. "Warren Buffett: Buy American. I Am." *New York Times*, October 16, 2008.

Buhayar, Noah. "U.S. Embassies Are Obsessed with Warren Buffett's Chocolate." *Bloomberg*, December 1, 2015.

Burck, Gilbert. "A New Kind of Stock Market." *Fortune*, March 1959.

Callahan, David. "Who's Who at the Secretive Susan Thompson Buffett Foundation." *Inside Philanthropy*, February 4, 2014.

Campany, David. "Allan Sekula: A Mirror to Fractured Times." *Financial Times*, March 8, 2019.

Cao, Sissi. "Melinda Gates Talks Her 'Big Test' with Bill Gates in Rare Interview." *Observer*, April 24, 2019.

Carlton, Jim. "They Coulda Been a Contender." *Wired*, November 1, 1997.

Chambers, Sam. "Bill Gates Joins Nuclear-Powered Shipping Push." Splash247.com, November 2, 2020.

Clark, Andrew. "Buffett Says Act or Face 'Economic Pearl Harbor.'" *Guardian*, September 24, 2008.

———. "She Was Working as a Waitress in a Cocktail Bar. Then She Met Warren." *Guardian*, September 1, 2006.

Cohen, Adam. "Microsoft Enjoys Monopoly Power . . ." *Time*, November 15, 1999.

Constantinou, Marianne. "Bill Gates Tries to Upgrade His Image." *Baltimore Sun*, May 4, 1998.

Consumer Federation of America. "Media Commentators Across the Country Reject Harsh and One-Sided Bankruptcy Legislation." Consumerfed .org.

Corcoran, Elizabeth, and John Schwartz. "The House That Bill Gates's Money Built." *Washington Post*, August 28, 1997.

Corr, O. Casey. "Melinda French Gates: A Microsoft Mystery." *Seattle Times*, June 4, 1995.

———. "Mr. X–Coupon King Bill Gates and Other High-Tech Tales." *Seattle Times*, February 27, 1992.

Crippen, Alex. "New Peter Buffett-Akon Collaboration Debuts at United Nations Concert." *CNBC*, March 25, 2009.

Daly, James. "The Robin Hood of the Rich." *Wired*, August 1, 1997.

Darlin, Damon. "He Wants Your Eyeballs." *Forbes*, June 16, 1997.

Deutschman, Alan. "Bill Gates' Next Challenge." *Fortune*, December 28, 1992.

Diamond, David. "Adventure Capitalist." *Wired*, September 1, 1996.

Dodge, John. "A Visit to Bill Gates' House a Decade Ago." *EDN*, July 3, 2006.

Doughton, Sandi. "Not Many Speak Their Mind to the Gates Foundation." *Seattle Times*, August 3, 2008.

Dugger, Celia W. "For Melinda Gates, Birth Control Is Women's Way Out of Poverty." *New York Times*, November 1, 2016.

———. "From U.S. to Africa, with a Fortune and a Tractor." *New York Times*, October 23, 2009.

Dzombak, Dan. "25 Best Warren Buffett Quotes." The Motley Fool, September 28, 2018.

Edgecliffe-Johnson, Andrew, and Billy Nauman. "Fossil Fuel Divestment Has 'Zero' Climate Impact, Says Bill Gates." *Financial Times*, September 17, 2019.

Egan, Timothy. "Bill Gates Views What He's Sown in Libraries." *New York Times*, November 6, 2002.

Eichenwald, Kurt. "Microsoft's Lost Decade." *Vanity Fair*, August 2012.

Einstein, David. "Gates Steps Down as Microsoft CEO." *Forbes*, January 13, 2000.

———. "The Lawyer Who Took on Microsoft." *San Francisco Chronicle*, March 20, 1995.

Elkins, Kathleen. "Warren Buffett Spends 8 Hours a Week Playing the 'Only Game' at Which He May Be Better than Bill Gates." CNBC, February 25, 2019.

Elliott, Philip. "Charles Koch Has Given $1 Billion to Charity." *Time*, October 3, 2018.

Ervin, Keith. "Federal Way Pares School-Chief List to Three Finalists." *Seattle Times*, July 26, 1994.

Eschner, Kat. "The Peculiar Story of the Witch of Wall Street." *Smithsonian*, November 21, 2017.

Feder, Barnaby J. "Rose Blumkin, Retail Queen, Dies at 104." *New York Times*, August 13, 1998.

Foroohar, Rana. "Warren Buffett Is on a Radical Track." *Time*, January 23, 2012.

Fox, Ben. "Warren Buffett Doubles Pledge to Kids' Foundations." *MarketWatch*, August 30, 2012.

Frank, Robert. "What Does It Take to Feel Wealthy?" CNBC, July 19, 2012.

Freed, Dan. "'King of Wall Street' Trader John Gutfreund Dies at 86." Reuters, March 9, 2016.

Gammon, Katharine. "What We'll Miss About Bill Gates—A Very Long Goodbye." *Wired*, May 18, 2008.

Gates, Bill. "Here's a Chapter from My Favorite Business Book." *Gates Notes*, July 13, 2014.

———. "25 Years of Learning and Laughter." *Gates Notes*, July 5, 2016.

———. "Warren and Me." *Gates Notes*, May 12, 2015.

———. "Warren Buffett's Best Investment." *Gates Notes*, February 14, 2017.

———. "Warren Buffett Just Wrote His Best Annual Letter Ever." *Gates Notes*, March 15, 2015.

———. "What I Learned from Warren Buffett." *Harvard Business Review*, January–February 1996.

———. "What Makes for a Good Bridge Partner?" *Gates Notes*, August 6, 2010.

———. "Why We Swing for the Fences." *Gates Notes*, February 10, 2020.

Gates, Melinda. "The Vacation That Changed Everything." AARP, November 28, 2017.

Geballe, Bob. "Bill Gates' Guinea Pigs." *Seattle Weekly*, October 9, 2006.

Gibbs, Nancy. "The Good Samaritans." *Time*, December 19, 2005.

Gibbs, W. Wayt. "Bill Gates Views Good Data as Key to Global Health." *Scientific American*, August 1, 2016.

Gillis, Justin. "Bill and Melinda Gates' Charities Go Far Beyond Writing Checks." *Washington Post*, October 3, 2003.

Goodell, Jeff. "Bill Gates: The Rolling Stone Interview." *Rolling Stone*, March 13, 2014.

Grant, Linda. "Taming the Bond Buccaneers at Salomon Brothers." *Los Angeles Times*, February 16, 1992.

Hanbury, Mary. "We Ate at Warren Buffett's Favorite Omaha Steakhouse—Here's What It's Like." Business Insider India, July 10, 2017.

Heath, Thomas. "Meet the Woman Who Gives Bridge Tips to Warren Buffett and Bill Gates." *Washington Post*, July 28, 2017.

———. "My Conversation with Warren Buffett about Bridge, Bill Gates and a Bus Ride." *Washington Post*, August 4, 2017.

Heilemann, John. "The Truth, the Whole Truth and Nothing But the Truth." *Wired*, November 1, 2000.

Helmore, Edward. "So Who's Crying Over Spilt Milk?" *Guardian*, May 9, 2001.

Hendrie, Caroline. "High Schools Nationwide Paring Down." *Education Week*, June 16, 2004.

Henican, Ellis. "Giving It Away: The Other Buffett Family Business." *Barron's*, June 18, 2018.

Herszenhorn, David M. "Gates Charity Gives $51 Million to City to Start 67 Schools." *New York Times*, September 18, 2003.

Hill, Paul T. "A Foundation Goes to School: Bill and Melinda Gates Shift from Computers in Libraries to Reform in High Schools." *Education Next*, Winter 2006.

Holm, Erik. "Warren Buffett Won't Quit Until He's 'Buried in the Ground,' His Son Says." *Wall Street Journal*, December 8, 2011.

Holt-Giménez, Eric, Miguel A. Altieri, and Peter Rosset. "Ten Reasons Why AGRA Will Not Solve Poverty and Hunger in Africa." Food First, October 2006.

Independent. "Office Romance: How Bill Met Melinda." June 27, 2008.

Isaacson, Walter. "In Search of the Real Bill Gates." *Time*, January 13, 1997.

Jewish Telegraphic Agency. "Long Before Israeli Deal, Warren Buffett Made His Mark on Jewish Community." May 16, 2006.

Johnson, Richard, with Paula Froelich, Chris Wilson, and Bill Hoffmann. "Buffett to Kin: You're Fired!" *New York Post*, Sept 7, 2006.

Johnston, David Cay. "Dozens of Rich Americans Join in Fight to Retain the Estate Tax." *New York Times*, February 14, 2001.

Kaufman, Frederick. "The Food Bubble." *Harper's Magazine*, July 2010.

———. "Let Them Eat Cash." *Harper's Magazine*, June 2009.

Kiersz, Andy. "Here's How Rich You'd Be If You Had Bet $1,000 on Warren Buffett Way Back When." Business Insider India, March 3, 2015.

Kimmett, Colleen. "10 Years After Katrina, New Orleans' All-Charter District Has Proven a Failure." *In These Times*, August 28, 2015.

Kinsella, Kevin. "Newsmakers: Tom Vander Ark." *Philanthropy News Digest*, October 15, 2003.

Kirkpatrick, David, and Brenton Schlender. "The Valley vs. Microsoft." *Fortune*, March 20, 1995.

Knight-Ridder Newspapers. "Microsoft Spoof: Microshaft Winblows 98 Bill Gates' Empire Is the Target of Latest Parody by CD-ROM Maker Palladium Interactive." *Spokesman-Review*, January 6, 1998.

Kolbert, Elizabeth. "Gospels of Giving for the New Gilded Age." *New Yorker*, August 20, 2018.

Lane, Randall. "Bill Gates and Bono on Their Alliance of Fortune, Fame and Giving." *Forbes*, December 1, 2013.

Levy, Steven. "Behind the Gates Myth." *Newsweek*, August 29, 1999.

Lewis, Michael. "The Master of Money." *New Republic*, June 3, 2009.

———. "The Temptation of St. Warren." *New Republic*, February 17, 1992.

Loomis, Carol J. "The Inside Story of Warren Buffett." *Fortune*, April 11, 1988.

———. "The $600 Billion Challenge." *Fortune*, June 16, 2010.

———. "Warren Buffett Gives It Away." *Fortune*, July 13, 2006.

Luckerson, Victor. "'Crush Them': An Oral History of the Lawsuit that Upended Silicon Valley." The Ringer, May 18, 2018.

Martin, Douglas. "Rabbi Myer Kripke, Early Buffett Friend and Investor, Dies at 100." New York Times, May 3, 2014.

Martin, Nina. "How One Abortion Research Megadonor Forced the Supreme Court's Hand." Mother Jones, July 14, 2016.

Matas, Robert. "The Man Who Gives Away Gates' Money." Globe and Mail, July 31, 2000.

Maxwell, Lesli A. "Foundations Donate Millions to Help New Orleans Schools' Recovery." Education Week, December 13, 2007.

McKibben, Sarah. "Foreclosed: 2 Million Homeless Students and Counting." News Leader, January 2009.

McNeil, Donald G., Jr. "WHO Official Complains About Gates Foundation's Dominance in Malaria Fight." New York Times, November 7, 2008.

Moeller, Kathryn. "The Ghost Statistic That Haunts Women's Empowerment." New Yorker, January 4, 2019.

Moorhead, Joanna. "Melinda Gates Challenges Vatican by Vowing to Improve Contraception." Guardian, July 11, 2012.

Munk, Nina. "How Warren Buffett's Son Would Feed the World." Atlantic, May 2016.
———. "It's the I.P.O, Stupid!" Vanity Fair, January 2000.

Myerson, Allen R. "Rating the Bigshots: Gates vs. Rockefeller." New York Times, May 24, 1998.

Nader, Ralph. "An Open Letter to Bill Gates." Nader.org, July 27, 1998.

Newburger, Emma. "Bill Gates Warns against Coronavirus Vaccine Going to the Highest Bidder—'We'll Have a Deadlier Pandemic.'" CNBC, July 11, 2020.

Norris, Emily. "Benjamin Graham, the Intelligent Investor." Investopedia, January 31, 2020.

Onion. "Bill Gates to Get Half." July 23, 1996.

Patel, Raj, Eric Holt-Gímenez, and Annie Shattuck. "Ending Africa's Hunger." Nation, September 2, 2009.

Pelline, Jeff. "Buffett Won't Invest in Tech Stocks." CNET, May 5, 1998.

Pemberton-Butler, Lisa. "Vander Ark's Exit No Surprise." Seattle Times, May 6, 1999.

Philanthropy News Digest. "Gates Foundation Commits $158 Million to Fight Poverty in the U.S." May 4, 2018.

Philpott, Tom. "Taxpayer Dollars Are Helping Monsanto Sell Seeds Abroad." Mother Jones, May 18, 2013.

Piller, Charles. "Gates Foundation to Keep Its Investment Approach." Los Angeles Times, January 14, 2007.

Piller, Charles, Edmund Sanders, and Robyn Dixon. "Dark Cloud Over Good Works of Gates Foundation." Los Angeles Times, January 7, 2007.

Piper, Kelsey. "Bill Gates Is Committed to Giving Away His Fortune—But He Keeps Getting Richer." Vox, April 23, 2019.

Ponsot, Elisabeth. "14-Year-Old Warren Buffett's First Tax Return Shows He Was Making Bank Even as a Teen." Quartz, June 27, 2017.

Premack, Rachel. "'I Missed a Lot': Bill Gates Regrets Not Partying and Going to Football Games at Harvard." Business Insider, April 27, 2018.

Provost, Claire, and Erick Kabendera. "Tanzania: Large-Scale Farming Turns Small Farmers into Mere Labourers." Guardian, February 18, 2014.

Provost, Claire, Liz Ford, and Mark Tran. "G8 New Alliance Condemned as New Wave of Colonialism in Africa." Guardian, February 18, 2014.

Read, Madlen. "Margin Calls Can Trigger a Downward Selling Spiral." Mercury News, August 18, 2007.

Reft, Ryan. "The Foreclosure Crisis and Its Impact on Today's Housing Market." KCET, September 20, 2017.

Rieff, David. "The Gates Foundation's Delusional Techno-Messianism." *New Republic*, November 1, 2010.

——. "A Green Revolution for Africa?" *New York Times*, October 10, 2008.

Robelen, Erik. "Venture Fund Fueling Push for New Schools." *Education Week*, January 16, 2007.

——. "Walton Family Puts Stamp on Education." *Education Week*, November 4, 2008.

Rondy, John. "The Human Cost." *Milwaukee Magazine*, February 2011.

Rubin, Elizabeth. "How a Texas Philanthropist Helped Fund the Hunt for Joseph Kony." *New Yorker*, October 21, 2013.

Schlender, Brent. "All You Need Is Love, $50 Billion and Killer Software Code-Named Longhorn." *Fortune*, July 8, 2002.

——. "The Bill & Warren Show." *Fortune*, July 20, 1998.

——. "The Billionaire Buddies." *Wall Street Journal*, July 21, 2022.

Seabrook, John. "E-mail from Bill." *New Yorker*, December 27, 1993.

Sellers, Patricia. "Melinda Gates Goes Public." *Fortune*, March 16, 2016.

Seymour, Jim. "Judge Richard Posner Enters Microsoft vs. Justice Negotiations." TheStreet, November 19, 1999.

Shah, Sonia. "The Patient Recruitment Bottleneck." Soniashah.com, October 3, 2007.

Sharwood, Simon. "Bill Gates Debunks 'Coronavirus Vaccine Is My 5G Mind Control Microchip Implant' Conspiracy Theory." *Register*, July 24, 2020.

Sherry, Allison. "Manual's Slow Death." *Denver Post*, May 5, 2006.

Singer, Peter. "The Logic of Effective Altruism." *Boston Review*, July 1, 2015.

Specter, Michael. "What Money Can Buy." *New Yorker*, October 24, 2005.

Spurgeon, Devon. "Warren Buffett Bids and Bill Gates Passes." *Wall Street Journal*, December 11, 2000.

Stannard-Stockton, Sean. "Gates-Buffett Example Worth Its Weight in Gold." *Chronicle of Philanthropy*, July 11, 2010.

Strom, Stephanie. "Gates Aims Billions to Attack Illnesses of World's Neediest." *New York Times*, July 13, 2003.

Strouse, Jean. "How to Give Away $21.8 Billion." *New York Times*, April 16, 2000.

Swisher, Kara. "Taming the Apex Predators of Tech." *New York Times*, May 21, 2019.

Thomas, June. "The Retreat Observation That Put Patty Stonesifer on Microsoft Leadership's Radar." *Slate*, March 28, 2019.

Udland, Myles. "This Is the Moment America Met Warren Buffett." Yahoo! Finance, April 30, 2019.

Vartan, Vartanig G. "Buffett's Low-Key Role in a High-Stakes Deal." *New York Times*, March 20, 1985.

Vidal, John. "Why Is the Gates Foundation Investing in GM Giant Monsanto?" *Guardian*, September 29, 2010.

Wathen, Jordan. "1 Stock That Was Pivotal in Billionaire Warren Buffett's Career." The Motley Fool, May 27, 2017.

Weise, Karen. "Warren Buffett's Family Secretly Funded a Birth Control Revolution." *Bloomberg Businessweek*, July 30, 2015.

Wilke, John R. "Billionaire Duffer Would Love to Belong to Storied Golf Club." *Wall Street Journal*, September 18, 1998.

Wilke, John R., and Rebecca Buckman. "U.S. Judge Calls Abrupt End to Microsoft Antitrust Trial." *Wall Street Journal*, May 25, 2000.

Winter, Greg. "Critical of Public Schools, and Poised to Take Action." *New York Times*, February 25, 2004.

Wired. "Gates, Microsoft Jump on 'Internet Tidal Wave.'" May 26, 1995.

Letters, Speeches, and Press Releases

Bill & Melinda Gates Foundation. "Purchase for Progress: Profiles of Progress." Press release, February 2012.

Bono. "Because We Can, We Must." Commencement speech at the University of Pennsylvania, Philadelphia, May 19, 2004.

Buffett, Warren. "Berkshire—Past, Present and Future." Letter to the shareholders of Berkshire Hathaway Inc., February 27, 2015.

——. Letter to Charles N. Huggins, December 13, 1972.

——. Letter to the shareholders of Berkshire Hathaway Inc., February 27, 1987.

——. Letter to the shareholders of Berkshire Hathaway Inc., February 29, 1988.

——. Letter to the shareholders of Berkshire Hathaway Inc., February 27, 2009.

Gates, Bill. Roundtable at the World Economic Forum, New York, February 2, 2002.

——. Speech at the National Education Summit on High Schools, Washington, D.C., February 26, 2005.

——. Speech at the Nigeria Human Capital Event, Abuja, Nigeria, March 22, 2018.

——. Speech at the World Economic Forum, Davos, Switzerland, January 29, 2001.

Gates, Melinda. "Educating All Children Well: Do We Want to Do It Badly Enough?" Speech at the National Conference of State Legislatures, San Francisco, July 25, 2003.

——. Keynote remarks at the London Summit on Family Planning, London, July 11, 2012.

——. Remarks at the Washington Women's Foundation Annual Meeting, Seattle, April 6, 2000.

"Microsoft." U.S. Justice Department news conference, May 18, 1998.

"Secretary-General Calls for 'Uniquely African' Green Revolution in 21st Century." UN press release, July 6, 2004.

Film, Music, Television

"An Hour with Warren Buffett, Bill Gates & Melinda Gates." *Charlie Rose*, PBS, June 26, 2006.

Becoming Warren Buffett (directed by Peter W. Kunhardt). HBO, 2017.

"Bill Gates and Warren Buffett." *Charlie Rose*, PBS, January 27, 2017.

"Bill Gates Must Die." Composed and performed by John Vanderslice, Barsuk Records, 2000.

"Blood into Gold." Composed by Peter Buffett, performed by Peter Buffett and Akon, Beside Records, 2009.

"Harm to Ongoing Matter." *On the Media*, WNYC, April 19, 2019.

"Melinda Gates." *My Next Guest Needs No Introduction with David Letterman*, Netflix, May 31, 2019.

Panic: The Untold Story of the 2008 Financial Crisis, directed by John Maggio. Vice/HBO, 2018.

"Remembering Susan Buffett." *Charlie Rose*, PBS, August 26, 2004.

60 Minutes, CBS, December 11, 2011.

INDEX